The ART of WINNING CONVERSATION

MOREY STETTNER

PRENTICE HALL
Englewood Cliffs, New Jersey 07632

Prentice Hall International (UK) Limited, *London*
Prentice Hall of Australia Pty. Limited, *Sydney*
Prentice Hall Canada, Inc., *Toronto*
Prentice Hall Hispanoamericana, S.A., *Mexico*
Prentice Hall of India Private Limited, *New Delhi*
Prentice Hall of Japan, Inc., *Tokyo*
Simon & Schuster Asia Pte. Ltd., *Singapore*
Editora Prentice Hall do Brasil, Ltda., *Rio de Janeiro*

© 1995 *by*
Morey Stettner

Library of Congress Cataloging-in-Publication Data

Stettner, Morey.
   The art of winning conversation / Morey Stettner
     p. cm.
   Includes index.
   ISBN 0-13-125774-9 -- ISBN 0-13-125766-8 (pbk.)
   1. Public speaking. 2. Persuasion (Rhetoric) I. Title.
PN412147 1995
808.5'1--dc20   94-49382
                                                      CIP

ISBN 0-13-125774-9
ISBN 0-13-125766-8

Prentice Hall
Career & Personal Development
Englewood Cliffs, NJ 07632
Simon & Schuster, A Paramount Communications Company

Printed in the United States of America

To Gene Safan,
the ultimate role model

ALSO BY MOREY STETTNER:

Buyer Beware: An Industry Insider Shows You How to Win the Insurance Game (Probus Publishing, 1994)

Contents

STEP ONE
Prepare to Persuade
1

CHAPTER 5
Three Steps to Designing a Dress Rehearsal Before Your Persuasive Encounter   89

CHAPTER 6
Package Your Points Persuasively by Thinking in Threes   111

STEP TWO
Listen to Learn
131

CHAPTER 7
How Listening Makes You a More Compelling Communicator   133

CHAPTER 8
How to Be More Persuasive by Showing Everyone How Well You Listen   155

CHAPTER 9
Unleashing the Power of Silence to Gain Knowledge
and Solve Problems   177

CHAPTER 10

Distortions: How to Avoid Listening for the Wrong Messages
and Crushing Your Persuasiveness   199

STEP THREE
Speak to Sell
221

CHAPTER 11

Plugging in Power Phrases to Easily Get Your Way   223

CHAPTER 12

Ask, Don't Tell: Posing the Right Questions So That Others

CHAPTER 13

Introduction
How This Book Will Help You Win Over Anybody

There is no magic to the art of persuasion. The rules are basic, the skills easy to apply. In fact, you probably already know how to persuade. You just may not be aware of what you do or how you do it.

The goal of this book is to shower you with awareness. With awareness comes knowledge; with knowledge comes power.

Let's get started.

First, three ground rules. Getting others to do, think, or feel what you want is a *process*—a series of cause-effect relationships. You will destroy your power to persuade if you let your fears, mood swings, or insecurities interfere. I have heard countless people explain their inability to persuade:

I hate when I know I'm right and someone stills says NO to me. It may take me a day or two to recover.

I tense up when I'm trying to convince someone of something important. The anxiety gets the best of me. I can't think straight or have a normal conversation.

I hedge a lot instead of just saying what I think. It's scary to be proved wrong. It also hurts when people ignore my opinion. So I play it safe.

Many of us set up roadblocks by serving as our own worst critics. We judge ourselves mercilessly. The result? We create a set of prerequisites before we feel we can communicate comfortably:

I like to persuade when I don't care what's at stake. If I don't care that much, I'm more relaxed.

I enjoy persuasion when I'm dealing with someone I like. I can't stand having to win over someone who's obnoxious.

I'm great in a one-on-one setting. Put me in front of a group, and I freeze.

Yet we cannot avoid important issues, obnoxious people, or audiences of more than one. By freeing ourselves from such prerequisites and replacing them with a mastery of the persuasive process, we become more flexible, formidable communicators.

The second ground rule involves the distinction between arguing and persuading. Arguments are rational discourses. *You can win an argument but still fail to persuade.* For example, you meet an auditor from the Internal Revenue Service at a party who tells you not to cheat on your taxes. You agree that you shouldn't fudge the numbers, but you do it anyway.

Persuasion requires more than logic. To gain allegiance or motivate someone to act, you must stir emotion and establish credibility. Aristotle wrote that a persuasive speaker must embody three elements: *logos, pathos*, and *ethos* (logic, emotion, and credibility). While arguments can be won on sweet reason alone, persuasion strikes a deep behavioral chord that makes us change what we feel. This book is not about winning arguments; it shows how to blend logic, passion, and credibility to win over anybody.

Finally, and most important, let us begin with a moment of silence. Look away from this book and take five seconds to relax, close your eyes, and keep quiet. You have just discovered what lies at the heart of persuasion: the ability to keep your mouth shut.

This book will show you how to spend quiet moments harnessing your mental and physical energy so that you truly listen. The goal: to treat listening with as much respect as speaking. This shouldn't come as a surprise. Pick up any book that promises to teach you how to sell yourself, and you will probably get a stern lecture from the author about the dangers of sloppy listening habits. My guess is that you have already been told a thousand times to *listen up*, to *pay attention*, to *follow directions*, to *read my lips*, to *put a lid on it*. You have surely been asked by a frustrated friend or colleague:

Are you finished yet?

Are you interested in what I have to say?

May I get a word in edgewise?

Admit it: at some point you've probably heard people (family, friends, bosses, coworkers, teachers) plead with you to stop talking and listen. Even the most attentive individuals, the ones who pride themselves on their unassuming manner (and insist that they "really prefer to listen rather than talk") still may rush to fill silence.

If you are like most of the people I have met, you will admit that you could stand to improve your listening skills. But that doesn't mean that you are willing to talk less. It's like dieters who know that they can lose weight by laying off fatty foods, but the sacrifice of giving up ice cream or chocolate is too much to ask. Many participants in my workshops nod impatiently when I praise the sweet sound of silence. They fidget in their seats and mutter, "Yeah, yeah, listening is important. Now tell me what to say."

Relax. I will not spend much time lecturing you about the beauty and benefits of silence. Rather than *tell* you to stop talking, I will *show* you what to do. Read on and you will gain plenty of tips, tools, and techniques that make you a more forceful, commanding communicator. Here's a preview of what you will learn:

- How to transform your fear of rejection or failure into positive energy so that you *want* to win people over
- How to overcome objections and regain the momentum of a conversation
- Three ways to build empathy and make it easy for others to say "yes"
- Three steps to rehearse your persuasive appeal so that practice makes perfect when it counts
- How to "think in threes" and wrap your ideas in an appealing package
- Four strategies that help you listen better and demonstrate to speakers that you actually *care* about what they have to say
- How to avoid the three biggest traps that block effective listening
- How to increase your attentiveness with two magic words: *teach me*

The best persuaders use a toolbox full of techniques to win over their audiences. They are curious, outgoing, and patient. They care about what they are saying, and they create the impression that they care about *us*. They know that the source of their persuasive power goes beyond the words they use, that the process of selling themselves begins hours, days, even weeks before they ever go face-to-face with others. Their voice, mannerisms, and word choice combine to produce a compelling message.

Consider how one of my students, Jan, persuaded her boss to change his work habits. An executive secretary, Jan tried to keep the chairman running on time through his hectic days. Yet she complained to me that he repeatedly neglected to keep her posted on his whereabouts. He would abruptly cancel meetings or extend trips without calling her. Jan asked him many times to change, but to no avail.

When I asked Jan what he liked to talk about, she said, "Sports. He's incredibly competitive. He comes in Monday morning and tells me how he won his golf game or lost a close tennis match. He loves to bet on games, too."

Bingo. Armed with this knowledge, I suggested that Jan propose to her boss that they "bet" that he could not go one week without getting "lost" somewhere. Convinced that he could win the bet, he agreed. Jan called me a week later with the happy ending: He won the bet and called her at least twice a day.

Jerry, engaged to be married, faced a different challenge. His fiancee's father, Carl, wanted to hold the wedding at a ritzy Manhattan hotel, while the couple hoped to marry at a romantic mountain lodge in upstate New York. Through gentle questioning, Jerry learned that Carl wanted to impress his friends by spending money on an expensive, prestigious hotel in the city. "We'll celebrate in style, I assure you, and everyone will see I've made it," Carl declared.

Rather than try to argue with Carl, Jerry learned that the mountain lodge hosted weddings for some of the wealthiest, most famous families in the world. Unlike a bustling Manhattan hotel, the lodge offered exclusivity and elegance. Jerry mentioned these facts to Carl, who liked the idea of "going one better than a big hotel ballroom."

Both examples illustrate how persuasion works. Jan and Jerry were aware of their roles—neither tried to do battle and turn potential allies into opponents. They were attentive—by listening and questioning they could redirect the conversation to their advantage. Finally, they took creative action. Jan initiated a fun wager with her boss, and Jerry researched the lodge and gathered the kind of information that changed Carl's mind.

You are about to develop a three-step persuasive program that applies to almost any personal or professional situation. We begin with an overview that helps you wash away any lingering fears that may inhibit your will to persuade. This book identifies three steps that each address an element in the sequence of persuasion: preparing, listening, and speaking.

More than two-thirds of this book covers persuasive strategies other than talking. Why? Because we plant the seeds of persuasion before we utter a sound. As long as you are willing to master the less glamourous but more powerful steps that precede talking, you are ready to derive the most benefit from what follows.

HOW TO MAKE THIS BOOK WORK FOR YOU

To make best use of this book, I suggest you read each part in order and not skip around. The chapters are designed as building blocks. Like circuit weight training, where you go from machine to machine isolating and strengthening different body parts, the book progresses in stages to help you develop your skills in a systematic way.

The overview in Chapter 1 will give you a better idea of how the three stages of preparing, listening, and speaking unfold. Many communicators fail to persuade because they launch into their sales pitch too early in the conversation. Their timing is off. They rush to talk us into something without properly laying the groundwork. In the absence of trust or rapport, we tend to tune out a speaker.

In my communication workshops, I conduct roleplays in which a participant tries to persuade a volunteer from the group to do something. Fran will try to talk Ron into buying her new jewelry. Stephen will ask his "boss" for a raise. Joyce will practice advising her teenaged daughter on how to handle peer pressure. Unfortunately, few participants begin by engaging the other person in a true dialogue with directed questions. I find that most would-be persuaders start by making statements or observations. They tend to proclaim what they think is right or what the other person should do. All too often, their stab at persuasion sounds more like dishing out orders or commandments. After the roleplay is over, I ask the participants, "Why did you keep *telling* the other person what you thought rather than *asking* questions to get a two-way conversation going?"

I usually hear one of these responses:

I figure the spotlight is on me to do the persuading and that I better come right out and say what's on my mind.

If I let the other person talk too much, it could throw me off. I mean, I know why I think I'm right and what I have to say. If I'm too quiet, then I could lose steam or wind up hearing what I don't want to hear.

It makes me nervous to ask a lot of questions. It feels fake to get someone else to do the talking when I'm the one who has something important to say.

Sound familiar? There is nothing wrong with wanting to state what's on your mind. If you have something important to say, it can be frustrating to hold it in and ask questions without caring about the answers. But if you bark orders at people, they may resist.

Memory Jogger

When it comes to effective persuasion, it doesn't matter how "right" you think you are. What matters is whether your audience understands and cares about what you have to say.

By sticking to the three steps of preparing, listening, and speaking, you can pace yourself and maximize your influence. You will avoid selling too soon if you know that you must prepare and listen *before* you give yourself the mental go-ahead to speak. This explains why you should read this book from the beginning: After the overview, I show you how to prepare your ideas, how to listen, and how to speak persuasively. My hope is that the prepare-listen-speak approach will, with practice, become second nature to you so that you treat each stage as a natural stepping stone to attain your goals.

This book is filled with information you can use. Dig in! Every chapter includes plenty of practice exercises, diagnostic tests, handy reminder lists, and other interactive features so that you can put the material to immediate use and become a stronger, more confident communicator.

Here are some of the unique features that you will find throughout the book to help you master the prepare-listen-speak approach:

Now Try This

Whenever you see **Now Try This**, go ahead and try it. These short sections introduce ready-to-use tools to help you prepare, listen, and speak with more confidence. They are meaty, how-to pointers that are designed to produce immediate, observable results. They are your action steps, so put them to work. Please do not skip these sections or tell yourself that you will "come back later." Treat every **Now Try This** as a fun experiment to expand your range of expression and sharpen your command of the prepare-listen-speak process. When you come to a **Now Try This**, I suggest that you read it and then *put the book down*. Consider how or when you can put what you are reading into practice. Ask yourself:

- What kind of situation in my life does this apply to?

- How can I modify this technique and make it work best for me?
- Am I ready to do this, or do I need to practice a related communication skill first?

If you are taking the time to read this book, you might as well capitalize on your investment by turning the text into your personal training manual. Make the material work for you.

Traps

This book exposes the traps that unwary communicators face when trying to persuade. Many of us fall prey to sloppy listening habits, lazy speech patterns, haphazard organization of thoughts, and other careless slip-ups that undermine our knowledge or good intentions. Pay attention to TRAPS and relate them to your daily experience. Have you stumbled into any of them? Have you noticed others who do? An awareness of these common pitfalls will help you avoid them in the future. The best defense against communication traps is knowing *how* to spot them and *when* they threaten to sabotage your persuasiveness. This book will teach you not only how to persuade, but how *not* to persuade. Be on the lookout for TRAPS.

Diagnostic Self-Tests

Each of us boasts a unique communication style and a distinctive personality. That's why this book includes some self-tests that are designed to help you assess your persuasive skills. These tests do not have right or wrong answers; rather, they serve as diagnostic tools to increase your awareness and point you toward specific aspects of communication that merit attention. Take these tests with a clear mind. Don't rush. Try to answer as accurately as possible. Remember, there's no need to impress anyone. You will not be graded.

Memory Joggers

You will find a memory jogger every few pages—a sentence or two that encapsulates the material and contains whatever pearls of wisdom I can offer. These pithy statements amplify the learning points and provide handy and memorable nuggets for your own private treasure chest of knowledge. As a reporter on my college newspaper, I was assigned to write "blow-up quotes" (those oversized snippets of an article that appear in bold and break up the small-print news copy). Similarly, the memory joggers throughout this book make it easier to extract key ideas from what you are reading.

Roleplays and Scripts

Through the use of roleplays and scripts, I illustrate the dos and don'ts of persuasive communication. Simulating a real conversation helps identify the interplay of speakers and issues. For example, a script can help you spot what happens when neither party prepares or listens. No persuasion occurs when speakers fight each other for the floor ("Now it's *my* turn to talk! You've had yours.") instead of demonstrating the patience and curiosity to exchange views and communicate for mutual benefit.

Quick Reviews

Every chapter closes with a Quick Review that highlights the main points covered in the preceding pages. These summaries, designed as checklists, provide a one-stop reference guide to the action steps contained therein. You may want to photocopy these Quick Reviews and post them in a prominent place (next to your desk calendar, on the refrigerator, in the car) as reminders of what it takes to master the art of persuasion. Do not pressure yourself to apply each and every tool for all occasions. The principles and techniques in the book will, over time and with practice, shape your instinctive response to interpersonal communication. The Quick Review makes it easy to remember the most important points.

THE IMPACT OF THIS BOOK ON YOUR DAILY LIFE

Why enhance your persuasive communication skills?

There is the obvious reason: You can sell more of the people, more of the time, on whatever it is you want them to do.

Specifically, this book will positively affect your daily life in a number of ways:

Your Personal Life

- Your relationships with family and friends will dramatically improve when you exert gentle, reassuring influence. Your insights, beliefs, and advice will be heeded even more by those nearest and dearest to you when you know how to maximize your persuasiveness. Participants in my workshops have often told me that they grow closer to family members once they apply such tools as Teach Me, Teach Me (see Chapter 7) and The 80/20 Rule (see Chapter 4).

- Your relationship with your spouse or partner will evolve in wonderful ways when you prepare and listen before opening your mouth to try to persuade. Instead of fairly trying to persuade each other with patience and sensitivity, couples sometimes resort to bickering or nagging to gain compliance. By following the precepts introduced in this book and developing your three-step persuasive program, you will more freely express your warm, nurturing side. You will bury any remnants of domineering, insistent, or arrogant behavior. Your persuasive expression will come across as caring, as empowering, as loving.

- Do you enjoy entering a room filled with strangers? Some find it harrowing to mingle among a sea of unfamiliar faces. By reaching into your persuasive toolbox and applying the techniques in the book, you will gain immeasurable confidence that spills over into all aspects of your life. Your shyness will fade. Your self-esteem—wherever it stands at present—will soar. You will meet people and radiate an appealing, charming mix of curiosity and good humor. You will lavish attention on others and take joy in remembering their names. You will no longer find strangers menacing; in fact, you will eagerly approach them and greet them warmly. When the time comes to persuade or lead them, you will do so with poise and dignity.

Your Professional Life

- Strengthening your influence skills will translate into all kinds of work-related success. You persuade almost continually at work, whether asking your boss for a raise or telling a clerk how to perform a task more effectively. If you run your own enterprise, then you must win over everyone from lenders to vendors, always putting yourself on the line in order to build your business.

- This book will prove particularly helpful when you must deliver bad news to your boss, colleagues, or staff. Your communication skills are sorely tested whenever you must tackle a delicate subject (layoff notices, faulty work, loss of a big account). As you will learn, the master persuader turns such jarring announcements into empowering calls to action. For example, I once helped a personnel manager prepare to notify his large staff that his department was about to be eliminated in a restructuring move. Before informing his employees of the situation, he prepared by finding other positions for as many staffers as he could and securing generous severance packages for those left without a job. We decided that he would use the horrendous news as an opportunity to motivate his staff to seek career advancement. When it came time for the big meeting, he promised to arrange for individual job counseling for anyone who requested it, and he went around the room praising each employee for some aspect of his or her performance. Because of his genuine concern for his staff and his appreciation for their years of service, he managed to instill a sense of hopefulness instead of mourning the demise of the status quo.

- Professional salespeople will gain a whole new approach to persuasion from this book. (Even if you do not depend on commission for an income, you probably "sell" yourself at work all the time.) Most salespeople have picked up some tips over the past decade about "consultative selling." This sensible approach ensures that the sale results from a low-key dialogue and fulfillment of a client's need rather than a hard-sell push to pummel a weary prospect into submission. I go one step further and give you a set of tools so that you know how to prepare, listen, and speak so that you send a powerful, irresistible message to even the most cynical prospects. Few salespeople, for instance, know how to use silence to their advantage. They might babble their way into oblivion instead of asking a question and then waiting patiently for an answer (see The Stop Rule in Chapter 9). They might be great talkers who just don't want to listen. Or, to take another example, they might skip the vital step of rehearsing their "pitch" using the three steps found in Chapter 5.

MEMORY JOGGER

Remember that to maximize your persuasive power, you must *prepare, listen,* and then, and only then, *talk.* Skip preparation or listening at your own risk.

Beyond the personal and professional benefits of improving your persuasive communication skills, you will grow more observant and tolerant of others. You will devote more attention to those around you and less to yourself. A participant in one of my workshops joked, "Before I took your course, Morey, I was self-obsessed. Now I'm obsessed with others."

In an age of information overload where overworked, exhausted people scurry around trying to manage their jobs, families, and friends, there is less time to step back and appreciate what others say or do. We may dwell so much on our own needs, worries, and fears that we fail to consider the ideas and opinions of those close to us.

This book shows you how to build your persuasive power on a base of mutual understanding, a foundation so strong that you can win over anybody.

STEP ONE

Prepare to Persuade

CHAPTER 1

The Art of Persuasion
Three Steps to Win People Over

Over the past eight years, I have taught thousands of people how to persuade. I begin by asking participants in my workshops how they do it, and I usually hear one of the following responses:

If I want something badly enough, I usually don't stop until I get it.

These are the hard-sell salespeople talking. The mouth does all the work. They operate with a "just keep talking and wear 'em down until they surrender" philosophy. It's persuasion by attrition.

I hate being pushy, so I just hint a lot.

This group feels that to come right out and ask for something is a sin. So they tiptoe around the topic, waiting for the day when others "catch on" and agree. It's persuasion by avoidance.

I come right out and say what I think is right.

Sounds like a sensible policy, but beware. Would-be persuaders can get into trouble when they think in terms of right/wrong or good/bad. It's persuasion by decree.

I pride myself on being logical and rational and making a sound argument.

Great, except that we do not operate in a purely logical world. Human interaction is filled with such irrational impulses as fear and insecurity. You may plead an airtight case only to realize that your listeners still reject your "perfect" argument. It's persuasion by pure reason.

I don't know how I persuade, but sometimes it just works.

This is the most common response. Most people engage in persuasion all the time, but they have no idea how they do it. When it works, great; when it doesn't, oh well...It's persuasion by chance.

Sound familiar? While these approaches may be fine for certain situations, the odds of successfully swaying others go way down when speakers bulldoze, sleepwalk, or stumble forward without a plan.

So here's the plan: Master the three stages of preparing, listening, and speaking. Prepare thoroughly for any persuasive encounter, listen raptly, and then speak with clarity and passion using a mix of questions and power phrases. That's the secret recipe. No fancy philosophy, no gimmicks, no puffery. And it works.

You will find this process so simple, yet so elegant, that with practice it will become second nature. It will help you adjust your communication style to fit any situation, from calming an unruly crowd, to negotiating a contract, to raising your kids. The circumstances may change, but the rules of persuasive communication remain the same. As you sharpen your ability to prepare, listen, and speak, you will unleash the full force of your confidence and envelop others in your charm and charisma.

You will win over anybody.

GETTING STARTED:
A ROAD MAP FOR THE CONFIDENT COMMUNICATOR

Before we examine more closely the three steps of preparing, listening, and speaking, you may be wondering why we will spend so much time with two skills—organizing your thoughts and listening to others—that may seem less important than talking. After all, you have to say something to persuade someone. You may think, "I can get by without bothering to prepare diligently or listen raptly, but there's no faking the moment of truth when I have to speak."

Talking, of course, counts for much of your success as a communicator. But the quiet tasks of organizing and listening are often overlooked.

A talker grabs attention. For some people, hearing their voice fill a room is a turn-on, a glorious sound that feeds an ever-hungry ego. Some people confess to me that they hate to listen because they feel powerless or inferior to others whenever they must keep quiet.

I used to put my faith in my ability to talk my way into anything I wanted. In high school, my experience on the debate team taught me that if you could talk smoothly and engagingly (tossing in bits of humor and irony), you could best your opponents. In college, I found that by adopting an authoritative voice (deep, dramatic, with lots of pauses for effect), I could impress professors without saying much of anything. It was only after I had to work for a living and experience more serious relationships that I realized the limits of glibness.

You see, the people who really matter to you—your closest friends, a trusted mentor, your family—will look beyond your words to unearth the true message. They know you. They cannot be fooled by a string of impressive-sounding words. They will not take you at face value. Nor should they. The more substantive our relationships, the more we must treat the art of persuasion as a holistic process that goes beyond mere words. So much needs to happen before we open our mouth.

We begin by establishing a baseline so that you can track your skill development. How do you communicate now? Take this self-assessment test and find out. There are no right or wrong answers.

Diagnostic Self-Test: Rate Your Communication Style

Rank each statement on a scale of 1 to 5.

      1 = Always

      2 = Almost Always

      3 = Sometimes

      4 = Rarely

      5 = Never

_____ If a speaker discusses a boring topic, I make every effort not to tune out.

_____ Before giving a speech, I rehearse (by taking notes, memorizing key points, performing in front of a friend or a mirror).

_____ I am more satisfied when someone says "I understand you" than "I agree with you."

_____ When someone interrupts, I keep quiet and wait patiently before continuing to speak.

_____ When I'm feeling angry or nervous during a conversation, I talk less.

_____ I enjoy asking friends for favors.

_____ I find it easy to ask questions in almost any conversation.

_____ I learn something useful even from the most talkative or unpleasant people.

_____ It is more common for someone to persuade me than for me to persuade others.

If your total score is less than 20, you are starting from a position of strength. You already demonstrate some of the discipline, patience, and curiosity necessary to communicate effectively.

If you scored from 21 to 31, you fall into the middle range. You have the potential to persuade with consistency, but you may not be using the best tools to accomplish your task.

If your total is over 31, you will benefit even more from this book. You are not doing anything "bad" right now, so don't worry about a personality overhaul. Your score indicates that you communicate in a more free-form, spontaneous style. The danger is that your judgments and doubts may interfere with your efforts to converse freely.

Let's hope your reason for persuading is not simply to prove you are right, to satisfy your ego, or to win at all costs. Your persuasive goal should be to spread good will and ample benefits around so that both you and your listeners come away winners. Why does this matter? If you get your way now, but you are proved wrong later, then you have no credibility for the next time. What's worse, if you leave people feeling resentful or remorseful, they can always change their minds and say no.

MEMORY JOGGER

Use each persuasive encounter to bolster your standing and lay the groundwork for exerting future influence.

INTRODUCING YOUR THREE-STEP PROGRAM TO SHARPEN YOUR PERSUASIVE POWER

Persuasion is more than saying the right words in the right way. Before uttering a sound, the best communicators have done their homework by preparing their thoughts and listening to those they want to win over. This book treats each stage separately, with parts devoted to preparing, listening, and speaking. All the pieces will fit together by the end. You will have a step-by-step persuasive program.

Step 1: Preparing. It's More than Jotting Some Notes on a Napkin

Do you believe you can change someone's mind?

Persuasion is more than a learned skill. It tests your convictions. You must carry within you a deep self-assuredness that you can guide people to think a certain way. This inner belief must not fade or crumble in the face of temporary setbacks. It should rest on a bedrock of self-knowledge, an unshakable faith in your ability to make yourself heard.

If you question your ability to sway opinion or change minds, then it does not matter how well you prepare your ideas. Investing the time and effort to plan your remarks should flow directly from your desire to help or support others. There is no room for self-doubt. If you catch yourself thinking "This isn't worth it," "It's not that important," or "Someone else will say something—I'll keep quiet," you denigrate yourself and weaken your will to persuade.

Less forceful persuaders open their mouths only if they sense an easy victory with minimal or no resistance. The confident communicator, by contrast, builds a strong case by bonding with others despite difficult odds. Preparation allows you to plan ways to connect to your audience, stir their emotions, and win their trust. You can also devise strategies that give others the chance to be generous at little cost to themselves. Flush with optimism and awareness, you are better able to appreciate others' wants and needs.

Memory Jogger

If you spend less mental energy dwelling on your own fears and insecurities, you have more energy left over to think about how you can bond with those you seek to persuade.

Top salespeople connect with customers by pressing "hot buttons" that trigger an affirmative response. They plant seeds so that a buyer thinks, "Yeah, I want a sporty car with a sunroof" or "A fountain pen *would* add a classy touch." You can prepare to persuade anyone by applying the same technique.

How do you find the hot buttons that will arouse others? It's easier, of course, when you know the person and are familiar with his or her attitudes and interests. Use the following worksheet to test your knowledge of the person you seek to persuade:

Worksheet: In Search of Hot Buttons

1. I want to persuade _____*[name]*_____ to _____*[your goal]*_____.
2. I have known [name] for _____ months/years.
3. The most excited I ever saw [name] was when _____*[describe]*_____.
4. The most upset I ever saw [name] was when _____*[describe]*_____.
5. [Name] tends to like people who are _____*[describe qualities or personal characteristics]*_____.
6. [Name] spends his/her free time _____*[describe]*_____.
7. When [name] buys something expensive, it is usually because the purchase:

    fills a practical need

    brings happiness

    makes him/her feel important or special

    offers a diversion from worry, stress or other problems

    other: _____.
8. [Name] likes salespeople who are _____*[describe qualities or personal characteristics]*_____ and does *not* like salespeople who are _____*[describe]*_____.

See how preparation pays off? This worksheet is designed to help you step into the world of the individual you want to win over. Once you know how to captivate someone and frame your persuasive message in an appealing way for that particular person, your chances of success soar.

Knowing what excites someone helps you plan what to say, but there remains the task of organizing your arguments in a coherent way. Sketchy outlines will not suffice. True preparation goes beyond scribbling random ideas on a napkin. You need to identify your best pieces of support from among all the reasons one could possibly have for agreeing with you. Through this filtering process, you are left with only the most relevant, irresistible benefits to attract your audience. These "gold nugget" reasons break down barriers and make it easy for others to say yes.

Memory Jogger

Organizing your thoughts *before* you speak allows you to focus on your listeners *when* you speak.

A final preparatory step is rehearsing what to say. Broadway stars spend months learning their lines before opening night. You can do the same by devising memorable phrases and growing comfortable with how your message sounds. Presidential candidates prepare for big debates by instructing their aides to throw tough questions at them. You can do the same by enlisting friends to help you anticipate objections and prepare crisp responses.

Through all these steps—empathetic bonding, selecting your finest supporting points, organizing your thoughts, and rehearsing out loud—you may wonder how much time it takes to properly prepare to persuade. It depends on what's at stake. In preparing a proposal to land a major client, I spent over two hours reducing my mishmash of ideas into a tight package of points. Then a colleague critiqued a trial run of my sales presentation while interrupting at will. Answering skeptical questions gave me a better handle on the issues and helped clarify what needed to be said. Add to that my research into the client's operations, and I invested over four hours to give a ten-minute pitch. After such intensive preparation, however, the actual presentation was a breeze.

Four hours is an extreme case. Expect to spend more time developing your persuasive skills in the weeks after you read this book, because the techniques will be new to you. Each time you practice these tools, you will learn to prepare with greater speed and efficiency. Your preparation will also vary based on the situation. If you are well acquainted with your audience, for example, then you may need to devote more time to rehearsing and less time to research.

Say you are asking the boss for a pay raise. It's not hard to predict the kind of pat excuses you might hear (budget cuts, poor timing, no raises this year). Executives hear so many salary requests that they may resort to automatic defense mechanisms to shut down further discussion. Rehearsing helps you tailor what you want to say to fight back objections without losing your cool.

Some participants in my workshops let their nervousness take control when they want to persuade. They may have a good point and the best of intentions, but their self-doubt and fear of rejection undermine their influence. As one dissatisfied salesman told me, "When the time comes to close the sale, I cannot help but hear the answer in advance, something nasty like *Absolutely not!, NO and I mean NO,* or *Get out of my office before I throw you out.*" He knew he was allowing fear to dampen his persuasiveness, but he could not figure out how to overcome his anxiety and ask for something.

I advised him to prepare what he wanted to say. We rehearsed a number of times, and I challenged him in both polite and less than polite tones. After thirty minutes of sample dialogues, he grew so comfortable with his message that he was able to respond to my objections with poise and patience. He did not lose his temper when I pretended to be angry, and he even maintained his calm when I exclaimed, "You don't know what you're talking about."

MEMORY JOGGER

The art of persuasion is a test of mental control. Careful preparation increases your command of the message and helps you conquer your fears.

Persuasion is less threatening if you have a road map to follow before you ever open your mouth. By organizing your points, you leave less to chance. In the absence of preparation, you may work yourself into a frenzy by worrying about what the audience will say or do to you.

Why exhaust yourself by dreaming up dreadful scenarios of what can go wrong? I know an entrepreneur who made dozens of presentations to venture capital funds asking for money. Instead of carefully preparing his remarks, he would dwell on the possibility of rejection. He would say, "It doesn't matter what I say. They'll use one of their turn-down lines such as *We aren't investing in your industry at this time* or *We cannot get committee approval* or *We are staying away from start-ups for a while.*"

It's bad enough to be a pessimist. But when you use "doomsday thinking" as an excuse to avoid what you want to say, you invite trouble. You can silence the negative voice inside your head that keeps repeating *You don't know what you're talking about* or *You're just gonna screw up* by adopting the techniques discussed in the chapters that follow. For example, staging a dress rehearsal (see Chapter 5) or establishing empathy (see Chapter 3) can work wonders to silence your internal critic.

The best way to continually sharpen your influence skills is to empathize with others. Empathy helps you understand the views and attitudes of those you seek to win over. We appreciate others making the effort to see things from our perspective rather than shoving their own biases or assumptions down our throat. Because so few communicators bother to empathize, those who do truly stand out.

When I first mention empathy in my seminars, the group often thinks that it is some abstract concept that does not directly affect how we communicate. It is only when I provide examples of how empathy increases persuasive power that the participants fully appreciate its role. In Chapter 3, we will explore empathy in detail so that you can use it to your advantage when you persuade.

Step 2: Listening. The Forgotten Persuasion Enhancer

In an ideal world we would listen all the time. Yet speakers drone on, distractions occur, and we wind up yawning instead of paying attention. Listening intently to every word we hear may be asking too much.

We can get by without listening. Most everyone does. It's like a massive conspiracy where we have all decided to pretend to care about what others say. We develop the nod of acknowledgment, the look of exaggerated concern, the grunt of understanding. These autopilot responses serve as our "listening" skills.

Listening is a vital element in persuasion. Unlike preparation, the second stage in your persuasive program can take place only with someone else. You can prepare on your own time at your own pace. Listening, on the other hand, depends on who's talking to you at any given moment. You must be ready to listen at all hours with little or no warning: the phone rings, a visitor bursts into your office, your friend suddenly appears at the door.

The best persuaders have tools at their disposal that make listening easier. You will be introduced to specific techniques that will not only make you a better listener, but will also help you persuade with clarity and force. You will learn how to:

- Distinguish between fact and opinion
- Arouse your curiosity
- Use nonverbal cues
- Retain messages with one-word tags
- Follow The Stop Rule

All these exercises produce immediate results by stimulating your mind to listen. A sharp listener is fully present in the here and now. Daydreams or distractions do not interfere. Nagging worries are shoved aside to make room for what others say. Your negative judgments do not hover above the conversation like dark clouds.

Why does listening play such a prominent role in winning people over to your way of thinking? Simple. We all yearn to be heard, to feel that others care about what we have to say. Like sunflowers that turn toward light, most of us are predisposed to those who make us feel special, who treat us as if what we say matters. We are more apt to say "yes" to someone who makes us feel important. And listening is a great way to earn a speaker's trust and respect.

Persuasion begins when you put your audience in a safe, secure position. Rapt listening sprinkled with well-placed questions and sincere praise produce free-flowing rapport. This helps you make friends and lay the groundwork to persuade. On the other hand, snap judgments, excessive interruptions, and dismissive comments send a threatening message. No matter how strongly you plead your case, you will not win out if you have already sabotaged yourself by alienating your audience.

MEMORY JOGGER

As long as you listen, you breathe life into a conversation. Nothing hurts more than someone who ignores us or brushes us off when we speak.

Listening enhances your persuasive power because it helps you gain credibility. Your comments hold more weight because you have made an effort to understand others first. People pay more attention to someone who talks only when necessary. Think of a Zen master who speaks sparingly but chooses each word with care. It is hard to imagine a Zen master babbling his way to enlightenment!

The quiet, observant communicator captures more information than the loudmouth does. Poker players appreciate the benefit of attentiveness. When a gambler at a card table speaks before anyone else does, the chance to learn from others is lost. In fact, many poker experts know the dealer has an advantage in betting last; this way, there is time to watch the faces, comments, and actions of the rest of the group. Same goes for regular conversation: The patient, silent listener speaks only when appropriate, using the remaining time to gather insight as others reveal themselves.

All this patience pays off in the form of knowledge. We listen to learn, and the more we learn about someone, the better our chances of persuasion. Effective communicators enter into conversations with a desire to extract useful information or to get to know another person better. Listening thus becomes a stimulating mental activity, not a chore requiring fake nods and smiles.

MEMORY JOGGER

The more we let others talk, the closer we come to understanding their point of view and identifying their hot buttons.

With so much to gain from listening, why does it remain so difficult for so many?

Human interaction is fraught with hazards that block clear communication. Consider the vanishing attention span of a generation weaned on MTV. Focusing takes patience and discipline. Even a momentary lapse in conversation can throw a dialogue awry. How many times have you stopped listening for a few seconds and then found yourself totally lost? Miss a sentence or two and you're stuck playing catch-up (What story is he telling? How did she get on this topic? What *is* the topic?).

What's worse, the following distortions threaten to make listening even harder:

Apathy The "I don't care so why bother" attitude. Indifference makes it tough to listen.

Exhaustion If you're like many people I know, you work long hours, sleep too little, and have almost no energy left to listen to your loved ones.

Runaway Emotions Unless you are related to Mr. Spock of *Star Trek* fame, you experience flashes of fear, anger, and excitement. It is a challenge to calm down and listen when your emotions shift into high gear.

Preoccupation How can you listen if you're worried about your next appointment or distracted by a stain on your shirt? In the ongoing battle for your concentration, the silliest anxieties can crush your ability to listen in the here-and-now.

Exaggeration We hear a remark that strikes a chord, dwell on it, and enlarge its meaning. We listen too much one moment and tune out the next.

Leveling The opposite of exaggeration. Instead of inflating or intensifying a particular message, we deemphasize what was said to the point where nothing stands out. We level off what others say.

Erasing Why listen if the message is unpleasant? It's tempting to screen out any harsh or hostile words simply by erasing them.

You may identify with some if not all of these roadblocks to effective listening. You're not alone. If you have trouble persuading people, it may have nothing to do with what you say or how you say it. All too often, poor listening habits are to blame. We will discuss distortions in more detail in Chapter 10.

Step 3: Speaking. Much More Than Mere Words

Our ancestors began speaking about 1.5 million years ago, when the base of the skull starting bending and the larynx started dropping. Hundreds of centuries later, we are still struggling to get our points across. So much for evolution.

Humans have made great progress in developing the physical ability to produce fully articulate speech. But somewhere down the line our priorities got tangled. Talking is the most overrated aspect of communication.

People enroll in my workshops wondering what to say to get their way. They think that if they could only come up with the right words, they could talk anyone into anything.

If you hold yourself to high standards of verbal expression, convinced that every word must be perfectly chosen to achieve the desired result, you ask for trouble. The most accurate, well-phrased statements in the world will not win over someone who tunes out. You've got to make people listen to you.

One of my students, a math whiz with the mind of a computer, complained that "people just don't listen to me." He added that he was all the more confounded by his inability to persuade because he approached every discussion in the same precise, logical way:

> I arrange what I say in five parts. I introduce the issue, provide some background details, state my position, give supporting arguments, and refute other views. I learned in school that this was how the Greek classicists expressed themselves.

If your college professor asks you to demonstrate the steps of introduction, exposition, proposition, partition and refutation, so be it. But trying to persuade in your everyday life with the precision of a Greek rhetorician hardly guarantees success. In the world outside academia, few will marvel at your airtight argumentation (and you may put people to sleep).

This book puts speaking in its rightful place as one element of your persuasive program, an outgrowth of diligent preparation and careful listening. All three stages—preparing, listening, and speaking—should blend together to maximize your persuasive power.

We will consider speaking holistically, moving beyond word choice to examine the inflection and tempo that influence any message. Your voice can produce a stinging rebuke, a loving coo, or a commanding speech. You can adjust the sound of your voice the same way you fiddle with the "volume" button on your television's remote control. But sometimes our emotions overpower us. Explosive yelling or seething fury can turn any dialogue into a free-for-all. We may not be able to hit the "mute" button in time to save ourselves from a temper tantrum.

The art of questioning saves the day. Asking the proper questions can:

- Defuse tension
- Release nervousness
- Show concern
- Build trust
- Chip away at any lingering resistance or skepticism

Use well-placed questions to suggest alternatives and solutions instead of telling people what to do. When we persuade, we tend to use declarative statements:

I want _____

 I think you should _____

instead of alert questioning

How about trying _____?

What would happen if _____?

Have you considered _____?

The secret of lively speaking lies in your expressiveness. A talker who rambles in a monotone or favors technical jargon over plain English wastes countless opportunities to persuade. Even the best listeners can grow weary of a dull speaker.

Expressiveness results when we bring dry, deadening comments to life. Think of a color scheme consisting of drab, dark shades versus a shimmering, fever-bright spectrum of fire-engine reds and glowing fluorescent yellows. We prefer speakers whose style radiates vibrancy and cheer like the rainbow of colors in a preschooler's romper room. We react less excitedly to a dreary talker who conjures up images of a rainy day with warship gray skies overhead.

Painting pictures with your words helps enliven your remarks. Sharp details, vivid imagery, and traces of irony or humor enhance almost any message. You need not show off your vocabulary or use a thick dictionary to speak in evocative language. Let your words flow naturally from your authentic personality.

It helps to establish a baseline, a beginning point where you and your audience stand side by side. People are more apt to be persuaded by someone who agrees with them. You can then reflect on the past and proceed into the future as allies. Below is a diagram of this persuasive technique.

Here's where we are now ➤ Here are our past successes ➤ Here's an idea for future successes

Launch your persuasive presentation by summarizing the present. Then recall the satisfaction or joy of shared memories (reminding your spouse of your first date, rallying your staff to perform as they did the first day on the job). End with a positive, forward-looking call to action.

The most persuasive appeals attract interest because they are perceived as flowing naturally from whatever is happening now. By framing your idea as a logical extension of the status quo, you can win over people who may fear change.

There is nothing less persuasive than proclaiming that you are "right.' Adults, like children, resist when told what to do. We do not like it when authority figures bark orders at us and we are expected to comply.

We also lose interest when speakers focus on themselves. If you want to win people over, involve them in the conversation. Avoid an overdose of *I*. Use the word that keeps on giving: *YOU*. Note the difference in these two approaches to persuasion:

I-FOCUS:

I know my plan will work.

Just do as I say and it'll be okay.

I need this to get done right away.

YOU-FOCUS:

With your input, the plan will work.

You wi'l be pleasantly surprised if you give it a try.

You can help make this a success.

There's nothing less persuasive (and more obnoxious) than spouting about *your* viewpoints, *your* reasoning, or *your* needs. The only way others will care about you, much less be swayed by what you say, is if they feel like a partner in the dialogue.

● **TRAP** If you state your demands and expect blind obedience, be careful. Don't confuse direction with persuasion. A parent can tell a child to "stop crying or you'll be sent to your room." A manager can tell a clerk to "get that office cleaned up or else." The subjects may comply, but they are left dispirited and angry as deeper problems fester. No one likes to feel subservient. Effective leaders—from parents to coaches to chief executives—use their authority not to issue edicts but to bring people together to achieve a worthy goal.

HOW TO HARNESS YOUR PASSION TO STRENGTHEN YOUR INFLUENCE OVER OTHERS

The best speakers rely less on power than on passion. They ignite us to act by tapping our self-interest. We forget that they are our parents, our bosses, our teachers. They make us feel like partners, not order-takers. They invite us to succeed. They speak with poise and confidence. We follow them because they seem to know what they are talking about. They empower us.

Nothing excites me more in my workshops than individuals who bury their passion. Why? Because I know that if I can show them how to unleash their pent-up feelings, they will thrive. It's that simple. Do you suppress your passion, or do you let it rise to the surface? Take this test and find out:

Diagnostic Self-Test: Your Passion Index

Answer each question and add up the numbers assigned to your responses.

_____ Do you express your feelings freely (1) OR do you prefer to withhold them (2)?

_____ Do you tell those individuals closest to you how you feel about them (1) OR would you rather not discuss your innermost feelings (2)?

_____ Do you allow yourself to get so excited that you act impulsively (1) OR do you prefer to maintain self-control (2)?

_____ Do you react with visible glee to very good news (1) OR do you take it in stride (2)?

_____ Do you find yourself crying or laughing while watching movies (1) OR do you generally not show any emotion (2)?

_____ Do you find that you can communicate comfortably with strangers (1) OR do you become shy and hesitant when meeting someone new (2)?

The lower your score, the more passion you exhibit. If you scored nine or more, then you could probably increase your persuasiveness by letting loose with more unfiltered emotion and expanding your range of communication. Try to stop restraining your passion. A caveat: In some work-related situations, professionalism dictates that you not burst out laughing at a colleague or act like a child, but this should not prevent you from speaking with honest, unbridled feeling.

We warm up to someone who speaks with candor. Honesty, coupled with a dose of vulnerability, works like a charm. Who can refuse to go along with an endearing, likable speaker? Think of the last time you agreed to do someone a favor. Did they ask for your help in a sincere, enthusiastic tone? Did they express appreciation when you agreed? Did you feel better about yourself as a result?

A dose of passion can carry you far. It's even okay to be needy. As long as you approach the issue from the listener's self-interest, you can plead for something and still maintain your dignity. Begging someone is not necessarily a mistake; it backfires only when you insist on getting *your* way. You can get away with quite a bit of nagging when your motives are to selflessly assist others to get what they want. Genuine enthusiasm and concern can penetrate the thickest veil of resistance.

Would-be persuaders often explain their reluctance to speak up by telling me, "I don't know what to say," "I don't like to be a pest," or "They'll just say no anyway." Hearing these comments over and over again led me to write this book. What you say matters. Your ideas and opinions deserve to be heard. But you must not take speaking for granted. Your job is to make others want to listen to you.

HOW THE PREPARE-LISTEN-SPEAK APPROACH PAYS OFF IN EVERYDAY CONVERSATION

To illustrate how the three stages of preparing, listening, and speaking unfold in a typical conversation, let's meet Bill and Mary. Bill, the vice-president of an insurance company, calls one of his underlings, Mary, into his office. Bill wants Mary to do a better job supervising Sam, an entry-level customer service representative. Example 1 shows what can go wrong when Bill fails to prepare, listen, or speak persuasively. Example 2 presents a new, improved Bill.

A Lesson in How NOT to Persuade

Bill: Mary, we still seem to be having a tough time dealing with Sam. Haven't you had that talk with him yet?

Mary: Yes. I sat down with him and discussed his attitude. He said...

Bill: It's not his attitude. It's more than that. He doesn't understand this place. He tells clients to call purchasing or p.r. or whatever...just to get rid of them. He shoves callers onto someone else without trying to help them. I don't know if he has any brains. His negative attitude just makes it worse.

Mary: He snaps sometimes, and that's what I'm wo king on with him. But he really wants to know ou operating procedures. He's new, and he's a slow learner. But I don't think he is deliberately rude to client˜ because he doesn't care.

Bill: Listen, you've got to control him better. Wꞔ talked about this last week, and I thought we agreed you would lay down the law. We've got to treat clients better. You know that's a top priority. I fear that Sam just is not motivated to do his job. You've got to keep an eye on people like him.

Mary: I know, I know. But with Sam, I think the situation calls for patience and encouragement. I keep explaining our procedures to him, and I've introduced him to the heads of each unit. In fact, I've had him practice ways to control his temper when things get crazy. Just last week he...

Bill: There you go again, Mary. Spending way too much time trying to teach your staff what they're not ready to learn. Just this once, put the cards on the table. Tell Sam he needs to learn our procedures NOW. Tell him that people have complained about his attitude. Tell him what we're trying to do in this business so that our expectations are crystal clear. Stop wasting your time making him your own personal reclamation project.

Mary:	I understand. But I've got my own approach, and it has worked for me before.
Bill:	Your approach doesn't work. We've got all these low-level people trying to get away with the least amount of work possible. You can't trust them. You've gotta watch over them and keep telling them what's right and what's wrong. You know how many of them are stealing stuff from us. It seems like every week I'm reprimanding someone else.
Mary:	I don't think they're really stealing anything. Actually, I think…
Bill:	Can you name one innocent person I have accused of stealing?
Mary:	No, I guess not. Listen, if you want me to come down hard I will.
Bill:	I've heard that one before, Mary. We both know you have trouble managing with muscle. You know you've got this reputation for protecting your people. Let's see if you can prove me wrong. Here's your big chance. I gotta run to a board meeting now. [Bill leaps up and races out the door.]
Mary:	[Suddenly left alone in the room] Whatever you say, Bill.

Would you want to work for Bill? No way. He gives bosses a bad name. Bill does almost everything wrong, from interrupting to barking orders to using hearsay as a weapon. He shows no signs of intelligently preparing his remarks or making an effort to truly listen to Mary. When he speaks, he issues commands rather than inviting input.

Bill starts off on an accusatory note ("Haven't you…"). We sense that Bill knows the answer to his opening question, and he is ready to pounce. He does not give Mary much chance to respond and interrupts almost immediately to contradict her ("It's not his attitude…"). Bill makes matters worse by ignoring Mary's next point (that Sam "is a slow learner"); instead, he plows forward with his own agenda. Rather than persuading by suggestion or gentle prodding, Bill blurts out, "Listen, you've got to control him better."

Bill suffers a speaking disorder that tends to afflict those who lack persuasive skills. He launches each sentence with a command (*"Tell* him…," *"Stop* wasting…"). He abuses his power by steamrolling over the thoughts and feelings of his subordinate. Ordering someone around like a servant does not qualify as persuasion.

But that's not all. Bill shows no evidence of preparing his thoughts before opening his mouth. He does not even try to empathize with Mary or organize his ideas in a persuasive manner.

How does he listen? Don't ask. His interruptions indicate that he really isn't interested in Mary's input. He neglects to paraphrase her points or acknowledge her remarks. He is quick to disagree, however, when she states an opinion.

As a speaker, Bill cuts corners instead of fostering a healthy dialogue. His dogmatic assertions ("You have trouble managing with muscle") and crude judgments ("You've got to keep an eye on people like him") sabotage his persuasiveness.

Bill's attempt to motivate Mary by issuing a polarizing challenge ("Prove me wrong") sets the stage for failure by creating a needlessly adversarial relationship. By having the last word and then heading for the door, Bill lets Mary know that her views and feelings are not important. The implicit message to Mary: I don't want to hear another word from you—just do as I say.

Poor Bill. He's a mess. Not only is he less than persuasive, but he's a bully. Mary probably resents him and plots her escape. Let's spruce up his personality and give him a second chance to persuade Mary.

The Right Way to Get Your Point Across and Gain Mutual Understanding

Bill: Mary, how's it going with Sam?

Mary: Well, I sat down with him and discussed his attitude. He said he would try harder. I told him a good place to start would be to learn our procedures.

Bill: That's for sure. What else did you two talk about?

Mary: I asked him how he liked the job. He seems to enjoy it here, but he gets frazzled easily and admitted that he has trouble controlling himself when ten things happen at once.

Bill: That must have made you feel good when he admitted that.

Mary: Yeah, it did. It saved me having to say it. But you know what else? I felt a bit frustrated. He says what I want to hear, but he doesn't follow through. I mean, he'll probably be back to his old self tomorrow.

Bill: Interesting. You may be onto something here. In checking Sam's work, I've found that just when he starts to show improvement, something happens and he's back making the same mistakes.

Mary: He sure requires a lot of attention.

Bill:	Maybe we should try a new tactic. Say you gave him a weekly production goal and left him alone to see how he performed. Promise him a reward if he meets the goal and warn him of the consequences if he doesn't. Dangle a carrot and a stick. I've found this approach prevents misunderstanding, increases morale, and focuses everyone's attention on results.
Mary:	Sounds good to me. I'll give it a try.
Bill:	Great. Keep me posted.

Meet the new, improved Bill. He's a nicer, more patient, sensitive guy. He understands how to communicate persuasively. Better yet, he can actually conduct a pleasant two-way conversation. What happened?

Reread both dialogues. Notice the differences in Bill's style. In Example 2, he talks less and listens more. When he does speak, he either encourages Mary to talk or offers positive ideas to assist her in handling Sam. He does not waste words, resort to confrontation, or interrupt. In fact, he appears genuinely interested in what Mary has to say.

Mary may not realize it, but Bill planned ahead of time to offer his suggestion to set a weekly production goal. He wanted to persuade her to adopt his plan, so he identified three benefits (prevents misunderstanding, increases morale, focuses attention on results) and waited for the right moment in the conversation to propose this solution. See how preparation works?

As a listener, Bill prompts Mary to speak. He asks questions instead of dishing out orders. He probes into Mary's feelings and lets her respond. He does not jump in while she talks. The new Bill listens for understanding, not agreement.

When he opens his mouth, Bill expresses himself clearly and provides constructive input. He does not ramble. He acknowledges Mary's remarks in positive terms ("That's for sure," "Great," "You may be onto something here"). He avoids criticism and steers the conversation toward a solution.

○ **NOW TRY THIS**   Barriers to clear communication make it harder to persuade. This exercise will help you identify key skills that we will develop further in the chapters ahead. Check all statements that describe you:

_____   I am more of a talker than a listener.

_____   I often find myself faking it: pretending to listen while I think about other things.

_____   I tend to use the time when someone else is speaking to think of what I want to say next.

_____ I am a selective listener (I pay more attention to a speaker whom I like or respect).

_____ My mind wanders when I must listen to a babbler.

_____ I often interrupt people who cannot express themselves in a concise manner.

If you checked any (or all!) of these statements, use this book as a resource to overcome these barriers. Just about everyone faces at least some of these same obstacles, so you're not alone.

Preparing, listening, and speaking will lead you to almost any persuasive goal. But not so fast. Sometimes we let fear get in the way. Before exploring each stage of your persuasive program in more detail, we will learn in the next chapter how to rid ourselves of the self-doubt that can undermine our confidence. We can successfully persuade only when we are willing to risk rejection. Shoving fear aside makes us truly unstoppable.

QUICK REVIEW

- Prepare to persuade with the firm belief that you can change someone's mind.
- Don't sell yourself short and weaken your will to persuade.
- Suggest ways for others to be generous at little cost to themselves.
- Identify what will motivate or induce others to act as you wish.
- Ask friends to help you anticipate objections and prepare crisp responses.
- Ask concise questions to increase your attentiveness, build rapport, and learn.
- Don't let a short attention span or distortions undermine your ability to listen.
- Speak to persuade only *after* you have taken the time to prepare and listen.
- Speak in visual pictures to enliven your remarks and increase expressiveness.
- Establish a baseline where you and your audience stand side by side.
- Speak in terms of YOU-FOCUS, not I-FOCUS.

2

Conquering the Fear of Asking for What You Want

The world is full of threats. As I write this, a major earthquake has just shaken Los Angeles. A severe winter storm blankets much of the rest of the United States. Today's newspaper reports that guns kill more people than cars. With so many serious risks lurking in our midst, it seems ironic that so many individuals are scared to ask for something.

Persuasion is hardly a matter of life or death.

But that does not stop some in my seminars from working themselves into a frenzy when faced with the challenge of verbal communication. Some of their comments:

I go to a lot of lectures, most of which are followed by a question-and-answer period. My heart palpitates when I contemplate asking a question, even though I'm seated in an audience where most people don't even know who I am. Raising my hand becomes tough because my whole arm feels numb.

My boss likes to get everyone's input at our weekly meetings. My mouth goes dry whenever I'm asked for my opinion. It's a little better when we're having a one-on-one chat, but I still feel so anxious. I don't want to say anything stupid or express an opinion that differs too much from everyone else's.

There's nothing worse than a job interview. I spent six months job hunting, and it was agonizing. Waiting to be called into an interview, I'd break out in an icy sweat. Beads would form all over my forehead. My underarms were soaked. My back stuck to my shirt. All this before I even entered the interviewer's office.

It's hard to discuss communication without coming right out and admitting it: We're all scared. Fear blocks concentration. With so much to worry about (fear of ignorance, fear of rejection, fear of misunderstanding, fear of manipulation), we need methods to handle these potentially devastating barriers to clear communication.

Erving Goffman has described personal encounters as situations that place both parties in jeopardy—at risk of "losing face."[1] We risk rejection of our message and ourselves whenever we try to persuade. We may worry about coming across as a pest, triggering a tirade, or suffering the humiliation and disappointment of having someone ignore us or prove us wrong. No wonder earthquakes and snowstorms seem tame in comparison!

I know what it's like to dread having to persuade, especially when it comes to asking for favors. I'm almost constantly asking for things, from input on my writing to a friend's help moving boxes. The fear is palpable. Rationally, I know the worst that can happen is others will say no. Tell that to my dry mouth and pounding heart. After years of experiencing this fear, I've learned that it is a necessary byproduct of persuasion. I cannot make it go away, so I transform it from an immobilizing force to a catalyst that ignites my energy and enthusiasm.

What causes all this fear to come raining down on us? Why worry about losing face? That's simple: All of us want *respect*, and all of us want to be *liked*. Credibility and liking are the two most important factors in persuasion. Just about everyone wants more of both. No matter how much we have, it is never enough.

Instead of worrying about being liked or respected, strive for authenticity. Just be yourself. People welcome any kind of genuineness, and most of us learn at an early age how to spot a fake. Your unbridled personality is your best asset even with its flaws and foibles. Any attempt to hide your real, believable self and present a false "front" to the outside world will backfire. Artificiality will not help you establish credibility or make people like you.

We are more apt to favor those who seem comfortable with themselves, who do not put on airs. We like individuals who carry themselves with the attitude, "Take me or leave me, but what you see is what you get."

There's nothing wrong with wanting to be liked. Whenever we try to win over a group, most of us wonder, *Do they like me?* To come up with an answer, we ask ourselves, *Do I like me?* or *If I were they, would I like me?* Then we project onto the audience our own standards, preferences, and biases. All too often, we serve as our own worst critics. We decide, *They must hate me. They see my phoniness, they hear my nasal voice, and...*

To make matters worse, some of us are well acquainted with that nagging inner voice that spreads self-doubt. As much as we want to communicate with charm and charisma, we wind up thinking *Boy, am I coming across like a jerk.* or *I'm not making any sense.* The solution? Shut off the radio inside your head that keeps putting you down. You will not conquer your fear by replaying the tape that begins *Your problem is...*

Anxiety can foil attempts at persuasion. Sometimes it's easier to keep quiet, to retreat into a shell where we can protect our fragile sense of self. But that means we pass up countless opportunities to speak up. Our ideas go unnoticed, our warnings unheeded, our strengths unrecognized.

Rather than succumb to the crippling role of fear and allow it to bury your will to persuade, this chapter identifies the major sources of anxiety and gives you strategies to fight back. You must not yield to sweaty palms or dizzying flashes of self-doubt. It's time to pull out all the stops and let loose with the full power and presence of your personality.

HOW TO OVERCOME RESISTANCE SO THAT PEOPLE SAY "YES" 90% OF THE TIME

You can fool some of the people some of the time, but you can't persuade all of the people all of the time.

No salesperson can win every order. No politician can earn every vote. No teacher can coax every student to study. Preachers, lawyers, doctors, counselors...they all fail to persuade some of the time. Every persuader, no matter how knowledgeable or passionate, confronts resistance and rejection.

There are no guarantees in human communication. Accept this fact, and you will save yourself a lot of fretting. I recall one disgruntled real estate agent who asked me how he could rebound from a terrible year. "I lost one sale after another," he complained. When I asked how he defined "terrible," he said that he had sold seventeen expensive homes, but that a handful of deals had fallen apart at the last minute. Most of his colleagues would happily have settled for such a year.

No one, with the possible exception of the Pope, is infallible. We all suffer setbacks and fail to persuade. Our best hope is to keep matters in perspective and play the percentages. If you succeeded all the time, you would probably become an arrogant bore. Better to settle for, say, a 90 percent success rate. Do not expect people to agree with your every utterance.

Leave room for differences in opinion or outlook. Realize that in some cases you can communicate masterfully and still come up short.

○ **NOW TRY THIS** Compute your persuasive batting average. Chart each attempt by listing the topic of your persuasive appeal, the audience, and the outcome. Here's an example of how one individual kept score during a typical day:

TOPIC	*AUDIENCE*	*OUTCOME*
Ask for lower rent	Landlord	Yes. Effective 1–1–95
Borrow van on Saturday	A friend	Yes
Sign up library volunteers	Speech to 40 community members	25 names on sign-up sheet
Ask for refund from antique shop	Owner of shop	No. Against shop's policy
Get insurance co. to cover claim	Insurance claim adjuster	Yes

Four out of five. Not bad. Rather than get upset at the shop owner for refusing to issue a refund, celebrate the four successes. Why dwell on the one encounter that got away? Perhaps you can learn something valuable from it (like never do business again with that shop, or always save your receipt). There is less to fear if you focus on the big picture and accept that a certain percentage of "at bats" will not produce "hits."

Salespeople often fear "closing," or asking for the order. Gabbing away with a friendly prospect is no problem, but when the time comes to seal the deal, the fear of failure can be overpowering. Although professional salespeople train themselves to expect yes and rebound from no, others scurry out the door without ever knowing what the potential buyer would have said.

Closing requires the intestinal fortitude to face rejection head-on. Whenever we ask for something, from a friend's forgiveness to a prospect's signature on the dotted line, we accept the possibility of a negative answer. The response may hurt, humble, or humiliate us, but we take that risk. Yet a salesperson's fear of hearing "no" can become a psychological barrier, a roadblock that can put the brakes on the most smooth, persuasive presentation. This fear takes on a life all its own and can serve as a particularly virulent form of self-sabotage.

If you grow uneasy asking for the order, try a bit of role reversal. Imagine that the prospect, Dan, has been listening to you sell for fifteen minutes. Dan spends this time considering the purchase, posing questions, and approaching a buying decision. Dan is no dummy. He fully expects you to ask for the sale, and he's waiting. The cruel irony of closing is that while you sweat and battle mental demons, Dan has already made up his mind to buy. He may be convincing himself to spend the money, or visualizing ownership of the product, or predicting what his friends will say when he brags about his purchase. After passing a certain point in the conversation, he wants to say yes, but you do not give him a chance.

Turn Nervousness into Energy and Excitement

It's normal to be scared in the moments before you open your mouth and try to persuade. But that does not mean your anxiety must become a liability. Turn your nervousness into raw energy and excitement. Drown your fear in a sea of optimism. Don't let it spill over into your conversation. As Morton Janklow, an attorney and literary agent, wrote, "Most people, when attempting to advance a point of view persuasively, become fearful that they will fail, and that fear is conveyed to the person they are trying to persuade. It is the surest way to fail."[2]

How do you hide your fear so that no one can see you sweat? Remember that your audience cannot read your mind. They have no way of knowing what thoughts rush through your head while you speak. By maintaining composure and presenting a confident, commanding face to the world, you can quiet your butterflies or at least get them to fly in formation.

Even if listeners detect a trace of nervousness, don't worry. They will forgive you for an occasional mistake, from loudly clearing your throat to an embarrassing Freudian slip. But if you muffle phrase after phrase or let a slight twitch turn into a raging flare-up, then the audience will grow distracted.

MEMORY JOGGER

It is okay to feel nervous when you try to persuade. But that's no reason to make your listeners nervous, too.

Those who anticipate they will be proved wrong sell themselves short. Instead of speaking with clarity, they swallow the ends of their sentences. Instead of establishing eye contact, they bow their heads or look away. Instead of boldly expressing their ideas, they use qualifiers or excuses that weaken their position. They slouch and appear self-conscious.

These are some of the dead giveaways that *fear* controls *you* rather than the other way around.

Your nervousness may peak in the minutes just before you launch a persuasive appeal. Whether as a job candidate waiting to be summoned into an interview or a home buyer about to negotiate the purchase price of a property, you surely have experienced the jitters. Some people tell me they cannot stand the stress of awaiting a big speech or an important meeting, because they think of everything that can go wrong. They focus on failure. Riddled with doubts and second thoughts, they convince themselves that their attempt at persuasion will prove a disaster.

Do not play this cruel waiting game. Approach the hours and minutes before you persuade by expecting the fear to reach a crescendo. Nerves are supposed to act up when you persuade. Your blood pressure will be higher than normal. You should be more worried if you do not experience any fear, because this may indicate you don't care about what you're saying. Treat the anxiety as a prelude to your remarks—an advance check that all systems are go. Remind yourself that once you start talking, the nervousness will subside as you establish a conversational rhythm.

Think of the last time you delivered a speech. In the moments before you were introduced, you were a mental wreck. But then you began to talk. With each passing sentence, you relaxed a bit more and eventually hit your stride. You were too busy connecting with your listeners to think about any lingering fears of failure. The worst part is scaling the steep hill that stands in the way of your presentation—the seemingly endless hours that tick away before the time comes to persuade.

Four Ways to Transform Fear into Positive Energy

How can you transform fear into positive energy? Each of you is different, so I cannot prescribe one foolproof strategy for everyone. Pick and choose what works for you from among these techniques:

Send mental messages.   In the moments before you begin speaking, give yourself a mental command such as "Let's go," "Win 'em over" or "Let's have fun." Rally yourself to victory by signaling that you are about to succeed. Sending an upbeat mental message can launch your persuasive appeal in a triumphant, supremely confident frame of mind.

Relax by breathing properly.   Beware of choppy panic breathing. Inhale and exhale as though guiding the oars of a rowboat. I use a mental image from when I rowed on my college crew squad; I recall the rhythmic stroking of the oars as the team paddled in unison, the joy of rowing evenly to gain speed. Regulate your breathing the same way you would pull that oar in and out of the water with long, smooth, relaxed strokes. We discuss proper breathing in more detail in Chapter 13.

Get the moves. Do not bottle your tension—unleash it! Tell your body that you are in control, and the same message will be sent to the brain. In the moments before you persuade, shake your body from head to toe, tilt your head back and forth, and drop your jaw and yawn a few times. Even while you are face to face with your listeners, you can wiggle your toes or twirl your fingers under the desk. This increases blood circulation and reduces anxiety. Do not cross your legs, or one of them might fall asleep. Every move you make will burn off excess nervousness and send bursts of physical vitality through your system.

Visualize positive images. You have probably seen weight-loss advertisements with BEFORE and AFTER photographs of satisfied customers. Before you persuade, imagine that you have already won over your audience. Smile like the happy people who have lost fifty pounds in the AFTER photos. This visualization exercise helps you feel victorious before uttering a sound. Other variations of this technique: Envision yourself gleefully heading downhill after climbing a mountain or walking off a winning marathon race. Or try conjuring up a peaceful scene in another part of the world. I sometimes recall a mental snapshot of a picturesque meadow in Amsterdam that I visited as a child. I think, "I wonder what's going on right now at that meadow." My frayed nerves cool off as my mind drifts to another time and place. Create soothing mental images to reduce your fear.

NO ONE'S ALWAYS RIGHT! HOW TO BOUNCE BACK AND WIN OVER ANYBODY EVEN AFTER YOU'RE WRONG

Some people just hate to be wrong. They stake their identity on their self-perceived "rightness." Any attempt at persuasion threatens their equilibrium, because they risk being exposed as having a poor command of facts or using faulty reasoning. Such a visible and embarrassing blow can ruin a carefully crafted reputation.

This kind of fear can entrap us in the snares of inaction, stalling, and rationalization. I have a few perfectionists in almost every one of my workshops whose desire for precise expression, while admirable at times, can produce a reluctant persuader who prefers to stay on the sidelines. Safe from rejection and protected from imperfection, they let life pass by and wait for that illusory perfect opportunity. It never arrives.

You cannot sell your ideas if you are convinced you are right and everyone else is wrong. Persuasion is not a zero-sum game. Subtle shadings of right/wrong and good/bad make it impossible to pick clear winners and losers in every conversation. Say a salesperson gives you the wrong information about a product. If she discovers the error, admits the mistake, and provides you with the correct information, you may trust the salesperson *more* than if the mistake had never happened. The ability to acknowledge a mishap and fix it can be the most persuasive move of all.

○ **Now Try This** If you want to conquer your fear of persuasion, look for opportunities to admit you are wrong. That's right—welcome a chance to say, "You know, you've made me see things differently," "I'm sorry for giving you incorrect information," or "Thanks for pointing that out." These kinds of comments demonstrate fairness and open-mindedness. Do not fear appearing human; after all, every mortal makes mistakes. None of us should be so proud that we cannot apologize for an error or admit when we screw up. People will respect your humility and honesty, and they will be more apt to heed your advice or listen to your views.

The fear of being wrong leads many politicians to lose the voters' trust. Instead of owning up to past indiscretions or admitting some bad judgment, public figures tend to hide behind legalistic explanations that no one believes. Lawyers read lifeless statements to the press, leaving the public even more convinced something is amiss. I keep waiting for a politician to say, "Here are all the facts. I was wrong. I'm sorry." That person would have my vote for life.

One politician who did not fear being proved wrong was Ronald Reagan. Reagan, like Abraham Lincoln, enjoyed telling anecdotes to illustrate his points. Yet Reagan's stories were often misleading or factually incorrect. David Gergen, a senior aide to Reagan (and later to Bill Clinton), described Reagan's anecdotes, like the one about poor people using food stamps to buy liquor, as "parables." He added that the public does not demand that Reagan be literally right "so long as the symbolic truth is defensible."[3] I guess Gergen was right, because Reagan was reelected in a landslide in 1984. The president's questionable command of facts did not affect his popularity or ability to lead.

Maybe the president can get away without apologizing for repeated verbal blunders, but most of us are better off admitting it when we screw up. I have had many sons and daughters tell me that their father "never says he's sorry" or "never admits he made a mistake." The same is occasionally said about a mother. Such a parent will not persuade children and will probably grow apart from them in later years.

In the corporate world, fearful managers may resort to bullying rather than persuasion. Instead of praising workers or leading by example, supervisors who insist on being right all the time will automatically poke holes in everyone else's ideas. Another ploy is to pose a question that they know their listener cannot answer, thus reinforcing their own sense of rightness at the expense of a colleague. This way, they never have to worry about the unpleasant prospect of being contradicted (especially by a lowly underling!).

MEMORY JOGGER

Individuals who are able to admit they are wrong win us over. Their honesty and humility are hard to resist.

Fear will crush your persuasiveness if you perceive the audience as a threatening, judgmental, adversarial force. You may hold yourself to an unrealistic standard of performance, convinced that you are being graded for every move you make. You will bury your authentic personality under all this stifling self-consciousness.

Think of the people you want to persuade (friends, family, clients, upper management). Do you tend to view these people as critics waiting to pounce on your every word? Your challenge is to see them for who they really are: individuals who hope to learn something useful from you. They are not going to attack you the moment you show vulnerability. Chances are they simply want to gain something from you, to derive some personal or professional benefit from what you say.

A young woman in one of my seminars, Sarah, disagreed when I made this point. A professional money manager and certified financial planner, she said that some people do not want to learn something from you and may not even listen to you. "I know someone who argues with me all the time, who seems to talk to me only when he thinks he can prove me wrong," she said. "I'm talking about my father-in-law."

"Why does he argue with you?" I asked.

"He never liked me, and he wanted his son to marry a different kind of woman—a gal who stayed home instead of having a career," Sarah explained. "So now, every time we're together, he tries to humiliate me in front of his son as if to say, 'See, I told you not to marry her. She doesn't know anything.' I dread being in the same room with him."

"How do you react when he does this?"

"I fight back," Sarah said immediately. "I don't back down and take it. Nothing gets resolved, but at least I let everyone know that I can stand up for myself. I'm operating partly out of fear, because I don't want my husband to start acting like his father."

Sarah and I devised a plan. The next time she and her father-in-law argued, she would resist the urge to return his verbal punches. "If you really want to win him over," I cautioned her, "you need to stop falling for the bait. Don't automatically start defending yourself. Even if you think you're right and you know he's wrong, you will exert more influence over him if you take control and come on over to his side."

Sarah returned to the seminar two weeks later with a triumphant look on her face. "Listen to this," she began. "The other day my father-in-law announces that I gave him poor advice on what to do with his pension money. For once, I didn't argue. I just sat back and said, 'You know, I guess I steered you wrong.'"

"What happened next?" I asked.

"We sat down to dinner. Over the course of the meal, he kept picking fights with me. He claimed I was wrong about a lot of things, from my opinion on the local schools to my views on the upcoming election. I refused to argue; I just kept quiet. My husband couldn't believe it! By the time we ate dessert, my father-in-law had run out of steam and stopped being so difficult."

"Have you spoken with him since then?"

"Yes. Once I learned to keep quiet and even admit he was right, he didn't attack me any more," Sarah reported. "Now he asks me questions! Suddenly, he seems to think I have something valuable to say. Yesterday he actually called to thank me for my input on a real-estate investment."

Sarah's experience reminds us that you can take charge of even the most unpleasant situations by transcending petty arguments that boil down to "I'm right and you're wrong." When Sarah was willing to be viewed as "wrong" by her father-in-law, she broke through a communication barrier. For the first time, she could persuade her father-in-law because he was finally willing to listen to her.

GOT A GOOD IDEA?
STEP UP TO THE PLATE AND SAY SO

Assertiveness-training seminars enjoyed much popularity during the sixties and seventies. Adults flocked to these sessions to develop more confidence and leadership skills. They learned how to express themselves in a direct, forceful way. Many participants left feeling on top of the world, as if their feelings and opinions really mattered for the first time.

So what happened? Here we are well into the nineties and some individuals still resist taking leadership roles, remaining in the background while others grab center stage. They might be frightened of giving a speech, meeting "important" people, arriving at a party alone, even making a phone call.

Each of us has a different threshold of fear. It often takes the form of a general feeling of uneasiness that forms in the unconscious recesses of our mind. In the presence of powerful or authoritative figures, we may turn to mush. Disagreeing with the boss sends shivers down our spine. Taking a stand at a City Council meeting proves harrowing. Picking a verbal fight with a formidable opponent sets off a physiological meltdown of irregular breathing and free-flowing perspiration. Persuasion can be off limits for unassuming types who would prefer to keep quiet.

It's your call, of course, whether to speak up or clam up. But when you choose to withhold your views or pass on the chance to sway opinion, you send the implicit message that your experience, insight, and ideas are less important than the speaker's. You devalue yourself. When you avoid exerting influence, you leave a vacuum that someone else inevitably fills. Persuasion swirls around you whether you like it or not. You might as well step into the batter's box and take a swing.

How to Overcome Fear and Boost Your Self-Image, One Day at a Time

To overcome the fear of making yourself heard, you need to develop a stronger, more rooted sense of who you are and what you believe in. Without a strong sense of self, your confidence will ebb and flow like gyrations in the stock market, depending on the amount of approval that you receive from others. A bright but unsuccessful insurance agent once complained to me, "I've had so many doors slammed in my face that I've given up trying to pretend I'm in control. I feel dependent on others. I've come to expect that prospects will treat me like dirt, that I must be subservient to survive."

Sounds depressing, and it is. He had become dislodged from his identity. Instead of accepting himself or at least drawing upon reserves of self-esteem, he let others call the shots. He lost or gained self-respect based on what someone else thought of him. The more he suffered rejection, the more he craved approval. Caught in this downhill spiral, he continually needed validation from the outside to convince himself he was a "good" or "successful" person.

MEMORY JOGGER

Never allow another person's opinion of you to be more important than your own.

Fear of taking charge results in part from the psychological survival mechanism known as "fight or flight." Put simply, this phenomenon has evolved in humans as a response to physical hazards. It began among primitive peoples when they realized that their very survival depended on others. Today, it manifests itself as a subconscious sense that our safety and security rest in the hands of outsiders who wield power over us (the boss, a parent, a big client). Our conscious mind assures us that these people do not pose an immediate danger to our life and limb, but that may not stop us from perceiving them as a threat to our well being.

By linking our survival to what others think of us, we set ourselves up for a fall. If we detect disapproval or fear rejection, we crumble. We feel like a piece of meat being inspected for excess fat. We can tell when we don't make the grade, and we panic. It hurts too much to talk, so we move to the back of the line while others shine in the spotlight.

Shy people, according to recent medical studies, tend to have higher than normal blood pressure because of the stress they experience in social situations. They are worried about what they are going to say next, so it becomes harder to calmly listen and enjoy the give-and-take of a conversation.

Coupled with the "fight or flight" response is our fluctuating confidence level. One day, we wake up ready to lead troops into battle; by dusk, we hide in the shadows hoping that no one notices us. Even when we assert ourselves, we are so busy wondering what our audience thinks of us that we neglect to concentrate on the message. A high school teacher confessed to me, "I like to think I can handle a room of thirty unruly teens, but every time I open my mouth in class lately I find myself thinking, 'They see right through me' or 'They see I'm a softie.'"

The road to a stronger self-image comes in increments. When fighting the collective force of centuries of human evolution, overnight cures will not work. Ideally, you want to set stages to measure your progress, from asserting a mild preference to expressing a controversial opinion to ultimately building a persuasive case. Each step requires greater leadership and self-reliance. Each challenge poses tougher obstacles that stand in the way of success.

Train yourself to handle nervousness by starting small. Practice overcoming anxiety in your daily life. With each step forward, you move closer to developing the mentality of a leader.

Take this diagnostic exam to help you pinpoint areas where your fears block your persuasiveness:

Diagnostic Self-Test: Pinpoint Your Fears

Answer yes or no to the following five questions:

_____ Do you feel uneasy showing up at a party alone?

_____ Are you reluctant to state a viewpoint that differs from what everyone else thinks?

_____ Do you have trouble refusing a friend's request for you to do something?

_____ Do you resist having to negotiate a purchase price or a contract?

_____ Do you avoid calling people on the phone to ask for something?

If you answered yes to any of these questions, identify the action you seek to avoid and DO IT. Make the effort and observe the results. The satisfaction that comes from taking a risk and testing your assertiveness will outweigh the initial discomfort. Each small win conditions you for a larger win. Conquering your fear of hearing no, for instance, will make you a better negotiator. When you champion an unpopular position that reflects your sincere beliefs, you enhance your ability to persuade resistant or hostile audiences. As your confidence and self-assuredness rises, so will your persuasive power.

○ **Now Try This**   If you want to sharpen your leadership skills, begin with word choice. Avoid talking in passive tenses, relying on qualifiers, or overdosing on dead verbs (such as *is, was, has*). Instead, infuse your remarks with immediacy and energy by speaking in the present tense with active verbs. Be direct; do not diminish your ideas with vague or ambiguous comments. This exercise requires that you fight the inclination to speak softly and carry no stick. Some examples:

- Replace "I thought it might be a good idea if we sat down and talked" with "I think we will both benefit by meeting each other."
- Replace "Perhaps we could get together sometime" with "Would you like to join me next Friday for dinner?"
- Replace "I'm not sure that is a good idea" with "That idea makes some sense, and I propose we _____."

By speaking clearly and using forceful words to drill home your points, you can conquer your anxieties and concentrate on the art of persuasion. This is one more step to help you control your fears rather than vice versa.

ABOLISH NEGATIVE THOUGHT PATTERNS TO REFRAME YOUR ATTITUDE

Each of us face nerve-wracking situations where we must stare down our fear. The test might come at any time:

- A manager must fire a loyal employee.
- A teenager stands up to an overprotective parent.
- A salesperson asks for a big order.
- A substance abuser admits the addiction and commits to breaking free.
- A bashful individual delivers a speech in front of a packed audience.

Routine communication is hard enough, but the challenge escalates when we find it hard to concentrate because we're agitated or frightened.

The obvious solution—to banish the fear—rarely works. Irrational feelings are not subject to rational laws. Good luck trying to deny or suppress anxiety: It will not go away. As a banking supervisor told me, "I was asked to lay off six of my clerks, and I told myself this was just part of the job. I was determined not to let it get to me. But it really hurt. As bad as they must have felt when I broke the news, I was a nervous wreck. I could barely eat or sleep the next few days."

Individuals respond to fear in different ways. Some people accept it and try to persevere. Others shove it aside and hope they can avoid whatever makes them uncomfortable. Like riders who fall from a horse, we can either jump back on the saddle or take up a safer hobby like gin rummy.

The worst way to handle fear is to let it dampen our attitude. Successful persuaders know how to harness the power of positive thinking even in moments of extreme stress. Do not allow fear to turn you into a brooding pessimist. Plagued by dark mood swings, you can talk yourself out of anything before uttering a sound. You may wind up projecting your own gloom-and-doom anxiety onto others in the form of negative judgments.

Think back to the last time you were truly scared to persuade. You probably worried yourself sick contemplating all that could go wrong. You went through one worst-case scenario after another, from the humiliation of failure to the embarrassment of appearing helpless, desperate, or incompetent.

Let's just hope you did not resent your listeners or blame them for your fear. Some of us lash out at others as a way of unleashing internal tension. In our search for a coping mechanism, we may greet the audience with an outpouring of ill will. Instead of appealing to the finer aspects of the human spirit, we stew in vengeful anger. This is clearly no way to treat the very people we seek to win over.

MEMORY JOGGER

Your odds of persuading people soar when you hold them in high regard. If you unfairly judge the individuals you want to persuade, your task grows harder.

Take the rough-and-tumble world of politics. When candidates begin sinking in the polls or losing faith in their campaigns, a typical response is a media blitz with negative commercials about the opponent. Instead of *Vote for me because I'm a winner,* the ads say *Don't vote for X because he's a liar.* Candidates with a commanding lead can afford to take the moral high ground and stick to uplifting messages. But when running scared, they fling mud and uncover sleaze—anything to denigrate the opposition.

The upshot of all this nastiness in a political race is that voters tune out. The more negative a campaign, the less likely that the candidates will draw supporters to the polls on election day.

You will not persuade anyone over the long haul by making your audience feel bad or appealing to their base instincts. Negative advertising sways a few fence-sitting voters, but it also leaves scars that will not soon heal. What's worse, you may find yourself using negativity to insult rather than to persuade your audience. As Alan Baron, a Washington pundit, warned unsuccessful Democratic presidential aspirants throughout the 1980s, "When you indicate to people that they are selfish and stupid, you lose two groups of voters: those who are, and those who aren't."[4]

The Three Most Destructive Mental Messages and How to Avoid Them

By identifying the most destructive attitudes that can sabotage persuasion, we can devise strategies to overcome them. To abolish negative thought patterns, feed yourself positive mental messages.

All or nothing Sloppy communicators favor simplistic either-or thinking. Fearful of engaging in a free-flowing dialogue, they prefer to establish boundaries and pick a side. They demand a "yes" or "no" without room for compromise or discussion. They leave no middle ground, no gray areas, and no flexibility. Examples:

- The union leader who declares "either you're with me or against me" instead of rallying widespread support by reflecting the views of diverse constituents.
- A mother who tells her teenage daughter, "If you don't earn a spot on the cheerleading squad, then you will have thrown away all your talent." A more supportive parent would encourage her daughter to sample a range of activities and then choose one to pursue to the best of her ability.
- The supervisor who tells a subordinate, "Either we do it my way or it just won't get done right." If you have ever worked for someone, you may have heard this line and snickered under your breath. A bank clerk told me, "My manager insists that I process business his way, but I've figured out another way that saves an hour a day. There's no room for innovation where I work, because the middle managers are so scared of losing their jobs. They just play it safe." Smart bosses do not dictate how work must be performed; instead, they set goals and motivate workers to achieve those goals.

Successful persuaders reframe the narrow either-or mindset in terms of opportunity or perspective. They would rather win over more people by remaining open to different opinions. They do not insist on having one "right" answer; instead, they reach consensus by considering a range of ideas.

Condescension We detest speakers who "talk down" to us. There is no better way lose friends and alienate people than to cast yourself as the font of all knowledge. The subtext of this dubious approach to persuasion is, "You do not possess my level of intelligence, so keep quiet and listen to me." Examples:

- A friend who attended medical school told me about the "smarty-pants guy" who was always showing off his knowledge in class. "The professor asked this know-it-all to lead a class project," my friend recalled. "But we rebelled against him and didn't follow his lead at all. We just could not stand his haughty attitude, and after a while we just ignored him."

- Some salespeople hit us over the head with the beauty and benefits of what they sell. They brag about their vast knowledge of the product. They regale us with windy anecdotes about other clients who "listened carefully to every word I said" and wound up happy. We resist buying from salespeople who insist that they know what's best for us.

If we stake our self-worth on our superiority over others (secretly living each day with the fear that someone will expose us as a fraud or a know-nothing), then we will try to win people over by proclaiming we know more than they do. When I was leading a workshop for a group of stock brokers, one participant kept interrupting the session to declare, "I see how all this might work for most people, but *I* can hold an audience's attention by telling them what to do. Without me, they're stupid—they don't know a thing." Would you buy stocks from this man?

Condescending speakers preach and pontificate at will. They fling insults and accusations at their listeners. Rather than connecting with others, they remain aloof and erect barriers that block mutual understanding We laugh when Archie Bunker patronizes his neighbors on *All in the Family* reruns, but when it hits close to home the consequences are anything but funny.

The best persuaders never boss us around. They know that in order to make a lasting favorable impression, they must make us think that it's our idea to adopt their plan or buy their product. They don't advertise their expertise or make us feel inferior. Like Benjamin Franklin, they play the role of the "humble inquisitor," asking gentle questions and engaging us in a nonthreatening dialogue that promotes mutual understanding. Even if they *do* know more than we do, they rarely let it show[1]

Labels   I'll spare you the lecture on prejudice. Some would-be persuaders, scared or intimidated by "different" people, are too busy attaching labels to others to actually listen to them. This negative thought pattern sounds like this: *you are _____ and all _____ behave that way* or *People like you are so _____*. With these sweeping judgments, a fearful or insecure individual can deny the legitimacy of someone with a different opinion or outlook. Resorting to overgeneralization offers an easy way out—a means of avoiding the issue. For example:

- The proliferation of talk-radio show hosts who spout opinions about "those crazy leftists" or "the far-right-wing lunatics." They are forever categorizing callers as pro-this or anti-that. Everyone gets labeled, but no one listens.

- The owner of a woman's clothing boutique confessed to me that she would "size up" shoppers the moment they entered the store. "I admit it—I was labeling like crazy," she laughed. "I would look at the way they were dressed, their jewelry, pocketbooks, shoes. Sometimes I caught myself judging them on their age or race. I'm ashamed to say that I would treat them differently based on whether I thought they would spend a lot of money in my store."

- When we ask a stranger for directions, the time, or change for a dollar, we tend to seek out someone who looks like us. We are generally more comfortable asking a favor from someone who seems familiar. We may stay away from people who look "strange" or who, because they are unlike the kind of people we are used to, strike us as threatening.

To avoid labeling, fight your fear of the "unknown." Welcome opportunities to interact with people from different backgrounds or cultures. Do not fall into the trap of assuming that an individual's behavior is representative of an entire group.

Here are some ways to feed yourself positive, open-minded messages about others:

- If you strongly disagree with a particular political party, religion, or general movement (whether it's feminism, gun lovers, or environmentalists), expose yourself to such views. You may not change your beliefs, but you can still strengthen your persuasive communication skills by learning to listen to positions far afield from your own.

- Whenever you give a speech, the inclination is to direct your eye contact at friendly faces. The next time you deliver a presentation, make an effort to look at people who do not strike you as particularly friendly. That's right, find the scowlers, the frowners, the ones whom you would not want to meet late at night in a dark alley. Find faces dissimilar to your own. You will soon find yourself feeling more at ease addressing even the most unhappy, menacing, hostile-looking members of the audience.

- If you are trying to persuade someone whom you have labeled unfairly, then you will not succeed. Step back from the conversation and establish a base of agreement. Like a shrewd negotiator who begins from a position of alignment (*We both agree that we want to arrive at a mutually beneficial outcome, right?*), find some way for the two of you to start on equal footing with a shared goal.

If you catch yourself adopting any of these negative thought patterns—from either-or thinking to condescension to labeling—reframe your mindset so that you fairly accept your audience.

MEMORY JOGGER

Persuasion is not done *to* someone but *with* someone.

Treat every encounter as a positive event. Develop a habit of talking to people, especially those outside your normal set of friends and work acquaintances. The simple act of initiating a conversation breeds confidence and helps you overcome fear. When the time comes to persuade, you will already see yourself as outgoing, curious, and friendly. Your engaging manner will lower defenses all around and make you a more commanding communicator.

Some people in my workshops resist the notion of planning how to act, what to say, and how to respond. They fear coming across as manipulative or insincere. They dislike my use of the word "strategies," insisting that it is a cynical use of mind games to get what you want. They do not like the idea of "practicing" how to persuade by applying "rules"—they prefer to "just be natural."

This book is not about teaching you how to fake it or resort to artiface to persuade. My intent is not to give you tools to flagrantly manipulate others; rather, the skills we discuss are designed to unleash your authenticity for all to see. The temptation to let your fears get the best of you can suffocate the finest aspects of your personality, undermining your persuasiveness and leaving you cut off from others.

As any marriage counselor will tell you, partners must practice relationship skills and establish rules to handle conflicts. Same goes for communication. If you don't hone your persuasive skills on a daily basis, your speaking and listening will turn sloppy and unconvincing. If you do not take steps to overcome your anxieties, you will be a reactive communicator who operates from a position of weakness. The tools in this chapter help you regain your momentum and command of the persuasive process.

You can conquer your fears and get what you want, and you don't have to lie or feel ashamed in the process. Remain fair and faithful to yourself. Get out there and take some risks. Turn enemies into friends. Admit when you are wrong and transform your fear into positive energy. You will always feel a bit scared when the stakes are high, but that should not stop you from winning people over.

QUICK REVIEW

- Don't bury or suppress the fear; use it to energize your persuasive style.
- To best establish credibility and be liked, let your natural personality shine.
- Keep persuasion in perspective. Realize that all of us occasionally fail.
- Strive for authenticity, not perfection, whenever you communicate.
- Think positive thoughts instead of worrying that you will be proved wrong.
- Expect your fears to peak just before you start to persuade. That's normal.
- Transform inner fear into outward power by unleashing your physical energy.
- Freely admit when you are wrong, to demonstrate your humility and honesty.
- View the people you seek to persuade as eager to learn something useful from you, not as critics eager to attack you.
- Control "fight or flight" fears by setting incremental goals to modify behavior.
- Abolish negative thought patterns by identifying and then correcting the source of your negativity.

NOTES

1. Erving Goffman, *Interaction Ritual,* Doubleday, New York, 1967.
2. *Parade* magazine, Parade Publications, New York, 12-29-85, p. 8.
3. *The Washington Post*, 8-22-93, p. C3.
4. *The Wall Street Journal*, 12-30-93, p A9.

Try On Their Shoes

Harnessing the Power of Empathy to Gain Support

Over 200 years ago, a fellow named John Woolman walked barefoot from Baltimore to Philadelphia. Why? He wanted to experience the pain the slaves suffered when they were forced to walk barefoot over long distances. As a result of his journey, he better understood what it meant to be a slave. He had empathy.

Empathy is the secret weapon that can help you win over anybody.

When I announce this in my workshops, most participants nod approvingly. "Sure, understanding others is very important," they say. Few people deny the power of empathy, but even fewer know *how* to harness that power for maximum benefit.

The word *empathy* is a translation of *einfuhlung*, which means "feeling into" in German. Also based on the Greek word for passion (*empatheia*), empathy is the understanding that comes from readily accepting the feelings, thoughts, or motives of another. This acceptance sends a comforting, supportive message of *I'm like you or You're safe with me.* Communicating these messages takes no magic, no special gifts, and no gimmicks.

Empathy, the most underutilized tool of persuasion, is actually a learned skill. Top salespeople use it. So does President Bill Clinton. A master at relating to people and their concerns on an emotional level, Clinton can sound credible talking to everyone from an angry protestor to a distraught earthquake victim. He expresses sensitivity to their needs. He places himself on their side by letting them talk—by keeping quiet and taking it all in. When aides try to keep him moving through his packed schedule, Clinton brushes them away so that he can spend more time listening to a distressed individual. He nods in understanding and contorts his face in expressions of sadness, sympathy, and satisfaction. He shows "connectivity" (a favorite word of political consultants who craft the public image of their clients), an elusive quality that voters admire in their leaders.

Take a lesson from Clinton and win people over with a generous helping of empathy. Without it, your chances of persuasion dwindle.

WHAT EVERY MAN AND WOMAN WANTS TO HEAR

People occasionally ask me how they can persuade someone to go out on a date. They want to know the best "pick-up lines." I tell them to forget about pick-up lines and work on empathy instead. Empathy helps you attract just about anybody.

A friend told me that he sees the same woman at the health club every night. The two of them chat while exercising. "I want to move to the next step and ask her out," my friend declared. "What should I say?"

The answer is to listen carefully and respond with sentences that begin:

I can appreciate...

I can identify with that...

I can understand...

I see that you...

Phrases like these signal to other people that you actually care about what they say and that you are able to understand them. This sounds like common sense, but surprisingly few individuals do it. Try empathizing with a new friend and watch how quickly you develop a comfortable rapport. Although you might still be nervous asking for a date, your chances of hearing "yes" are much better if you have already demonstrated your ability to empathize.

If everyone took the trouble to empathize, we would have far fewer negative or lonely people out there. We cry out for affirmation, and there is no better way to affirm the feelings of others than to make an attempt to understand them. Empathy is the ultimate form of acceptance. It lets speakers know that you are willing to see things from their point of view, that you are more concerned with understanding than with agreement.

If you empathize with enough people, you soon realize what almost all of them crave: to feel special. The best persuaders know this. They know how to communicate *You count in my eyes, You're important to me, Your thoughts and feelings matter.* These messages are often expressed implicitly through responsive listening, animated facial expressions, and the ability to transcend petty personal squabbles in order to arrive at a larger understanding. Appeal to a person's need to feel special, and you will move mountains.

● **TRAP**　Beware of deluding yourself into thinking you're full of empathy when you're really full of self-obsession. Empathy does not mean trying to predict how others view us. It does not consist of thoughts such as, *Gee, I wonder if she likes me.* Empathy means unconditionally focusing on another person's feelings, even if those feelings do not involve *you* at all!

What happens when we fail to empathize? You can probably recall a time when you tried so hard to persuade, and *you knew you were right,* but somehow your words fell on deaf ears. You spoke eloquently, tactfully, sincerely. You looked people right in the eyes and appealed to them with sound arguments. You were nonthreatening, insightful, even funny. In short, you offered a charming, sensible voice of reason—but you did not persuade.

What went wrong? Perhaps you did not establish a bond with your audience. Despite your smooth presentation, you probably gave them no reason to believe that you understood their point of view. Cast as the outsider, you did little to break down barriers and build trust.

Peggy Noonan, a political speechwriter, wrote about a "problem with some Republican men" that results from lack of empathy, "There is a kind of heavy-handed dorkishness in their approach that leaves them unable to persuasively address questions requiring delicacy; they always sound judgmental when they mean to show concern."[1] Her observation can apply to some parents or teachers; indeed, many of us may undermine our persuasiveness by burying our concern for others under layers of unwelcome moralizing or lecturing.

Even worse, consider how a speaker's insensitivity toward an audience may sever any potential for harmony or understanding. Peter Ueberroth, a hero in planning the 1984 Los Angeles Olympics, could not replicate his success when asked to lead a coalition to rebuild Los Angeles after the tragic riots in 1992. His mission was to persuade the private sector to help reconstruct riot-torn areas. In a highly publicized speech, he suggested that many burnt-out businesses were "not of any great, huge value" and that some of the city's community leaders would do best to "get out of the way" and not participate in rebuilding.[2] He thus alienated the very constituency that he was brought in to assist: small business owners, mostly minorities, in need of financial assistance.

The quality and intimacy of our personal relationships largely depends on our willingness to empathize, to foster the kind of unconditional trust and respect that only comes when two people make concerted efforts to understand one another. In their book *American Couples,* Philip Blumstein and Pepper Schwartz interview couples about how they relate to their partners. One man describes the level of communication in empathetic terms, "We have a lot of 'I' dialogues. For example, 'I feel down' or 'I feel wonderful,' and then, of course, the other person is supposed to say, 'Why?' and that helps things get talked about on the right basis."[3] By asking *why,* the individual attempts to dig deeper in a search for understanding.

MEMORY JOGGER

Armed with at least some knowledge of others' feelings and motives, the odds of successful persuasion soar.

THREE WAYS EMPATHY ENHANCES YOUR PERSUASIVENESS

Failure to empathize can wreak havoc, but you may wonder how empathy pays off. When we establish a base of understanding, persuasion becomes far easier. The audience feels closer to us because we have taken the trouble to step into their shoes. Listeners are then ready to accept our input or guidance. Psychologist Leslie Maxson, who answers letters for a magazine advice column in *L.A. Parent,* told *The Los Angeles Times,* "I try to imagine as well as I can what position the person is in, what their life situation is."[4]

Let's look at three ways empathy can strengthen a persuasive message.

The "Me, Too" Effect: Sell Yourself by Helping Others Identify with *You*

When I lived in New York City in the late 1980s, David Liederman was a celebrity. His David's Cookies chain baked the best chocolate chip treats in town, and his newly opened Broadway Cafe was a smash. This guy knew food. Yet, he topped 300 pounds. So he lost 100 pounds over three years and wrote a weight-loss book to trumpet his success. A journalist heard him make a wonderfully empathetic statement while he was promoting his book, "My goal in life is for someone to say, 'You look terrible, David. Eat something.'"

With half the adult women and 30 percent of adult men on diets, and Americans spending $30 billion trying to lose weight in 1991, Liederman captured their frustration and identified with their longing to slim down. His endearing comment, tinged with humor and humanity, gives us a vivid example of empathy in action.

Take a lesson from David Liederman and sell yourself by drawing your audience into your world. Make them say, *Yeah, I can identify with that* or *Me, too.* Here are two examples:

- You want your friends and colleagues to make a small investment in a new business venture. To prepare to persuade them, you ask yourself, "What can just about everyone identify with when it comes to working for a living?" Most people yearn for an enjoyable, challenging job. So you decide to use empathy to tap this universal craving for interesting work. "This business represents my dream job, the kind of work that would make me wake up on Monday morning with a big smile on my face, raring to go to the office." It's a safe bet that your listeners want the same thing, and they may consider the prospect of investing in such an enterprise.

- You manage a team of supervisors that needs to learn how to praise the support staff more freely. You want to persuade them to routinely recognize the fine work that their clerks perform. So you ask yourself, "What do my supervisors identify with when it comes to getting and giving feedback?" You realize that, like their subordinates, the supervisors thrive on compliments. You say, "Each of us from time to time has gone beyond the call of duty to deliver great work, and has not heard a word of thanks in return. It has happened to me, and I'm sure it has happened to you, too. It hurts. Let's make sure that does not happen with your people."

Memory Jogger

To take advantage of the *me, too* effect, you need to step into your listeners' lives and capture a shared experience.

Your objective is to express a common feeling that shows how similar you and your audience are. This explains why empathy is so important: It bridges gaps and builds trust by demonstrating your understanding of the audience. One salesman who dreads asking for the order tells prospects, "You know, we've reached the point in the conversation where my heart starts beating the way it does before I have to give a speech. I always get nervous when I ask, 'Are you ready to sign the papers? [long pause] Well, are you?'" How's that for a funny, effective way to close a sale with a dose of empathy? Virtually everyone goes through a bout of sweaty anxiety when the time comes to deliver a speech, so potential buyers can appreciate the salesman's nervousness as the time comes to close the sale.

A Gentle Way to Elicit Information and Create Rapport with Friends or Strangers

A sensitive interviewer can establish empathy with almost any subject. Barbara Walters recalls the comment she made to Mike Nichols, the film director, during the release of his first movie *Who's Afraid of Virginia Woolf?* She started off, "Mr. Nichols, I'm not interested in hearing about Elizabeth Taylor or Richard Burton. I want to know about you." While other interviewers kept asking the young director about his famous stars, Walters figured that Nichols may have had some interesting opinions of his own.[5]

When you meet someone for the first time and you want to generate a lively conversation, remember how Walters used empathy with Mike Nichols. Think about what the other person wants to talk about. Take a good look at those you wish to win over and consider what interests, hobbies, projects, experiences, or plans may relate to them. Then ask non-threatening, open-ended questions that elicit the kind of information that will bring you closer and increase understanding.

Personal relationships evolve in wonderful ways when each partner tries to step into the other's shoes. Whenever you hear your mate repeatedly raise a topic, it makes sense to follow up with some questions about that topic. Ignore the subject at your own risk! For instance, participants in my seminars often complain that their spouse does not listen when they discuss their favorite pastime (from football to knitting to collecting antiques). "I just love talking about ___, but I guess I'm the only one in the house who does," is a common refrain.

If you want to enliven your relationship (not to mention increase your persuasiveness), show interest in what your mate shows interest in. It may be a struggle at first to care about something that you find boring, but your efforts will not go unnoticed. The two of you will have much more to talk about, and your ideas and opinions will carry more weight if you demonstrate that you want to learn more about a subject near and dear to your loved one.

Overcoming Objections by Finding Common Ground

In a persuasive encounter that changed modern history, a lifelong friend of Harry Truman's named Eddie Jacobson visited the President in the White House on March 13, 1948. Jacobson's goal was to persuade Truman to meet with Chaim Weizmann about the Palestine issue (this was in the months leading up to the creation of Israel). Although Jacobson knew Truman did not want to talk about the Middle East mess, he brought it up anyway, and they argued. Truman was adamant: He would not meet with Weizmann. Then, rather than give up, Jacobson noticed one of Truman's prized possessions, a small bronze of Andrew Jackson on horseback. As a last-ditch effort, Jacobson pointed to it and delivered a final persuasive plea:

> Harry, all your life you have had a hero....I too have a hero, a man I never met, but who is, I think, the greatest Jew who ever lived....I am talking about Chaim Weizmann. He is a very sick man, almost broken in health, but he traveled thousands of miles just to see you and plead the cause of my people. Now you refuse to see him.[6]

Jacobson placed himself in Truman's shoes. He realized, in a split second, with his emotions at a peak, that Andrew Jackson's heroic status in Truman's mind was analogous to Chaim Weizmann's status as a hero to the Jews. In the heat of the moment, Jacobson's sincerity and ability to empathize with his friend overpowered everything else. Truman, after a long silence, muttered, "You win." He agreed to see Weizmann and supported the formation of Israel months later.[7]

Even if you do not know the person you wish to persuade as well as Jacobson knew Truman, you can still find common ground with the help of empathy. The secret is to find something—an idea, an interest, or an outlook—that you and your audience share. If you attend the same church or shop at the same stores, that's a start. If you graduated from the same school or your children are the same age, that's even better.

MEMORY JOGGER

The first step in persuasion is to find a base of agreement, a shared perspective that allows both parties to proceed with the underlying belief that "we understand each other."

Empathy breaks down barriers between potential adversaries. Looking beyond a person's objections to find common ground ("We both agree that___") makes it easier to persuade.

Managers often ask me how to keep morale high in a department battered by layoffs and consolidation. "I've got a nightmare on my hands," an administrative director told me. "My people are scared for their jobs, and they see things going on around them that make them worry that they have no security."

In this situation, an effective leader must find a base of agreement among all in the department. Here are some ways the empathetic manager can persuade anxious staffers to stay the course and keep their heads up high:

- "While there's no denying the fact that this organization is undergoing some painful cutbacks, I realize the value that each of you brings to this company. I know many of you are concerned. I am, too. But we all share the same goal of keeping our jobs and performing them to the best of our ability. Now more than ever, we need to keep that goal in mind and focus on what we can control: taking pride in a job well done."

- "Many of you have told me that you find it hard to concentrate on your jobs when you are fearful of losing them. I understand, because I've been in your shoes. Five years ago, I was in the same position and arrived at work every morning just waiting for my pink slip. It was a terrible time for me. Like many of you, I decided to ride out the down cycle and kept showing up and doing my job as well as I could. We're all in this together, so let's help pull each other up and make it through these times."

If you must win over a resistant audience, remember to empathize. Ask yourself, "What do they feel right now? What are their priorities, fears, hopes?" By addressing these issues directly and showing that you care, you are well positioned to exert influence.

● **TRAP**   Don't fall into the tempting trap of making excuses not to empathize. Parents may throw their fearful youngsters into pools as a sink-or-swim exercise, rationalizing that their children's terror is somehow good for them. Managers may humiliate their employees publicly, thinking that an angry outburst will send a strong message to workers that mistakes will not be tolerated. Sports coaches or military drill sergeants may deliberately push their squads to exhaustion to prove a point about mental toughness. While these measures may work in isolated cases, they are hardly empathetic. Don't fall for the "tough love" argument. The frightened child may learn to swim, but will not understand (and may even resent) your method of teaching. Employees' work may temporarily improve, but their morale will not. When you create an adversarial environment that blocks mutual understanding, you will not persuade over the long haul.

We are more interested in ourselves (our dentist appointment, mosquito bites, dinner plans, golf game) than in what others have to say. This makes it harder to pay attention to a persuader. Here's where empathy steps in. If you describe a shared experience with someone who is otherwise distracted, you will suddenly find a willing conversational partner.

USING EMPATHY TO TURN ACQUAINTANCES INTO FRIENDS

I recall a senior executive who would not hire me for a consulting project (and was about to end our meeting) when I happened to mention that I attended college in Providence, Rhode Island. He perked up and said with a warm smile, "Oh, did you go to Brown?" It turns out we both graduated from the same university, and we suddenly found ourselves comparing notes on our collegiate experiences.

Since then, I have made an effort to lace my conversations with references to my past—where I grew up (Southern California) and where I have lived (Los Angeles, New York, Providence, Sacramento, Idaho, Washington, D.C.). Almost everyone I meet has either lived in one of these places or knows someone who has. This gives us something familiar to discuss—a bond that brings us closer.

Empathy results when you establish connections. Peppering your remarks with biographical facts such as your hometown, your favorite movies, or vacation spots can result in a more fulfilling, revealing dialogue. When people ask me how to start a conversation with a stranger, I advise them to search for something you have in common. Examples:

- "I just bought a pair of shoes like yours but I haven't had a chance to wear them yet."
- "I like your earrings, and I'm always looking for ones with creative designs. Where did you get them?"
- [At a break during a seminar] "I noticed you were taking notes like crazy. Me, too. What do you think of the meeting so far?"

MEMORY JOGGER

You cannot depend on the other person to find what the two of you have in common.

With shared references, feelings, or experiences, you will enjoy rewarding conversations and turn acquaintances into friends. Better yet, you will send a reassuring message that *we're alike.*

● **TRAP**   When another person begins to discuss a personal experience, soak it up. Find time to listen. Don't cut in, or you may lose a golden opportunity to build empathy. People enjoy relating their experiences. They are often hurt when interrupted, so let them finish. Never insist on tugging the conversation back to yourself. For example, a colleague sits back and begins, "I recall way back when…" You notice his eyes lose focus because he is generating internal imagery, and his voice captures the flavor of the experience. Keep quiet, follow the story, and try to picture the setting along with the speaker. Better yet, ask a question or two so that you can better visualize the scene:

What did your office look like?

Did you put in long hours?

Where did you live at the time?

HOW EMPATHY DEFUSES TENSION AND REDUCES CONFLICTS

Empathy comes in particularly handy when you are faced with an antagonistic or apathetic person. One young insurance agent told me about his very first sales presentation. "I was reciting benefit after benefit, just as I was taught to do in sales school. Then I notice my prospect reaching for the phone. He says, 'Excuse me, I have to make a call.' He just expected me to ramble on. He wasn't listening anyway. I never connected with him."

Seasoned persuaders take such situations in stride. When Alabama's governor lured Mercedes, a German company, to open an auto plant in his state, he did not let Mercedes executives' concerns about the state's racial history scare them off. Instead, he confronted their resistance head-on with an example that hit close to home. "We tried to tell them that Alabama is no more the state it was in the 1950s and 1960s…than Germany is the same country it was in the days of the Hitler regime," he told *The Wall Street Journal.* "They kind of nodded their heads when I said that."[8]

It is hard to disagree or maintain an adversarial stance with someone who strives to understand you. Say you are making an important sales presentation to a company president. After waiting in the reception area for thirty minutes, you are escorted to her office. She is screaming into the phone, a look of frustration on her beet-red face as she finishes the call. "Come on, not now. We've had three weeks to plan this. Why all the last-minute problems? Listen, fix everything and let me know when the system is up and running again." She slams down the phone and looks at you.

"Didn't mean to keep you, but I'm putting out all kinds of fires today," she says with irritation in her voice. You try to cheer things up with a few pleasantries, but you notice she is making notes and shuffling papers while you're speaking. "Now I'm ready," she says without conviction while fiddling with a file and glancing at her watch.

You realize the timing is not right for your sales pitch so you say, "It looks like one of those days. I can see you're busy with some urgent matters. Let's set another time to meet."

"Oh, this is just a typical day at this crazy place," she responds with disgust. "You're here. I'm ready. What can I do for you?"

Her secretary interrupts with a knock at the door. "Sorry to bother you, but Meyer says there's an emergency downstairs."

Here's where empathy counts. Knowing how it feels to get caught knee-deep in crises, you wait for her to finish talking with her secretary and then you say, "Thanks for your willingness to make room for me today, but I can see you've got a lot going on." Then, before she can insist on rushing through your meeting, you add, "How about if I arrange with your secretary on my way out to pick another day that looks good for you?" You shake hands and offer a look of supreme understanding and sensitivity to her full plate of problems. She agrees to your suggestion.

When you return a week later, she does not keep you waiting. Her voice is warm and welcoming as you enter her office. She greets you like an old friend. The phones are quiet, and the secretary does not burst in with bad news. You are now ready to persuade, and she is ready to be persuaded. Your empathetic patience and appreciation of good timing save the day.

You also need to develop keen observational skills to empathize. Get in the habit of arousing all your senses when you communicate. Don't just dwell on what *you* say or how *you* look. Watch what's going on around you. Take it all in. Master persuaders detect when someone starts shaking a foot (a sign of impatience, tension), rubbing the eyes (exhaustion), or fingering a wristwatch band (boredom). They spot these nonverbal red flags and realize it's time to wrap up whatever they are saying.

A top insurance salesman who earned $1 million a year in commissions told me how he empathized with people. "What I'm about to tell you is a secret," he cautioned. "It'll sound crazy, but it works in both my personal and professional life."

"Okay," I said. (Let's hope he forgives me for revealing his secret.)

"I've learned that you have to show people you are capable of seeing things from their point of view," he began. "They will listen to you once they feel you have put their feelings before yours. So what I do is take a good look at what they're wearing. I study their clothes from top to bottom, the fabrics, the fit, everything. Then I pretend *I'm wearing the same stuff*. While we talk, I start to feel that turtleneck around me or the tightness of that belt. What happens is you step entirely into their world. Everything they say takes on added importance and hits closer to home. And believe me, they can tell they are talking to someone who really cares, who understands them."

"What happens if you're talking with a woman?" I asked.

"Same thing," he replied. "The first time I laid eyes on my wife, she was out on the patio at a friend's house. We started talking. It wasn't that cold out, but this breeze kicked in. I noticed she was wearing a thin little dress, and she started shivering. I imagined myself wearing the same thing, and I got cold just thinking about it. At the same moment, we both said, 'Let's go inside.' It was uncanny."

Give it a try! The reason this exercise in "clothes reversal" builds empathy is that it forces you to pay close attention when someone else speaks. It activates at least two senses—sight and touch. The more attuned you are to the thoughts and feelings of others, the better. Don't let life pass by in a blur. If you are too self-absorbed to observe what goes on around you, then you will have trouble reaching out to those you seek to persuade.

CREATE A MENTAL DATA BANK
TO STORE YOUR OBSERVATIONS ABOUT OTHERS

Maintaining a positive, attentive, nonjudgmental attitude will propel you forward, but empathizing requires another step. Take mental notes of what others say.

Masters of persuasion know how to ask questions and, better yet, they actually care about the answers. Every time they hear someone state an opinion or preference, they pay attention. Political views and social habits are fair game. Phrases that begin *I think, I feel,* and *This makes me so_____* signal that valuable information will soon follow. Capture and retain these revealing statements. Put them in your mental data bank. Search for clues that indicate how someone's experiences or memories influence their outlook.

As you take mental notes of speakers' preferences and opinions, tune in with special care when you hear talk of contradictory motives. Many people are pulled in opposing directions when making choices. By learning how they resolve a mental tug-of-war, you will get a better idea of how they arrive at a tough decision. This insight can help you prepare your persuasive appeal.

For example, a colleague confessed to me that after years of voting Republican, she intended to vote Democratic. I asked why. After a long pause, she identified the sick national economy, the abortion debate, and a documentary film about the homeless as "things that made me question why I was always so far right." Her response shows that she is open to new ideas and swayed by macro issues (the economy, abortion, the homeless). When the time comes to persuade her, I will discuss grand, evocative themes rather than getting bogged down in details.

Another example: A friend took six months considering what kind of car to buy. He read consumer guides, visited dealers, and even checked insurance rates for different types of vehicles. When he finally made a decision, he confessed that "after all those months of research, I discovered all of a sudden that I wanted to impress everyone by buying an expensive sports car." He ended up making a spontaneous purchase of a red convertible that he spotted in a showroom window. This tells me he can be persuaded on impulse and that he cares about others' perceptions. If I ever try to win him over, I will focus on how my idea preserves or reinforces his self-image instead of merely listing reasons or justifications for him to act.

Why are mental notes so important in helping you build empathy? They force you to pay attention to what others say and how their minds process information. Stop whatever else you are doing and listen carefully when others tell you any of the following:

- how they resolved a dilemma (such as handling a friendship on the rocks, dealing with a troublesome neighbor, meeting with the boss to discuss problems on the job)
- their shopping habits (such as how they select birthday/holiday gifts, whether they use coupons in the grocery store, whether they are comfortable returning merchandise or writing a manufacturer regarding a product)
- how they reacted to an emergency (after the January 1994 earthquake in Los Angeles, everyone had a here's-what-happened-to-me story)
- how they responded to a personal or professional setback (such as the breakup of a marriage, a lost promotion at work, a failed business start-up)
- how they devised a solution to a problem (from managing their time better to improving their relationship with their kids)

Whenever speakers reveal how they behaved in a certain situation, you get a window into their psychological make-up. Their thoughts help you understand how they operate. You can spot their strengths and weaknesses, their likes and dislikes, their greatest dreams and worst fears. All this information should be filed in your mental data bank for use when you want to persuade them.

○ **NOW TRY THIS** Keep a notepad in your car or desk. Immediately after you meet with someone, jot down your observations about the individual. The act of writing your impressions will help you "enter" this information in your mental data bank. Following a meeting last week with a potential business partner, I sat in my car and wrote, "Gets excited by new technologies, likes to predict trends, avoids discussing past mistakes or old jobs, flashy floral tie, vague on educational background, most comfortable when I let him show me his new computer." After recording these observations, I drove off. These random scribblings will undoubtedly help me empathize with him in the future. (Alternative: Keep a pad by the phone to record your thoughts after you hang up.)

Top salespeople are often the best mental notetakers. They are always trying to figure out what makes prospects tick. One real estate agent told me:

> I get listings to sell houses by treating every house I go in as an extension of the owner. When I first tour a house, even if the purpose is entirely social, I enjoy chatting with the owner about the layout, the design, the furniture, and so on. I try to find out what they like most or least about the place. Whatever I learn gets stored in my head, so that when the day comes to list the property, I'm already familiar with how the owner thinks.

Don't forget to ask follow-up questions. People will give you plenty of clues as to how they made up their minds. Catalog the clues and keep jotting those notes so that you increase your understanding of why and how they act.

The lesson here is to lay the groundwork to persuade well before you ask for something. Approach every conversation as an opportunity to fill your mental notepad with observations on how others think and behave. When they express an opinion or share an anecdote, do not simply nod and smile. Ask yourself, "What does this reveal about how they reach decisions?" When they complain about poor service or praise something, ask yourself, "What does this tell me about them?"

SEE YOURSELF STEPPING INTO SOMEONE ELSE'S SHOES

Along with taking mental notes, increase your ability to empathize through visualization. Visualization is using your imagination to see. This process involves replacing your personal frame of reference with another. Taking such a mental leap requires detachment so that you can gain an objective view of how you communicate and how others respond.

In one of my first communication workshops in 1985, I taught a group of Rhode Island suicide-prevention volunteers how to persuade troubled callers to stay on the line. Individuals would dial the hotline number, mutter a few words, and then hang up before the counselors could respond. The volunteers felt impotent when faced with these calls, and they desperately sought ways to sustain the conversation.

I developed a visualization exercise. Grabbing some masking tape, I asked a participant to peel the tape and apply it along the floor to form a straight line.

The group wondered what this had to do with suicide prevention. I had their attention! Then I asked a volunteer to stand and approach the line. "Before you cross that line," I instructed, "you are to think of one of your recent callers. It doesn't matter which caller, but think of a specific conversation you have had this week. When you step over that line, *you become that caller.* You will then tell us what you, as the caller, feel or think. Remember, the first thought you have once you step over the line is from the point of view of the caller."

Stepping over the line served as a psychological crossing as well. Each participant visualized the line as a kind of entry into another world, and some crossed the line with trepidation. With beads of sweat, shaking hands, and even a few teary eyes, the volunteers forced themselves to enter the mind of a suicidal person awaiting them on the other side of that tape.

Their comments from the "other side" ranged from smooth-talking rationalizations (*I'm really fine. Why I am calling?*) to outright despair (*I need help*). In replaying a tape of their remarks, participants could hear how successfully they managed to empathize with their callers. The hopes, doubts, and fears that plagued their callers hit close to home, and the pain that the volunteers experienced allowed them to better understand and appreciate the emotions rumbling inside the callers' heads. The result was that the group persuaded more callers to "hang in there" during those peak moments of crisis when just staying on the phone was a first step toward recovery.

You can visualize in smaller, simpler ways in your daily life. How? Detach yourself from your everyday conversations and view them from a different perspective. Keep tabs on one or two persuasive encounters each day. Then, as you tuck yourself into bed at night, mentally review these conversations in your most relaxed, nonjudgmental state of mind. Assess both your speaking and listening. Did you demonstrate a high degree of empathy? Were you surprised by any of the responses when you tried to persuade?

Even better, visualize persuasive exchanges the night *before*. Let's say that it is Sunday night, and you are scheduled on Monday to deliver an academic paper to a group of highly distinguished leaders in your field. In the peace and unhurried calm as you drift off to sleep, imagine the following day's presentation from the point of view of a detached observer. What do you say? How does the audience respond? After the first minute of your presentation, how do they *feel* about you and your message?

Empathy comes from disengaging yourself from the rush of daily life, with its constant distractions that make even momentary concentration a monumental challenge. This is why I recommend that you visualize when you are about to fall asleep. All this talk of empathy may sound nice, but it is unrealistic to expect that we fully relate to others while phones ring, our head throbs, and we still need to stop at the bank, the cleaners, and the pharmacy (to get aspirin, of course) in the next hour!

Visualization produces insight. With this newfound understanding, we can maximize our persuasive power.

NOT EVERYONE IS PLEASANT: HOW TO WIN OVER DIFFICULT PEOPLE

Techniques such as taking mental notes and visualization build empathy. These steps work particularly well when we converse with pleasant people. We are well positioned to persuade when we have established connections with a friendly audience. They are predisposed to trust us and follow our lead once we demonstrate that we understand them.

Cynics may roll their eyes and shake their heads when they hear words such as empathy and understanding. They think, *Empathy and understanding...more sensitive words for the sensitive '90s? All this talk of shared experience sounds nice, but I have to persuade difficult people—stubborn, nasty, impatient types. I can't stand them, and the last thing I want to do is take the trouble to empathize with them.*

Fair enough. Empathy becomes a chore when we do not like or respect the individuals we meet. But difficult people exist. We cannot ignore them or choose to interact only with our "favorites." We may not like our boss or our biggest client, but we are stuck with them.

○ **NOW TRY THIS**   Select a negative person whom you wish to persuade. For example, choose a colleague from work who can be described as rude, cynical, pessimistic, or just plain sad. The next time you converse with this individual, flood the dialogue with empathy. How?

- Ask open questions such as *How did you feel about that? What did you do when that happened? What are your thoughts on this morning's meeting?* Such questions may encourage your colleague to unleash feelings that need unleashing.

- Let the person answer. Resist the urge to judge what you hear. Stop muttering to yourself *I can't stand this, how can you say that? That's the wrong attitude to take.*

- When the other person stop talking, surprise him or her by asking a follow-up question or prompting the person to continue *(You really think so? Go on).*

- When the person accepts your invitation to continue, note how much more he or she reveals about his or her outlook, biases, or fears. In most cases, you will find that even the most negative person will open up to such an attentive, responsive listener. Better yet, you will start to see a fully dimensional human being lurking inside a brittle outer shell. You may not suddenly like the speaker, but at least you will dig deeper and expose layers of personality that may help you establish empathy.

Empathy, as demonstrated in this experiment, helps you treat even the most unpleasant people with a dose of fairness and dignity. These types are not used to having someone attempt to understand them. They enter conversations expecting to argue or complain, and they rarely meet anyone who takes a genuine interest in what they have to say. If you make an effort to step into their shoes and share their concerns, they will be more apt to heed your advice or accept your persuasive appeal.

Perhaps the most challenging situations involve people who are doubly difficult because of their oversized egos. An empathetic persuader considers the other person's inflated self-esteem and communicates accordingly.

John Calley, a Hollywood motion picture studio chief accustomed to dealing with egomaniacs, tells the story of how he persuaded Irwin Allen, co-director of *The Towering Inferno,* to abandon a costly project called *The Walter Syndrome.*[9]

Calley, who viewed Allen as "an ego running utterly amok," had to figure out a way to convince the director not to pursue the new movie without ruining the working relationship they had established. He knew he had to appeal to Allen's huge ego, so he said, "Irwin, I wouldn't presume to talk story with you, because of who you are—because you are Irwin Allen. I am just not that brazen."

Allen smiled and said, "I understand."

Calley responded that he merely wanted to ask a question.

"I can't say I'm not intrigued," Allen said. "What is the question?"

Calley then hit the nail on the head. "My question is this," he began. "Would Cecil B. De Mille have made *The Walter Syndrome?*"

As Calley recounts the conversation, Allen immediately tossed the script in the trash and declared, *"The Walter Syndrome* is a closed issue." The two men concluded their chat by standing and hugging.

Breaking Through Negativity with Empathy

When I first moved to New York City, I asked favors of just about everyone. *Do you have a spare desk for me to use? Can I borrow that computer? Can you help me carry these bundles of mail to the post office?* Many kindly souls agreed to help, from my neighbors to friends of friends, and I was soon spending lots of time with people in a position to assist me. Although I usually enjoyed their company, I grew bored when hearing a steady stream of complaints about New York. Some could not believe I chose to leave sunny California for messy Manhattan. They expressed their displeasure by listing their many reasons for plotting an escape (crime, filth, crowds, expenses, crazy cabbies, muggers, "the subway urine thing," Con Ed explosions, the incompetent mayor).

On one hand, I was a wide-eyed newcomer thrilled that people helped me start my dream business. But in between my heartfelt thanks, I found myself stuck in conversations that made me want to leap off the Brooklyn Bridge. At first, I resented all their negativity. *Sour grapes*, I thought. *The only reason they're being so nice to me is because they need someone to listen to their complaining.* Their torrent of doom and gloom sank my spirits.

Then I remembered…empathy. Instead of biting my lip and burying my anger when forced to listen to yet another cynical "I hate this godforsaken city" speech, I made an effort to understand their point of view. I asked why they stayed. I wondered aloud whether their friends and fellow workers felt the same way.

Through gentle questioning, I found that their negativity faded and they began to open up to me. My printer admitted that his frustration with

New York was actually a result of the city's high commercial tax that prevented him from reinvesting his profits in new binding equipment. My lawyer told me he was so exhausted from the long commute each day that he could barely stay awake. As they shared their deeper concerns with me, I could better appreciate why they loved to hate New York. Uncovering the source of their anger brought me closer to them. I no longer found myself searching for excuses to flee.

Our mission as persuasive communicators is to build alliances. This explains why preparation is so important. Every human encounter represents a chance to gain understanding, to learn something about the values, fears, and feelings of those around us. When we come across difficult people, the same rules apply, but empathy becomes tougher. You will occasionally need to empathize with people whom you do not like or respect, and you will not enjoy having to step into their dreary or topsy-turvy world.

Sharpen your empathetic skills now so that you are ready to persuade later.

QUICK REVIEW

- Affirm the feelings of others by making an attempt to understand them.
- Use empathy to appeal to others' need to feel special.
- Don't engage in unwelcome lecturing or moralizing.
- Don't fall for the "tough love" argument and find excuses not to empathize.
- If someone is visibly preoccupied or distracted, describe a shared experience and you will capture his or her attention.
- Let others relate their experiences and anecdotes. Don't interrupt them.
- Don't dwell on what *you* say or how *you* look. Observe others' behavior.
- Take mental notes of what others say.
- Use visualization to help you empathize.
- Empathize with even the most difficult speakers by making an attempt to understand them.
- Build alliances by learning about the values, fears, and hopes of others.

NOTES

1. *Forbes,* 9-14-92, p. 69.
2. *The Los Angeles Times,* 12-13-92, p. M6.
3. Philip Blumstein and Pepper Schwartz, *American Couples,* William Morrow & Co., New York, 1983, pp. 542–543.
4. *The Los Angeles Times,* 7-11-94, p. E3.
5. John Brady, *The Craft of Interviewing,* Vintage Books, New York, 1976, p. 60.
6. David McCullough, *Truman,* Simon & Schuster, New York, 1992, pp. 606–607.
7. Ibid, p. 607.
8. *The Wall Street Journal,* 11-24-93, p. A6.
9. Calley's story is told in *The New Yorker,* 3-21-94, p. 82.

Flexing Your Personality Muscles to Strengthen Your Appeal

When you flex your personality muscles, your natural range of expression expands. This helps you communicate authentically with different types of people.

Persuasion offers a litmus test of our sensitivity. We need to pick up on what others say and adjust our response to best match their outlook. Maintaining a pliable personality can benefit us in both our personal and professional lives.

Gifted persuaders can tell whether we prefer to hear just the facts or lots of small talk, whether we like fast or slow talkers, whether we make decisions gradually (*Give me time to think about it*) or in a burst of theatrics (*Stop right there, I'll do it!*). Once they determine our preferences, they vary their style accordingly. This doesn't mean they fake it; rather, their elastic personalities enable them to adapt to others while remaining true to themselves.

In addition to your empathetic understanding of others, you can prepare to persuade by developing a more flexible approach to communication. It's all in the tone of your appeal. With some individuals, you must forcefully assert your proposal. Others respond more favorably if you humbly suggest that they consider your input. Your job is to customize your persuasive strategy to fit a particular audience.

WHO'S YOUR AUDIENCE?
HOW TO EXERT INFLUENCE BY GIVING YOUR LISTENERS WHAT THEY WANT

One of the first things a student of public speaking learns is *audience analysis*. This means don't curse to a group of nuns, don't try to sell funeral plots to a group of teenagers, and don't talk to law enforcement officials about your fondness for illicit drugs.

If you overlook the values and preferences of your audience, then you may lose more than the opportunity to persuade. You may make enemies. I am forever warning executives not to open their talks with an obligatory joke. "I need to make a long presentation," they tell me, "so I want to get 'em laughing first so they're in a good mood." Then they launch an opening story that borders on being offensive and alienates half the room. In an effort to release tension, they raise it.

Two listeners may respond to the same message in totally different ways. That's why humor is such a risky device with which to try to curry favor with an audience. Moreover, your goal in any persuasive presentation is not to make people laugh, but to make them feel comfortable. You want to generate positive emotions and put them in a receptive frame of mind. You can achieve this without the hit-or-miss gamble of a joke.

How? Try describing an experience that you and your listeners shared (last night's gala dinner, the storm that blew through town, the previous speaker) so that the audience comes together to reflect on the same event. When you discuss a topic that relates to everyone, you are assured of holding their interest. If you insist on relying on humor, keep it self-deprecating and let others relax at *your* expense.

In one-on-one conversations, your ability to persuade depends on what your listener wants. A college professor might be persuaded of your intelligence by your ability to spot a complex problem. A corporate executive, on the other hand, will not be impressed if you run around saying, "This is wrong, this is wrong." Leaders in business respect those who *solve* problems rather than merely point them out.

Beware of those who resist your idea not on its merits but because they perceive your success as a threat. When you plan to persuade people, think through what they stand to gain (or lose) by saying "yes." Will they be unlikely to admit their true reason for opposing you? Will their egos prevent them from accepting your input? Will they refuse your advice out of stubbornness or spite? Will they expect something in exchange for going along with you?

MEMORY JOGGER

Never try to persuade until you know your listeners' top priorities.

Just because you are certain you have an excellent idea, don't assume everyone will agree. A recommendation that seems obvious or brilliant to you may not prove self-evident to everyone else. You must identify what motivates your audience and stir that desire.

How can you tell what motivates others? In some cases, they'll come right out and tell you. Your challenge is to adjust your persuasive approach to fit your audience. Some examples:

- I know a successful salesman who provides printing equipment to business owners. He says that he continually modifies his pitch depending on his prospect. "When we're first getting to know each other, I casually ask whether they like a salesperson who spends time with them and educates them about the equipment, or would they rather work with an order-taker who keeps the advice to a minimum," he explains. "Some people look to me as a resource, while others do their own research on what to buy and then expect me to process sales." He works happily with all types of customers, and he will not offer his input unless clients ask for it.

- When the chief financial officer of International Business Machines toured a software production facility, he was subjected to a long meeting and slide show in which an executive spoke about delivering software electronically. The CFO, however, had not come to hear the details of the cost-per-megabyte of zapping software over phone lines. His intent was to discuss broad strategy and identify opportunities for cost-cutting. Impatient with the presentation, he interrupted the speaker, "Where do you want to take this business? Get me to the end and tell me where you want to go."[1] Even after this warning, the speaker returned to the mechanics of networking tools. A flexible persuader would have responded by focusing on the big picture, transforming a nuts-and-bolts lecture into a forward-looking call to action.

- In some personal relationships, one partner is overly sensitive to criticism or to making mistakes. A woman in one of my seminars said, "My husband knows that I'm not very good at handling criticism and that I come down hard on myself when I mess up. Yet when he wants me to do something, he'll lash out or reel off what I did wrong." Her husband's behavior was hardly persuasive, because his focus on criticism only made her less responsive.

Do not force someone to change his or her personality just for you. This reminds me of toddlers who repeatedly try to shove triangular shapes into square holes. When I conduct role plays in my workshops, some participants attempt to persuade with the underlying message, "You can accept my advice—which is good; or you can ignore it—which is bad." Few listeners are swayed by such a simplistic approach. If you sermonize, explaining what's "good" and "bad," you lower the odds that your message will be heeded.

If you want to persuade, then the burden rests on you to deliver your message in the most appealing manner for your particular audience.

● **TRAP**   Never launch your persuasive salvo unless the other person appears receptive. It's sometimes better to lend a sympathetic ear or to simply postpone your selling than to blindly charge ahead with your agenda. If you do not remain flexible to your audience's needs, you may wind up talking to a wall. Ask yourself, "Are they interested in my input right now?" Don't overlook what your listeners want from you. If they want you to keep quiet and listen, then comply. Although you may be temporarily frustrated, your patience will pay off when the timing improves and you have a window of opportunity to persuade.

Motivate Others by Internal Factors or External Stimuli

Some of us base our decisions mostly on internal factors such as self-esteem or intuition, while others are influenced more by external stimuli such as advertising or peer pressure. By knowing whether your audience is led by internal or external motivations, you can frame your message in the appropriate manner. Examples:

- Health officials find that young adults are more successfully persuaded not to smoke by social and environmental influences than by reason. Antismoking campaigns thus promote the idea that it's "cool" not to smoke. (But persuasion works both ways. One cigarette brand ties its identity to a hip cartoon character, a camel that wears sunglasses, to attract buyers. Even though the company insists it is not trying to lure teenagers to smoke, watchdog groups are not so sure.)

- Job recruiters try to fill positions with the best candidates, and this requires that they emphasize the right aspects of the work. Some candidates care more about external rewards such as a high salary, a big office, and a company car with a private parking spot. Others might welcome intangibles such as stability, harmony, and the chance to unleash their creativity.

Your persuasiveness will improve if you can determine whether the other person pays more attention to internal or external motivators. The following exercise will show you how.

○ **Now Try This** Whenever people tell you how they overcame an addiction (to drugs, smoking, food, etc.), note whether they were guided by internal or external drives. Examples:

Internal

I just couldn't live with myself anymore.

I hated to look in the mirror.

I lost all respect for myself.

I was so sick all the time I just had to get better.

External

My friends made me quit.

It seemed to go out of style after awhile.

I got so tired of everyone giving me a hard time about it.

It became too expensive.

When the time comes for you to win over this individual, use internal or external support depending on what has worked best for them in the past. Here are examples of how you can respond persuasively:

Internal

Dig deep inside yourself. I know you can do it.

You've got such a strong sense of decency, and this is the decent thing to do.

Only you can improve things. I'm suggesting a way for you to get there.

Here are the pros and cons. I'm sure you will weigh them fairly and make a decision.

External

You don't want to let everyone down, do you?

Thousands of people are already happy doing it. You should, too.

With the bad economy and all, this makes sense.

Get advice from your friends and family and you'll see I'm right.

CONNECTING WITH THE PARENT, ADULT, AND CHILD IN ALL OF US

There are three communication styles—parent, adult, and child—that help us win over others. There is a time and place for each role. Sharpen your persuasive skills by identifying each style and responding in an appropriate manner when you want to get your point across.

The Parent   The parent instructs and passes judgment, using phrases such as *always, never, if I were you*. Eager to dish out criticism and tell others what to do, the parent is comfortable playing a bossy, I-know-what's-best role.

The Adult   The adult avoids judging and respects the rights of others, asking lots of *how-when-why-what-where-who* questions to gather facts and assess others' actions. The most admired leaders, usually gain consensus and "buy in" by seeking the opinions of others and listening attentively.

The Child   The child, while creative, wants to be led and speaks in terms of *I want* and *I guess*. Less apt to take responsibility or work independently, the child will await instructions and enjoy being coddled by a "parent" figure.

Whether we realize it or not, we assume the guise of the parent, adult, or child when we communicate. Our natural personality provides room for all three behaviors, although we tend to play up one aspect of our behavior more than the others. I met a supervisor during one of my consulting assignments who could never quite escape the "child" mode. He seemed to thrive on helplessness and wide-eyed wonder at how life swirled around him. He would frequently yell for help from his office, and someone would run to the rescue to turn on his computer or fix his stapler. He was demonstrative with his emotions, stomping his feet and slamming his door at the least provocation.

When I asked his boss how he managed to tame such a demanding personality, he smiled and said, "Oh, it's so easy. He behaves like a child, and I behave like a parent. We get along great."

MEMORY JOGGER

The best persuaders choose the style—parent, adult, or child—that appeals to a particular audience. If you want to persuade a "parent" or "adult," speak like an "adult." If you are dealing with a "child," then you may need to play the role of "parent."

A vice-president of a public relations firm said that when a client started screaming at her and lashing out with insults, she interrupted, "Hey, time out. Let's not get petty here." She explained later that she treated him "like a mother treats a child," and he apologized.

On the other hand, an aide to the President may adopt the communication style of the child, properly deferential but proposing a steady stream of "what if" ideas.

● **TRAP**   Some of us exhibit the worst aspects of the parental role, *overdosing* on judgments and criticisms instead of persuading gently. We tend to want to control others—to tell them what to do and how to do it. We may treat all audiences alike. Their opinions mean little to us because we think we know better. A clue that you are relying too much on this controlling side of your personality is if you frequently use words like *should, ought to, supposed to,* and *have to.* The gestures of a parent include pointing fingers, a wagging head, hands on hips, folded arms, and a glaring or disapproving facial expression. If you recognize any of these behaviors in yourself, give the other parts of your personality—especially the nonjudgmental adult—a chance to rise to the surface.

Ironically, parents may persuade their children more readily by *not* acting like a "parent." The traditional parent views children as youngsters who need to be managed, but a new school of parenting advises that kids be treated as partners in growth. Communicating as an adult (with lots of fact-finding questions) instead of exercising judgmental authority (with lots of *I-know-what's-best* lecturing) may be more effective.

A Father Who Befriended His Son by Shifting Gears
from Parent to Adult

In one of my workshops, a fellow named Bob gave a practice speech enti-tled, "My Son Steve." He began by discussing how far he had progressed in "dealing with" his teenage son. Steve never wanted to do the household chores or even keep his room clean. His father, rubbing his hands togeth-er while recalling his exasperation, told us he tried everything from with-holding Steve's "movie money" to "just plain yelling."

At wit's end, Bob then embraced the opposite strategy. "Instead of fighting and pleading and knowing the kid wouldn't listen, my goal was to get *him* to do the talking." Bob actually befriended his son, taking Steve to his favorite pizza parlor every few days. By making Steve comfortable, his father found his son talking more and arguing less.

"It turns out Steve was preoccupied with a girl," Bob told us with a laugh. "At the time, it wasn't so funny to the poor kid. His nerves were shot. He could barely study, much less help around the house. He just didn't have any experience with this sort of thing, and he felt worse because he was making me mad. Over pizza one night, he actually apologized for let-ting this girl get in the way of his responsibilities around the house. Let me tell you, that just floored me when he said that."

Bob could have kept yelling, but in his wisdom he shifted gears from the angry "parent" to the more patient "adult." A smart, sensitive father, Bob understood how to flex his personality muscles to persuade his son to open up.

UNLOCKING YOUR PERSUASIVE POWER BY IDENTIFYING OTHERS' PREFERRED COMMUNICATION STYLES

When I ask soft-spoken participants to stand in front of the group and deliver an extemporaneous speech, I may videotape the presentation. Later, after the speakers watch themselves on video, I draw a straight line about a length of a yardstick on a flip chart. I ask the subject, "If this line repre-sents the full range of your personality, how much of yourself did you show us in your practice speech?"

The truth, as so many speakers discover, is that they are burying vir-tually their entire personality. Blame it on nerves, stress, or fear; whatever the cause, the effect is a flat, crushingly unpersuasive presentation. Participants repeatedly hear me say, "Be flexible—shift gears whenever you feel like it." The many hues and shadings of our personalities need to find expression. With free-ranging room to roam, we uncover facets of our char-acters that enable us to win over a wider range of audiences.

How can you flex the biceps of your personality? Where do you find this room to roam? You can take an acting class, but keep in mind the aim is to let loose the full force of your *natural* personality (not create layers of falsity). It's better to try varying your vocal tone, tempo, or volume to tap the highs and lows of your voice. Use energetic, sweeping gestures to visually accent your points. Communicate your empathy with open, honest facial expressions. When Jimmy Carter occasionally applied these skills to enliven his homespun authenticity, he could be persuasive (as in the 1976 presidential campaign). But more often than not he buried his passion. Pundits joked that when President Carter gave a Fireside Chat, the fire went out.

Consider what top salespeople or charismatic preachers do so well: push our hot buttons. They know how to shake us from our torpor, to appeal to our preferences or biases with searing, stinging immediacy. Their timing, word choice, and tone of voice reinforce the impact of the message, and we are aroused by their passion. They knock away our doubts and objections so that we want to say "yes."

Sounds good, no? Wish you could wield such influence to get what you want?

You *can* harness this power with a wonderfully simple technique: identifying preferred communication styles. Adjust your speaking style to best relate to others. Slow your tempo if they speak slowly. Pump up the volume if they speak louder. Sift through what you want to say and express only those points that will most appeal to your listeners. Shift the spotlight away from you and your needs onto others and their needs.

How to Align Your Selling with the Audience's Needs

When I first arrived in New York to establish my consulting business, much of my time was spent selling my training services to anyone who would meet with me. I would confidently stride into an executive's office and launch into a pitch describing all my accomplishments. My mouth was a steamroller flattening everything in its path. Few companies hired me.

Then I saw the light. Instead of talking about my resume, I began thinking in terms of my audience. These executives wanted results: more effective salespeople, more productive service representatives, more motivated employees. I came up with a short, sweet way to deliver those results by offering a "pilot program." Skeptical managers agreed to "sample" my service at no risk, and profitable contracts soon followed. Instead of rambling on about my credentials (which were of limited importance to them anyway), I used every precious minute to show how I could specifically address their business needs.

A friend who works as a fee-only financial planner faced a similar challenge in his search for affluent clients. His background was impressive, but he promoted himself through direct mail and local advertising in his community. This led to a poor response even when he offered a free "financial check-up."

Then, as a result of diligent research and preparation, he concluded that his audience wanted personal service, not some anonymous promise of free help. So he held financial seminars at the local college where he explained the difference between commission-based investments and his noncommission service. His ability to adopt what he called his "personal outreach" strategy paid off handsomely when new clients came marching to his door.

● **TRAP**   Beware of *octopus persuasion*. When overly aggressive people try to sell their ideas, they may come at the unsuspecting victim from all sides like an octopus on the attack. The octopus salesperson recites reason after reason, bouncing from the low price to the two-for-one deal to the tug-at-the-heartstrings approach, "I gotta make more sales to pay my daughter's hospital bills." The listener, suffocated and surrounded, hunkers down to resist the onslaught and awaits an opportunity to escape. When you set out to persuade, do not pelt others from all directions; instead, select the best approach based on your sensitivity to their preferred mode of communication.

From Decision Trees to Bottom-Line Analysis: A Look at How Different People Like to Communicate

In order to adjust your communication style to fit your audience, you must first identify how others speak and listen. Gender, for instance, offers some clues as to how individuals process information. Women are more likely to be persuaded by personal examples where they can observe behavior and draw connections. Men, by contrast, may not view anecdotes or experience as sufficient evidence to support an argument. Many recent books discuss how gender affects communication; the bibliography lists some of them.

Beyond gender differences, professional training shapes our preferred communication style. Doctors, lawyers, computer programmers, and other highly trained technicians often use decision-tree thinking—a sequence of small judgments that leads to a diagnosis or larger decision. They think in flow charts, moving from point to point with each new answer. To best explain a theory, they might reach for a napkin and diagram their idea. You have probably known people who enjoy sketching or drawing schematic representations of what they're thinking. This helps them communicate a concept without relying solely on words.

When you ask questions, technical types provide precise, deliberate, cautionary responses. They are not afraid to temper their comments with qualifiers (*maybe, however, possibly*). They squint, rub their chins, play with their pencils, fiddle with paper clips, and pace back and forth while deep in thought.

To persuade technicians, let them affirm each step of your reasoning. Sell them on your ideas one piece at a time. As they put the pieces together, they will inch closer and closer toward agreement. Do not jump ahead and rush to the conclusion or you will trigger resistance. Remember that they have invested years of advanced schooling to learn to think in a specific way, whether as a lawyer, doctor, or physicist. Adopt to their style, and you will persuade.

The Doctor-Patient Encounter: A Clash of Communication Styles
You can appreciate the importance of how different groups like to interact by examining how doctors treat patients in interviews. Dr. Elliott Mishler, a social psychologist at Harvard Medical School, finds that doctors may dominate the interaction with questions based on their technical understanding of the treatment, while the patient, often in vain, tries to get the doctor to pay attention to the personal side of the illness. Studies show that when doctors allow their patients to share their stories and explain their concerns, then the patient is more apt to comply with the doctor's instructions and feel like a collaborator in the treatment.[2]

In a separate study, patients were found to have three different problems on their mind, on average, when they entered the doctor's office. But they found themselves cut off by the physician within the first eighteen seconds of the interview, thus never getting a chance to raise all of the topics they had hoped to discuss. Patient compliance fades when questions or concerns are left unanswered.[3]

Most patients want their physicians to give them large doses of information and explanation. In a study of 336 doctor-patient encounters by Harvard Medical School and U.C. Irvine, two thirds of the doctors were found to have underestimated their patients' desire for information. In encounters averaging twenty minutes, a little over one minute was devoted to the doctor giving information to the patient, although the doctors later estimated that they had spent almost half of their consultation time doing so.[4]

For physicians eager to gain patient compliance, revealing more information may help. Patients will pedal the bike or lay off the linguini if they are persuaded by a doctor who gives them plenty of facts and answers all their questions in a supportive, empathetic tone.

Climbing the Corporate Ladder by Talking About "Efficiency Ratios" and "Load Factors"   Like doctors, senior executives have their own preferred communication style. Corporate chieftains are accountable to such groups as the board of directors, shareholders, employees, and customers. They speak a language filled with *return on equity, earnings per share, consolidated revenue, allocated expenses, assets and liabilities,* and *investment income*. They think in terms of numbers, from sales or staffing projections to quarterly results. They reach conclusions by comparing different units of measure, from region-by-region results to productivity per salesperson to earnings per law partner. Although you may not understand such measurements (or even have access to the same data as senior managers), you can frame your arguments to appeal to such individuals.

A young executive at a bank told me how she finally persuaded her division head to adopt her plan to streamline office procedures. For months, she had submitted memos to no avail and proposed inexpensive changes in the way the back office processed data and generated financial reports. "I got tired of hearing no response, so I paid closer attention to how the senior management reached decisions," she said. "As I sat in meetings with them, I noticed that they kept looking at something called an 'efficiency ratio,' or expenses as a percentage of revenue."

Armed with this knowledge, she calculated how her recommendations would lower expenses and improve the company's efficiency ratio. Now she was talking in a language that her bosses could understand! Suddenly, her suggestions were adopted and she earned a promotion for her fine work.

Another manager, this one in the airline industry, shared with me the secret of persuading senior executives in his business. "Talk in terms of 'load factor,' and they'll listen to you," he advised. "The load factor is based on the number of seats filled with paying passengers on flights. Once I learned to tie everything to this number, I was taken more seriously by management."

Going One-on-One with the Head Honcho   If you wish to persuade a chief executive or some other "Very Important Person," your personality will have to stretch like a rubber band to sway the volatile, high-powered, and often egotistical individual that awaits you. Not all presidents are intimidating, of course, and you have no reason to feel inferior (but admit it, you will anyway). Take it from me, a guy who was once all too eager to please people in power: Don't worry about being liked. Avoid slavishly agreeing to everything you hear. Just make your point in the most persuasive way that you can, and then shut up.

MEMORY JOGGER

When you interact with important people, spend less time worrying about making a good impression and more time ensuring that you listen attentively and speak clearly. Communicate effectively and the rest will take care of itself.

Prepare yourself for unexpected questions or comments. Many chief executives make unpredictable or outrageous statements to throw others off guard, especially during a negotiation. They also tend to use analogies to make points, comparing a task such as hiring the right manager to sports or marriage. They usually know how to translate corporate jargon into easily accessible sound bites for journalists, shareholders, and others outside their industry. You can influence top executives by expressing yourself with snappy analogies (*This is like driving a car/shopping for new clothes/making a recipe from scratch*). Finally, never agree with someone (no matter how powerful the speaker) unless you truly see things the same way. Think for yourself at all times and draw your own conclusions.

Whether it's decision-tree thinking or bottom-line financial analysis, your success in getting what you want depends on your ability to speak your audience's language.

Chop Your Remarks into Easy-To-Digest Chunks When Explaining Complex Ideas or Interviewing for a Job

How about everyone else—the nontechnicians, the generalists? How can you persuade *them*? If you must convey technical information, break it into steps, stages, or chapter headings. This works whether you are giving a formal presentation or engaging in casual conversation. Most listeners will grasp dry or fact-heavy material if you feed it to them in digestible chunks.

○ **Now Try This**   Stuck with a tough assignment of having to persuasively communicate complex ideas? Try to fit your material into an organizational structure that will appeal to your audience. Examples:

We're facing three major problems.

Let's look at this process in three distinct stages.

I'd like to talk with you about the three steps ahead of us.

If we break down this issue into its component parts, we can best decide how to proceed.

We must overcome a series of obstacles before we finish to project. They are...

You will learn more about organizing your thoughts in Chapter 6.

Another way to present information in a simple, persuasive manner is to assemble your ideas in a tidy framework such as past/present/future or problem/cause/solution. Many conceptual thinkers will latch onto your message if you make it easy for them to categorize or classify your data. Tossing out too many facts without placing them in the proper context will weaken your persuasiveness.

To prepare for a job interview, consider the task of the interviewer you seek to impress. A typical recruiter will look for certain traits in a candidate, including the ability to communicate persuasively and organize thoughts effectively. When you answer questions during the interview, make it easy for the interviewer to jot notes. Provide bullet points to highlight your remarks. If you are asked, *Why should I hire you?* your answer can pinpoint the three strongest qualities you bring to the position (*You should hire me because I'm persistent, independent, and extremely driven*). Interviewers appreciate when candidates express themselves clearly and answer all questions specifically.

TAPPING YOUR NATURAL RANGE OF EXPRESSION SO THAT THE "REAL YOU" SHINES THROUGH

You may be thinking, *I don't want to adjust my personality to fit in with everyone around me. Sounds too much like I'm trying to make people like me. Why can't I just be myself and persuade in my own way without being phony?*

Answer: you are right. You should not change your personality to copy everyone else. This smacks of falsity and will destroy the authenticity you need to make a genuine appeal.

Instead, tap your natural range of expression to relate effectively to others. Be yourself, stay within your comfort zone, and do not put on masks or resort to artifice.

○ **NOW TRY THIS**   Many of us do not appreciate the full range of expression that flows naturally from our multifaceted personalities. To increase your awareness of how you communicate, get a pen and paper.

Describe the last time you were truly furious, ecstatic, remorseful, and commanding. What triggered each response? How did your communication change (for example, did you stutter, giggle, yell, cry, talk faster/slower, keep quiet)? If others observed your behavior, how did they react? If you are uneasy with the notion of flexing your personality muscles, realize that you do it anyway whenever your emotions change.

The purpose of this exercise is to reacquaint you with your richly diverse personality. If you are convinced you talk in a monotone, then think about the last time you said good-bye to a loved one at an airport or when you first cradled an infant. Your demeanor surely changed to reflect your emotions. You can sweeten your voice, strengthen your tone, vary your pitch, pause for dramatic effect, even scream—as long as it comes naturally. Don't pretend you are powerless when you have the power to adapt.

Tap your natural range of expression. Select which part of your communication arsenal to use based on what will appeal to your audience. Persuaders are animated. They hold our attention and make us care about what they say. Through a keen awareness of their audience, they control how they speak and listen while the rest of us may fire shots in the dark.

The best persuaders have access to the full spectrum of their genuine personality. They shift from animation, to silence, to curiosity with ease. They are continually expanding, not contracting, the boundaries of their personalities by varying their voices and experimenting with new gestures or expressions.

Persuasive speakers unleash their personality in all its glorious colors for another reason. They know what they are up against when trying to persuade. Salespeople see far too many prospects doze off. Public speakers watch some audience members slump over and fall asleep. Lecturers will tell you of the time they dimmed the lights for a few minutes to show slides, only to find that a few tired souls fell asleep in their chairs. Listeners will not always listen.

If your range of expression is too narrow, you increase the odds that those you seek to persuade will tune out. Why should they go along with you if they must struggle to stay awake while you are speaking?

Stirring the Emotional Urge to Buy

Boredom results when our emotions shut down. We inhale vapors of apathy and grow indifferent to the chatter whirling around us. Think of the last time a telemarketer interrupted your dinner to pitch magazine subscriptions or a new long-distance phone service. Before you could count to three, you were already plotting ways to hang up. The caller read from a script, waiting for and perhaps expecting you to interrupt. You probably did not even care what they were selling—you just wanted to escape.

Top salespeople know that decisions are often driven by the emotional and psychological character of the buyer. Logic serves to rationalize the decision in the buyer's mind *after* the mental purchase has been made. Consumers thus look for logical reasons to buy things that satisfy emotional urges. As one chief executive officer observed, "Ask executives why they ultimately make many of their decisions and in the end they'll say it wasn't the facts, it was how they felt about it. Emotion drives decisions probably more than anything."[5]

As a result, master persuaders do not simply memorize a bunch of dry facts and then blurt out a canned speech or recite a stale script. Instead, they engage others in a lively, mutually beneficial exchange. They communicate energy through intensity, passion, humor, imagination, enthusiasm, or some other powerful force of will.

It is not enough to learn your lines and repeat them with robotic sameness. True persuasion requires a bolt of lightning, a splash of icy water, a tremor that shakes complacent audiences off their foundations.

● **TRAP**   You love logic. You expect others do, too. As you build a persuasive argument, you strive for an open-and-shut case that is so beautifully, undeniably logical that you cannot lose. But despite all your sound, well-reasoned positions, you find your audience detached, uninterested, and largely unimpressed. What went wrong?

You fell into the I LOVE LOGIC trap, thinking that pure, sweet, unfiltered reason always wins the day. Although you may hold yourself to this high standard, do not assume others are equally enthralled by your show of logic. They may lack emotional involvement, or they may not view you as a credible spokesperson. We persuade by incorporating logic, emotion, and credibility into our remarks. Logic alone will not suffice.

How can you prepare to speak with more emotional impact? Practice applying one of the following techniques to your everyday conversations:

Tantalize   To activate your audience's emotions, begin sentences with *Think how relaxing it would be to...* or *Imagine for a moment that you....* Loosen up your personality so that you allow yourself (and your listeners) to dream of an ideal state, a problem that vanishes, a future better than the present.

Appeal to greed   That's right, give greed a chance. Network marketers recruit new members to sell their products by promising vast wealth

(*You, too, can triple your income in six months*). Infomercials stoke our emotional fire by showing us how much better our lives will be if we (1) buy that juicer, (2) attend the no-money-down real estate seminar, or (3) send away for the free sampler kit. How can we refuse? You can do the same by saying, *One year from now, you can enjoy...* or *If you think you could never* ___, *think again.*

Appeal to fear If you show someone that the price of not heeding your advice or acting as you wish is too high, then you will persuade. Questions that begin *What happens if [describe worst case scenario]?* or *Are you prepared if...?* are hard to answer with cold logic. Why? When an emotion like fear is aroused, logic loses its steam.

Infuse your comments with a dose of excitement. Make it a habit to speak with more vigor and enthusiasm. Broaden the natural range of your personality so that you can stir the emotions of those who listen to you.

● **TRAP** In order to tap your full range of expression, avoid feeding yourself negative mental messages. I have worked with many people who insist that they cannot help speaking in a dreadful monotone or who refuse to raise their voice. They repeat *I am stuck with a droning voice* or *I never raise my voice* or *I don't like to wear my emotions on my sleeve.* As a result, they are less apt to experiment with vocal variation. Every time they tell me that they are "born with a terrible voice" or that they don't "believe in" showing too much expression, they reinforce a rigid, inflexible self-image that inhibits their persuasiveness. Their refusal to expand their natural range of expression often stems from a lack of confidence. Don't neutralize your personality; energize it. Put down this book right now and start yelling, laughing, whispering, ordering, pleading. Hear yourself break free from the confines of your own self-imposed limits.

DON'T LET THEM IGNORE YOU: USE THE SPEAK-LISTEN RATIO TO CAPTURE YOUR AUDIENCE'S ATTENTION

Yin and yang.

Chinese dualistic philosophers devised this cosmic principle long ago. They were on to something.

My grandmother once told me that anything in moderation is fine, but that the extremes could get us in trouble. She was on to something.

Balance. In the boxing ring, they call it *mixing it up.* On the talk shows, they engage in *give and take.* In the courtroom, they uphold *scales of justice.*

Persuaders are balancers. They maintain a healthy mix of speaking and listening. They do not talk too fast or too slow. They measure risk-reward, cost-benefit, or cause-effect to explore both sides of an issue. They blend logic, emotion, and credibility in packaging their persuasive idea. Their voice, gestures, expressions, and words combine to deliver a clear, consistent message.

The most important aspect of balance is the speak-listen ratio. A crucial component of a flexible personality is the ability to ration your words, to persuade with a generous helping of listening along with a side order of speaking. Adding too much speaking to the recipe will ruin the flavor of your personality.

People commonly use at least 30 percent more words than necessary to express their ideas. This wastes time and causes audiences to tune out. What's worse, we live in the midst of an information explosion. Deluged with data, we are less apt to listen when a speaker heads in a direction we do not want to go.

MEMORY JOGGER

Never waste words when you want to persuade.

Prepare to persuade by monitoring how much of the time you spend speaking and listening during your daily conversations. Get what you want by cutting the time you spend talking. Keep your remarks brief, resist the urge to go off on tangents, and end with a question.

Consider the speak-listen ratio in terms of a thirty-minute job interview. You can try to sell yourself by talking for twenty minutes or more, eating up time by giving long, chatty answers. The downside, of course, is that the interviewer will get to talk for only ten minutes at most. Most people fade fast and lose interest if they don't feel like an equal partner in a conversation. Talking too much is like weighing down a seesaw so that you cannot bob up and down with your playmate: It takes all the fun out of the activity.

If you balance the amount of time you spend speaking and listening, you can enliven a dialogue by limiting yourself to specific, focused answers. This ensures that both parties actively participate in the conversation. Like a long tennis rally, a good exchange progresses smoothly as the participants keep hitting the ball back over the net. They do not hog the ball or miss their shots. They work in tandem to sustain a consistent, mutually enjoyable interaction. They talk *with* each other, not *at* each other.

○ **NOW TRY THIS** Introducing The 80/20 Rule. This rule, which I first developed for my sales training programs, states that you should listen 80 percent of the time and limit your speaking to the remaining 20 percent. This applies to any encounter in which you seek to persuade. Salespeople may talk themselves out of a sale by rambling on when they should keep quiet. Arguments erupt when two explosive personalities lock horns and talk over one another instead of each letting the other person blow off steam. The rule even relates to a first date, when you want to learn about your friend and not monopolize the conversation. This does not mean you should carry a stopwatch around with you and treat the 80/20 ratio too seriously. As long as you strive to listen most of the time and speak only when you have something to say, then you will wield more persuasive power.

The 80/20 Rule underscores the difference between talking *with* someone and *at* someone. When engaging in a satisfying, revealing conversation, chances are you allow the other person to do most of the talking. You listen attentively and speak only when appropriate. This way, when you *do* speak, the other person does not ignore what you say.

This kind of conversational balance promotes persuasion. By keeping your remarks concise, you guard against overselling. People will pay more attention to what you say when they believe you have listened to them. They will be more willing to accept your advice or buy your product if they feel that you have taken the time to understand them. Best of all, by limiting your speaking you need not worry about being interrupted by an impatient listener.

If Others Interrupt You; Say Less But Make It Count More

An accountant in one of my workshops complained about how her colleagues interrupted her all the time. "It seems that whenever I open my mouth, someone cuts me off," she said. "So I speed up and string all my words together to make my point before it's too late."

The solution? I advised her to prevent interruptions by grabbing listeners' attention so that they kept quiet. By adding drama to her remarks and following The 80/20 Rule, she found that her co-workers actually invited her to elaborate. When asked a tough question, she would pause, establish eye contact, and deliver the kind of compelling answer that made even the least patient listeners want to hear more.

During our follow-up session a few months later, she told me of one instance in which she made the speak-listen ratio work to her advantage.

Her boss asked her how to improve employee morale during the stressful tax season:

> I told him, "Try chaos." He just looked at me wondering what I meant. I kept quiet. So he asked me to explain, and I said we needed to liven up the office, scale back bureaucratic rules, and let employees decorate their work space. In short, we needed to offer relief from the grinding routine. That was my point, but had I just come right out and said it he would have interrupted me.

● **TRAP** Never compete for a listener's attention. Do not try to make yourself heard over the ring of a phone or the blare of a siren. Instead, stop talking and wait for the noise to subside. Some listeners will distract you by lighting a pipe, cleaning their eyeglasses, or shuffling papers while you are speaking. Whenever you see someone engage in another activity while you are trying to make a point, shift to the listening mode. Pose exploratory questions to gauge your progress:

Are you with me so far?

Are you ready to move to the next step?

Do you have any concerns about what I've said?

Beware of letting your mouth run.

How to Let Others Persuade Themselves You Are Right

Another benefit of limiting your speaking is that you can give listeners a chance to persuade themselves. Rather than telling them what you think they should do or prodding them to act in a certain way, you can gently lead them in the direction you wish. This suggestive approach frees you from having to talk too much. It also allows your audience to come up with their own ideas and win themselves over to your way of thinking. You sway opinions by dropping subtle hints that give others the chance to persuade themselves. Then you let them talk.

When I advise mid-level managers, they often tell me that they persuade their boss by planting seeds "so that the chief can claim credit for the idea." They know if they talk too much they will waste time and possibly bore their superior. In his book *How To Sell Your Ideas,* Jesse Nirenberg gives a humorous example of a fictional chat between brainstorming executives:

"I'd like to propose to you a great idea you're suggesting."

"I like it already."

"I haven't told it to you yet."

"But it's mine, isn't it?"

"Yes, and that's why it's so good."

"I can hardly wait to hear it."[6]

Although Benjamin Franklin never had to persuade modern chief executives, he also favored the hint-your-way-to-the-top approach. He took the stance of "the humble Inquirer and Doubter." Franklin, one of America's great persuaders, was a master of balance. Despite his inventive vision and vast intellect, he resisted the urge to talk more than necessary or tell people what to do. Instead, he expressed himself in terms of "modest Diffidence," a habit that he confessed in his autobiography "has been of great Advantage to me, when I have had occasion to inculcate my Opinions and persuade Men into Measures that I have been from time to time engag'd in promoting."[7]

Abraham Lincoln shared Franklin's fondness for gentle prodding over pontificating, for listening over speaking. As young Lincoln advised the Springfield Washington Temperance Society in 1842, "When the conduct of men is designed to be influenced, *persuasion,* kind, unassuming persuasion, should ever be adopted. It is an old and a true maxim, that a 'drop of honey catches more flies than a gallon of gall.'"[8]

Memory Jogger

The moment you win people over is the moment when they talk themselves into believing you are right.

If You Talk Too Much, Your Pitch May Backfire

Another reason to balance your speaking and listening is to remind yourself to periodically check in with your audience to assess your progress. Consider a team of American marketing representatives sent to deliver a key sales presentation to an influential group of foreign investors. The Americans give a three-hour presentation replete with sophisticated sound effects, state-of-the-art visual technology (screens mounted strategically throughout the room, multi-color handouts with fancy graphics), and a well-rehearsed, finely tuned script. Sounds like a sure winner?

They forget one thing: to let the audience participate. After a seemingly flawless three hours of talking away, the Americans confidently ask their listeners what *they* think. After sitting in a dark room for the same length of time as a screening of *Heaven's Gate,* the audience is finally asked to respond.

This is not the way to persuade any group, especially foreigners who may already face language barriers. A member of the audience might smile and say, "We do not understand."

Imagine the Americans' panic, "W-W-What part didn't you understand?" The answer hurts like a slap in the face: "All of it."

The foreigner's response may in fact be a savvy attempt to turn a weakness into a strength. If the Americans are forced to repeat their long performance, their enthusiasm will fade and their persuasive power will plummet. And they have no one to blame but themselves. Had they stopped every so often to ask, "Would this interest you?" or "How do you think your employees would benefit?" they could have fostered a dialogue to ensure the audience followed the presentation.

To take a real-life example, a curator at the Smithsonian felt that the 1994 Japanese exhibit explaining the history of the United States should reflect America's racial diversity. He gave an impassioned speech to a Japanese audience, leaping to his feet, shaking his fist, and pounding on the table as he described how America's racial conflicts were critical to its modern character. When he finished speaking, the Japanese were silent until one of them asked if he was feeling sick. For a culture used to self-restraint, hearing a thundering speech seemed out of place.[9]

Do not overestimate the power of words. Sounds may come from your mouth, but whether anyone cares to listen is another matter. Even if you are a recognized expert in your field who is paid thousands of dollars for a one-hour speech, please (for the sake of audiences everywhere) do not pontificate at will.

The worst approach you can take is "the longer I speak, the better." A good example is leaders with big egos who neglect to balance their speak-listen ratio. They grow fond of the trappings of power and inflate the importance of their remarks. As a writer observed of Benito Mussolini, "If he did not become great it was because he let himself be drugged by a poison which is more dangerous than opium or hashish—by words. He talked so much and so often at length he took his own words for reality and lost contact with the world."[10]

● **TRAP** Imagine you are the most knowledgeable person in the room about the topic at hand, and it's your job to persuade others of your idea. You are the expert. Everyone looks to you for answers. You possess a wealth of statistics, examples, and illustrations to support your point. You open your mouth to talk, and something goes wrong—*you cannot stop talking.* You begin harmlessly, "Let me just say..." A few minutes later, you realize that you have so much MORE TO SAY. Your comments turn into a lecture, involuntarily pinning your listeners into submission. Your vast knowledge works against you; even your enthusiasm for the topic betrays you. You have lost your speak-listen balance, and one by one people tune out.

When placed in a collaborative situation (such as a team project or a family outing), you will persuade by listening far more than by speaking. Better yet, each word you utter will have added significance if you are known for brevity. As Harry Truman fondly described his secretary of state, General George Marshall, "He never made any speeches at you. Sometimes he would sit for an hour with little or no expression on his face, but when he had heard enough, he would come up with a statement of his own that would invariably cut to the very bone of the matter under discussion."[11] When Marshall spoke, the President listened.

If you treat words as a precious resource, people will listen to you.

QUICK REVIEW

- Customize your persuasive strategy to fit your audience.
- Before you persuade, think through what someone stands to gain or lose by saying yes.
- Know whether your audience is led by internal or external motivations.
- Select the side of your natural personality—parent, adult, or child— that will best appeal to your audience.
- Tame your judgments. Don't overplay the role of parent.
- Flex the biceps of your personality with vocal range, gestures, and expressions.
- Present information in a way that is easy for your audience to comprehend.
- Tap your natural range of expression to relate effectively to others.
- Use The 80/20 Rule: Limit your speaking to 20 percent of a conversation.
- Let the audience participate in the persuasive process. Win them over with suggestions, not orders.

NOTES

1. *The Wall Street Journal*, 1-26-94, p. A6.

2. *The New York Times*, 1-21-88, p. B10.

3. Ibid.

4. Ibid.

5. *Inc.*, March 1992, p. 48.

6. Jesse Nirenberg, *How To Sell Your Ideas*, McGraw Hill, New York, 1984, p. 118.

7. Quoted in Kenneth Silverman's introduction to *Autobiography of Benjamin Franklin*, Penguin Books, New York, 1986.

8. Donald T. Phillips, *Lincoln on Leadership*, Warner Books, New York, 1992, p. 39.

9. *The Los Angeles Times*, 8-2-94, p. F3.

10. Wallace C. Fotheringham, *Perspectives on Persuasion*, Allyn & Bacon Inc., Boston, 1966, p. 110.

11. David McCullough, *Truman*, Simon & Schuster, New York, 1992, p. 534.

Three Steps to Designing
a Dress Rehearsal Before
Your Persuasive Encounter

While empathy and flexibility help you prepare to persuade, there's more. This chapter tackles the nitty-gritty steps of rehearsing what to say and how to say it.

Why rehearse? When you seek to persuade someone of something important, your odds of success soar if you have already practiced what you want to say. Professional actors and athletes do it, and so should you. The three steps are fun and do not require much time. Best of all, rehearsing gives you the confidence to win over any audience.

Your rehearsal should take into account your comfort level with your audience. When you prepare to persuade an individual, you need to assess your relationship with that person. The task of winning him or her over becomes much easier if you already enjoy open lines of communication. To determine the quality of your communication with those you seek to persuade, use the following exercise.

DIAGNOSTIC SELF-TEST: MEASURING YOUR RELATIONSHIP WITH A FRIEND OR ACQUAINTANCE

Read the following statements and circle either A, for agree, or D, for disagree. (Replace X with the name of the person you want to influence):

A   D   X strikes me as an open, fair-minded individual.

A   D   I can ask X for help without feeling embarrassed.

A   D   X values my input and treats what I say seriously.

A   D   X recognizes when I make a good point.

A   D   X wants me to be successful and takes joy in my triumphs.

A   D   X has been there for me in the past when I was in need of help.

A   D   I am aware of the reasons for X's major decisions.

A   D   X tells me when I make a mistake, but does not insult me.

A   D   I feel free to disagree with X.

If you circled A at least seven times, you are well positioned to persuade. If you circled A less than seven times, your communication with X needs work. Rehearsing is a must. You may want to develop more rapport with X before attempting to persuade.

● **TRAP**   Don't skip this chapter because you think your knowledge is sufficient to bowl over anybody. Also beware of treating your vast experience as an excuse for lack of preparation. Knowledge or experience do not persuade. Communication does. You can have the greatest proposal in the world based on years of impressive research, but none of that matters unless you speak and listen effectively.

WHY MEMORIZATION IS THE WORST KIND OF REHEARSAL

Veteran persuaders, such as longtime salespeople, sometimes think they are exempt from rehearsals. They might conclude that after so many years of communicating the same message, they have "heard everything." Rather than continually refining their persuasive skills, they fall back on old habits and hope for the best.

Rehearsals are invaluable. They help you sharpen your communication skills and strengthen your mastery of your subject. I recall a spry senior who volunteered as a docent in an art museum. She told me that she spends every Sunday night "playing a little game" with her husband in which he would try to stump her by asking arcane questions about the museum's art collection. This exercise made her fresh for the next week of tours and helped her achieve her goal of educating visitors so that they would enjoy their visit and donate money to the museum.

Rehearsing involves more than learning lines from a script. Memorization can lead to trouble. An orator plans a big speech by reciting it over and over in the mirror, but that's not the kind of rehearsal that produces persuasion. A canned delivery will shut off your listeners' minds and bury your passion. Your message will fall upon deaf ears.

Speakers who rely on memorization appear to push the words out of their mouths. Their heads lurch toward the audience, and their eyes widen. They adopt the helpless deer-in-the-headlights look that afflicts so many political candidates during staged debates. Ironically, their attempt to take command of their presentation by memorizing it serves only to enslave them. They worry so much about spouting their preprogrammed phrases that they have no mental energy left to *feel* their message.

Memorization strips you of your best persuasive asset: authenticity. Instead of practicing your "lines," use your private rehearsal time to test different ways to express your ideas. Decide where to place verbal emphasis, how to organize your points, and what words sound most enticing. This makes memorization unnecessary. You will grow so familiar with your remarks that they will roll off your tongue when the time comes to persuade.

With so many unpredictable forces at work during human interaction, you should strive to reduce uncertainty. Here's where rehearsals help. The three steps you are about to learn lower the risk of a mishap interfering with your persuasiveness. You want to be ready for anything.

STEP 1: GO AHEAD AND TALK TO YOURSELF! EXPRESSING YOUR IDEAS OUT LOUD HELPS CLARIFY THEM

Come on, admit it. You talk out loud in the car, sing in the shower, and smugly answer those *Jeopardy* questions when no one else is around.

Yes, you talk to yourself. You are not a nut. No reason to be embarrassed. My guess is just about everyone does it, including me, so there's nothing to worry about.

Talking to yourself can provide some excellent training as you prepare to persuade. Hearing your own voice can affirm your beliefs and help you express those beliefs to others. You will strengthen your resolve and build confidence.

Sometimes just the act of reading out loud to yourself can produce a powerful effect. A participant in one of my speech workshops told the group about the day he decided to become a literary agent. He flipped through a paperback collection of Shakespeare plays and stumbled upon a passage that moved him. Alone in the room, he recited the passage in his normal tone of voice. He repeated the words, this time with more feeling. The drama and beauty of the language overwhelmed him. By bringing the

words to life, he understood for the first time how much he loved literature. He knew from that moment that he wanted to make his living from
the world of books.

Talking in private offers a magic all its own. We experience catharsis,
a dose of humility, perhaps an epiphany, as we verbalize the emotions and
observations that may otherwise remain unspoken. As Wallace
Fotheringham wrote in *Perspectives on Persuasion,* "...every speaker...is his
own most affected eavesdropper, and that is why the art of talking to ourselves is one that we may not neglect save at the ever-present risk of growing self-distortion."[1]

Why talk out loud when quiet, calm thinking may serve the same purpose? Talking lets you hear your message as others hear it. You put the
sense of *sound* to work for you. Better yet, rehearsing lets you assess the
pros and cons of your message objectively. You will know when you
sound disingenuous or deceptive. You cannot fool yourself when you are
alone in a room talking to the walls. Whether you call it your *inner voice,*
your *soul,* or your *conscience,* you need to let it run free. This way, you
can avoid becoming so close to your own point of view that you lose perspective on how others may interpret what you say.

Another advantage of talking to yourself is the flood of fresh ideas
and emotions that rush forth as you speak. Translating what you think into
clear, crisp words distills your message. You may even identify ways to
solve thorny problems. Some people find that by rehearsing in a free-flowing, stream-of-consciousness fashion, they uncover emotions that had been
suppressed. By conversing freely with yourself, you may be flooded with
unbridled feelings.

So spend some time alone with a tape recorder, vocalizing your
reflections on why you want to persuade, what you hope to achieve, and
how others will be affected by your proposal. Rid yourself of self-consciousness. You may feel a bit silly and embarrassed at first, but keep going
until you grow comfortable with the sound of your own voice.

● **TRAP** As you talk to yourself, do not judge your remarks or continually edit what you say. Do not allow self-criticism to interfere, especially
if you tend to hold yourself to ridiculously high standards. Resist the urge
to think how terrible your voice sounds (*So squeaky!*), how weak your
points are (*They'll rip me apart!*), or how your message may spark contro-
versy (*They'll hiss me! They'll heckle me!*). Instead, record your remarks and
pretend you are another person listening to you. Most people do not sit in
cruel judgment waiting to attack your every word. What are you offering
the audience? How will they gain? Are the benefits clear and appealing?

Steer clear of self-sabotage by asking yourself these questions and focusing your attention on the audience.

What exactly should you say when using this Talk to Yourself approach? A useful starting point is to imagine your listeners asking *What should I do? How should I think?* or *What are my options?* Respond to these concerns (with the tape running). These questions probably resemble the ones that your real audience will be asking as you try to persuade them.

○ **NOW TRY THIS**   With the tape recorder on, rehearse your persuasive message by completing any of the following sentences:

All of us...

What would happen if...

There's something you need to know...

You and I both know that...

There's so much to gain by...

What a pleasure it would be if...

These phrases can help you develop compelling statements or questions that will grab your listeners' attention.

Talking out loud lets you experiment with different verbal strategies. You can win someone over by making a declaration, asserting your point of view, issuing promises, or posing questions. Try framing your persuasive point using each approach.

Say you want to persuade a friend to join you for a date. You can rehearse by speaking in a variety of ways and then deciding which sounds best:

1. DECLARATION—you declare something as true or possible without evidence.

    We could have a great time together next Friday.

2. REASON—you offer evidence to support your interpretation of the truth.

    Since we both like movies, I'm sure we could have a great time together next Friday.

3. PROMISES—you promise an outcome or action.

    I promise it will be a fun evening.

4. QUESTIONS—you skip statements and jump right to asking for what you want.

    What do you say we get together next Friday?

You can prepare for almost any persuasive encounter by sampling each of these approaches and selecting the one that sounds best to you. Worksheet 5–1 diagrams how you can plan what to say.

Four Ways to Express Yourself

Prepare your next persuasive appeal by completing this worksheet.

First, know what you want:

I want to persuade _____*[name of person/audience]*_____ to _____*[desired action]*_____.

With your goal in mind, construct sample phrases using each of the following types of statements:

*   DECLARATION (come right out and directly state what you want):

    _____.

*   REASON (offer evidence, such as something you and your listeners have in common, to back up what you want):

    _____.

*   PROMISES (promise a desirable result or reward if audience complies):

    _____.

*   QUESTIONS (pose a question that leads the respondent to say "yes"):

    _____?

The safest approach is usually to ask a question (which we discuss in more detail in Chapter 12). When mobilizing a group to act as you wish, you may want to use strong arguments. Declarations tend to work well when you "mean business" and do not wish to waste time on "small talk."

Promises are particularly useful during negotiations when both parties jockey for position and try to exert leverage to achieve their goals.

STEP 2: HOW TO HANDLE OBJECTIONS— ANTICIPATE AND DISARM

After you complete the first step and talk to yourself, your rehearsal gets nasty. That's right, now you must think in terms of conflict or confrontation. By planning for the worst, you enter into any persuasive situation ready to defuse hostility. The more you practice handling objections, the stronger your command of your audience and the less you have to fear.

If you are a top salesperson, you surely rehearse responses to common questions or objections. Customers will complain about the price, question the quality of the product, or compare your terms with the competition. Some people will procrastinate to avoid making a buying decision, others will sling objections your way as a diversionary tactic, and still others will nitpick or negotiate in an effort to cut the best deal. You know how to handle any of these situations. At no point do you give in to their resistance or resent their unwillingness to buy. You enjoy the persuasive jousting and *expect* to win them over.

Rehearsing helps you plan for such situations, to anticipate resistance and disarm the audience with your gracious, patient, nonthreatening response.

MEMORY JOGGER

You gain credibility and sharpen your leadership skills when you are able to listen to objections and respond without defensiveness.

Respond to Disagreements with a Verbal Embrace

No matter how many angry attacks or stubborn refusals greet you, respond to what you hear with a verbal embrace. When someone objects to your ideas, always acknowledge what's been said:

That's one way of looking at it.

I understand where you're coming from.

You might be hot under the collar, but maintain your composure and strike an outward pose of equanimity.

Salespeople are trained to handle objections by saying,

I'm glad you asked that.

or

My other satisfied customers initially expressed that same concern.

Such statements disarm those who expect either an escalation of hostilities or your immediate surrender.

Prepare Yourself for Objections Disguised as Questions

Knowing what questions to expect can improve your rehearsal. Not everyone will respond to you like an outraged lawyer by proclaiming, "I OBJECT!" You are more likely to hear a question such as *Why should I do this?* than an outright objection such as *I will not do this.* Think of the most likely questions your listener might ask. For example, when you ask for a raise, the boss might shoot back:

Why should I give you a raise when profits are down?

How can I agree when you are already the best-paid person in the department?

Do you think it's fair for you to get a raise when we've just had lay-offs and no one else is getting raises?

Caught unprepared for such questions, you might fumble for something—anything—to say in defense. Your nervous tic will flare up. The boss's arms are folded, and the full force of authority presses against you like a stiff, icy wind. You regret getting yourself into such a mess in the first place.

If you are expecting the boss to erect these roadblocks, however, you can rehearse cogent answers. Here are some sample responses:

To successfully rebuild this firm and return to profitability, we need to maintain competitive salaries for those people who have a future here.

I see your point, but I don't measure my pay against my colleagues. That's not my business. You have always told me that pay should reflect the level of service we give the company and how much we produce to improve the bottom line.

We both want what's fair. I think it's fair to pay people what they are worth, especially now that we're in a restructuring stage and we want to generate momentum to operate as a leaner organization.

Questions often serve as thinly disguised objections that may carry an undercurrent of anger or accusation. Shrewd negotiators will often intimidate those seated across the table by posing questions in a hostile, cynical, or furious tone. Job interviewers will resort to outlandish questions to see how a candidate responds. Law school professors will direct tough "hypotheticals" at those notorious students who love to fill the room with the sound of their own voice. "Turning a pompous know-it-all into a fool in front of one hundred of his peers works like a muzzle on a dog," one law professor told me with glee.

Okay, you wonder, I'll be grilled when I try to persuade. But how do I ready myself for the kinds of questions that may come my way?

Grill yourself first. It requires two simple steps:

1. Anticipate the Questions   List questions that *you* would ask if you were on the receiving end of your persuasive appeal. Consider the factors that will influence whether your proposal is adopted. Identify any budget constraints, office/family/personal politics, past promises, future events, or other distractions that may enter into the discussion. Questions usually spring from concerns that threaten to block acceptance, so try to pinpoint any worries or reservations that may preoccupy the other party.

2. Draft Effective Answers   Now devise specific answers to these questions. Write down what you deem an Ideal Response. Use a pencil with an eraser, because you should experiment for at least ten minutes with a variety of possible "comebacks." By anticipating questions and planning satisfactory answers, you reduce the anxiety that comes when you are "put on the spot."

MEMORY JOGGER

You can overcome any objection if you rehearse smart answers to the toughest possible questions.

Here are some techniques to help you anticipate questions and disarm the questioner with a trenchant response:

Leap Ahead and Look Back   A useful method for preparing winning answers to tricky questions is to imagine that you can jump ahead one week, looking back on the successful persuasive encounter and telling a friend what happened ("It was great. I said ___, then she said ___, then I said ___"). This frees your mind to come up with creative responses. The pressure suddenly lifts if you pretend the conversation has already occurred. You are no longer preparing for some future event, but reflecting on the past. You now have a "second chance" to deliver your Ideal Response in the live action of real life.

Humanize Your Facts   Tackle tough questions by humanizing your facts. Steer clear of dry analysis. Piling one statistic on top of another will not suffice. You will need facts to address a questioner's immediate concern, of course, but persuasion also requires an emotional charge. If a friend angrily questions your suggestion that he should break off an engagement (*What gives you of all people the right to say that?*), try this, "The fact is I've gone through the same thing." After pausing, continue adding personal information, "You may be surprised to hear me say this, but I speak from two long, hard years of experience. When I was in your shoes, I heard the same advice and I didn't believe it, either."

Talk about people, not things or abstract concepts, in your Ideal Response. Share what motivates or inspires you. No matter how brutal the interrogation, you can bounce back by responding with poise and genuine feeling. This will bring audiences closer to you. You will awaken their emotions and soften their hard edges.

MEMORY JOGGER

Just because the questioner shows no emotion, do not feel obliged to behave the same way. Let loose with passion and energy, even when you feel as if you are talking to a tree.

Hold a Press Conference for Yourself   Holding your own private press conference, replete with tough questions and penetrating answers, will lead to new insights and a more balanced understanding of your topic. You will enjoy an added dose of confidence as you rehearse how to persuade. Preparing Ideal Responses heightens your awareness of the subject matter.

○ **NOW TRY THIS**   Think of a specific persuasive challenge ahead of you. Consider your audience (spouse, supervisor, community board). Imagine yourself in their shoes. Put your empathy skills to the test and identify the three questions you would most likely ask the speaker. If your remarks include technical details or complex formulas, expect fact-finding or clarifying questions. If the topic is controversial, expect loaded questions that sound more like objections. List the questions and rehearse your answers. Practice a question-and-answer exchange with a friend. Even if these anticipated questions do not arise, the boost in your confidence will more than justify the investment in preparation time.

How to Prepare for a Hostile Audience

If you face hostile listeners, confront their objections right away. Never evade the core issue in the hope that it will disappear on its own. It probably won't. You need to fairly describe your audience's position, acknowledge their right to an opinion, and then clearly and concisely express your view. Make every word count. Try not to repeat yourself.

MEMORY JOGGER

You can persuade a hostile audience if you first demonstrate that you understand the source of their hostility.

In my sales training programs, I often lead a brainstorming session in which participants identify all the objections they commonly face. We list them on a flip chart, and the group shares their preferred responses. This activity produces from twenty to thirty objections and a "trophy" response to match each one. The trophy goes to the best comeback line as voted by the group.

Get in the habit of anticipating questions and preparing concise, meaty responses. Welcome objections as a positive sign that your listener takes you seriously. Although you may dread the prospect of getting into a verbal scuffle with a resistant or hostile opponent, consider the truly dreadful alternative of silence. One who voices no objections and greets your comments with a face of stone can pose far greater challenges.

At least with objections, you know where the other party stands. Their position is clear, and you have a fair chance to address their concerns. Most salespeople will tell you they prefer dealing with an outspoken loudmouth than with a silent zombie.

If you are preparing to persuade a potentially explosive audience comprised of individuals with divergent and deeply felt opinions, then try to characterize their range of views as reasonable but slightly less advantageous alternatives to your idea. Do not disagree outright; find a way to "agree up to a point." By accepting opposing positions as sensible, you create the impression that you are a wise, objective judge with the ability to examine pros and cons in a fair-minded manner.

Sometimes, you can easily predict what your listeners will say (*That's too expensive; We've never done it that way before; I thought we already covered this in detail and made a final decision*). Don't wait for the obvious objection: Beat them to the punch! Prepare to raise the objection *before* they get a chance. Rehearse such lines as, "If I were you, I'd be concerned about [objection]." This lets you address the objection at your own pace while sending a message of supreme empathy. Rather than hide from objections, come right out and face them head on.

Even if you are wrong in what you presume the objections will be, you still win because the other party will tell you if any real objections remain (*I'm not so concerned about price, but I am worried about your company going under and losing my money*).

MEMORY JOGGER

Never show resistance to an objection or you will polarize others. If you push, they will push back.

○ **NOW TRY THIS** Looking for a foolproof way to respond to any objection? Try the *feel, felt, found* approach. Listen to what the other person says. Wait for them to finish discussing their reasons for not going along with you. Resist the urge to interrupt. Then, when the time comes to address the objection, fit your response into this format:

I know how you feel. Others have felt the same way. They have found that...

A salesperson who hears someone dither about making a decision to buy might say, "I know how you feel. Many of my best clients have felt the same way at first. They have found that this product has saved them hundreds of dollars—not to mention headaches and aggravation."

STEP 3: CHOOSING THE BEST WAY TO SUPPORT WHAT YOU WANT TO SAY

Remember as a kid when you grabbed some crayons and went crazy with a coloring book? Each page offered a bare black-and-white sketch of a beach scene or a baseball game or a backyard barbeque. Your choice of colors and your skill in staying within the lines gave the picture your own personal touch.

The final step in designing your dress rehearsal works the same way. Talking to yourself and anticipating objections lay the groundwork for any persuasive encounter. They help you speak up and address the toughest questions. All you need now is to assemble your facts and support—to get out those crayons and bring color and flair to your message.

How do you add color? By choosing a lively mix of supporting material to uphold your main point. If you want to talk someone into doing something, you need to supply reasons for them to act. These reasons can consist of:

- Facts
- Statistics
- Other evidence (such as studies, empirical data)
- Personal experiences
- Anecdotes
- Third-party endorsements

By rehearsing your persuasive appeal using a range of supporting devices, you can launch your sales pitch with all the ammunition you need to win over anybody.

How the Three Steps of a Dress Rehearsal Unfold

Say you want to persuade a friend to devote less time to her day job and more time to her painting. You feel she has great talent as an artist, and you want to encourage her to realize her potential and produce more ambitious works of art.

Step 1 You begin by rehearsing out loud to yourself. After listening to yourself on tape, you decide you sound too preachy, so you settle on a more down-to-earth approach (*You know how I feel about your gifts as a painter, and I think you can benefit by juggling your priorities a bit so that you can pursue painting even more*).

Step 2 Then you anticipate her objections (*I need to make money with my day job; I don't agree that my painting shows much promise; I prefer to dabble in painting rather than treat it too seriously*) and prepare sensible responses (*You can still make the same money and work a bit less; Let others judge whether your painting has promise; Keep dabbling but just do it more often!*).

Step 3 Now you need to fill in the blanks, to support your point so that it carries more weight. This involves brainstorming. Generate a list of all the reasons you can think of why she should follow your advice. Separate the list into facts and experiences. Let your mind run free. After a few minutes, you fill a page with your ideas. A sample:

> FACTS: Her art professor has offered to exhibit her work; two of her paintings have sold for $700 each; her painting was featured in a prestigious gallery last month.
>
> EXPERIENCES: Her love of painting since early childhood indicates an innate gift; her tendency to stay up all night completing a painting reveals her true passion; encouraging words from a famous mentor shows she has what it takes to succeed.

These pieces of support supply the finishing touches. Your rehearsal is over. You are now ready to persuade.

Leave Room for Improvisation

Hold on, you say. *How do I remember all these facts and experiences? I have a long list of supporting points, and I'll never be able to memorize them all.*

You're right—you cannot remember them all. Nor should you. The point of rehearsing is not to memorize a script. Instead, your goal is to strengthen your command of your subject and enter into a conversation on a note of confidence and preparedness. You can then draw upon your supporting facts and experiences as needed without having to recite every piece of evidence.

When the time comes to persuade, leave room for improvisation. A spontaneous flash of insight might prove more powerful than all the reasons you have identified during your rehearsal. In fact, the best way to train yourself to be more spontaneous is to diligently rehearse. All those hours spent planning what you want to say bring you closer to your persuasive goal. Your mind will already be well acquainted with the topic when face-to-face persuasion occurs.

Improvise within limits by remaining faithful to what you rehearsed while accommodating any last-minute alterations. Just as a child draws in a coloring book by staying within the lines, you want to keep your remarks from straying too far from your persuasive point. Add all the color you want as long as it contributes flavor and richness to your central message. Draw upon the best support: the most compelling examples, the strongest set of facts, and the most relevant personal reflections and anecdotes.

Experiment with a mix of examples, facts, and illustrations during your rehearsal.

MEMORY JOGGER

Use your dress rehearsal to mix soft anecdotes and hard data. For instance, blend stories with statistics to drill home your message.

Although your word may be gold, do not rely on it alone to persuade. Toss in enough evidence to buttress your goal. Document the validity of your idea with testimony, precedent, and documented facts.

During one of his most important speeches in the 1860 presidential campaign (at the Cooper Institute in New York), Abraham Lincoln attacked the pro-slavery views of Stephen Douglas. When Douglas claimed the Founding Fathers approved of slavery, Lincoln responded that twenty-one of the thirty-nine signers of the Constitution had at some point voted to prohibit slavery. The audience cheered Lincoln's skill at debunking his opponent's claim. It is hard to argue with speakers who research a topic and produce clear, convincing evidence to support their position.

MEMORY JOGGER

The more your audience cares about your topic, the more energy they will invest to critically examine your points.

When you assemble evidence and test it out during your dress rehearsal, make sure it is relevant to your goal and based on credible sources. You can probably get away with a few third-party endorsements (*Your neighbor likes it, so should you*), but strengthen your position by sticking to precise data that relates directly to your main idea. For example, persuading a group of investors to fund your drugstore business expansion will prove more successful if you prepare a thorough analysis of retail sales for specific stores in targeted regions.

Experts Say...

Journalists will often turn to consultants, pundits, or think-tank gurus for quotes to support a point. These quotes often consist of generalizations that are meant to persuade you. It astounds me how many news articles revolve around unsubstantiated "insights" from alleged experts. The reason? Most editors think that such comments legitimize a story. What's worse, readers eat this stuff up. For instance, a business magazine publishes a story about consumer trends and notes that baby boomers have been raised on entitlement and instant gratification, so sacrifice is a staggering notion for them to grasp. Oh. As one of the 78 million men and women born between 1946 and 1964, I was not raised this way and easily grasp the concept of sacrifice.

Just as you should beware of generalizations, pay attention to the role of statistics. Statistics only have a short-term effect on persuasion because cold numbers, on their own, rarely plant visual pictures in listeners' minds. It's your job to create a vivid image to make the numbers come alive and mean something to others. Statistics work best when they contain some element of surprise, mystery, or drama. They need to make listeners curious so that they want to learn more.

Here are some examples of the best way to integrate statistics into your persuasive communication:

- In the seven seconds it takes you to read this, four children died from the effects of malnutrition or disease.
- By using this software program to do your taxes, you can pay yourself $70 an hour for the money you save not hiring an accountant.
- Americans spend over 6 percent of their annual household budget on their personal insurance; that's more than they spend on clothing or entertainment.

Notice in these examples how the statistics themselves do not stand alone; they are tied to another, more immediate idea that is aimed squarely at triggering audience reaction. Numbers may be easy to ignore, but by comparing them to something that hits closer to home, they lend strong support to a persuasive case.

● **TRAP**   Examples are not proof. Do not assume that your wonderful illustrations give you an open-and-shut case. Speakers can find examples to support almost any point, and opponents can dismiss or refute them just as easily. Conclusive proof, by contrast, includes scientific research or hard data that lend weight to your analysis. In the absence of proof, do not spend too much time on any one example. Provide a range of short, simple illustrations that support your conclusion.

You want to enter a persuasive dialogue with plenty of evidence to back up your point. Even though you may not need to use it all, allow yourself the luxury of improvising within the limits set by your supporting material. Arming yourself with anecdotes, examples, and proof gives you the confidence to win people over, because you have already laid the foundation for a persuasive case.

Preparing an Airtight Argument

Another benefit of staging a dress rehearsal is that you can evaluate the logic used to support your point. Crafting an airtight case takes time, and you do not want to leave this task to the last minute.

There are two types of logical argument: deductive and inductive. Deductive logic, which moves from the general to the specific, draws a conclusion from a set of premises (*We need a new car. This loan will help us buy a new car. Therefore, we should arrange this loan.*). Inductive logic operates in reverse by identifying a host of specific problems and then offering a general conclusion (*Profits are down: The machinery is broken: Our workers' compensation premiums have doubled due to on-the-job injuries. Therefore, we need to consider radical changes in our entire operation*).

In the absence of deductive or inductive logic, some desperate speakers resort to dogmatic assertions or groundless accusations. For example, Senator Joseph McCarthy would infuriate his critics by insisting that he had documented proof that communists had infiltrated the top ranks of American government. But when asked to support his claim, he did not provided any physical evidence or logical reasons to strengthen his case.

Use your rehearsal to line up the best evidence to strengthen your arguments, and demand that others provide logical support when *they* try to persuade *you*.

Ethos, or credibility, flows from a speaker who shows good moral character and who is qualified to address the topic at hand. You should always seek to establish your expertise. You can do this with phrases such as "In my seven years of experience, I have found..." or "During my five-year investigation, I spent much time..." Credibility statements need not sound like bragging. Reinforce your credibility by drawing a conclusion based on your experience:

BAD: I have been doing this for eighteen years.

BETTER: After eighteen years in this business, I have learned...

Establish credibility without fanfare. There is no need to sound pompous. The best persuaders add a dose of humility (such as admitting mistakes and showing how they have learned from them). Extracting lessons from past errors can bolster your appeal as a credible spokesperson. Politicians often turn moral transgressions into image-enhancing "learning experiences" to attract forgiving voters. (The next time a candidate tries to win your sympathy by admitting a personal "mistake," ask yourself whether he or she volunteered the admission or whether the speaker was caught red-handed before going public with an apology.)

● **TRAP**   Do not equate an appeal to common knowledge with evidence. Poor persuaders may cite conclusive "evidence" based on what they perceive as a universally acknowledged truth, only to find out that the audience does not accept this seemingly self-evident "truth." Be careful when you make a general statement such as "every shopper hates waiting in line." All it takes is one shopper to say "I like to read the gossip magazines in line without having to buy them," and your evidence turns to mud. Declaring that "the numbers speak for themselves" means nothing, because people can conclude almost anything they want from a set of figures. During my year as a newspaper editor in college, I marveled at how vitriolic columnists "supported" their opinions by manipulating statistics to their advantage. Link evidence tightly to your persuasive goal, and don't accept the arguments of others who play fast and loose with logic.

The Best Way to Structure Your Persuasive Appeal

If you want to give yourself broad parameters within which to improvise, create *constructs* to house your persuasive message. A construct provides a loose structure for your remarks so that you can fit your supporting points into your overall goal. During your rehearsal, experiment with these constructs and determine whether any of them enhance your persuasiveness:

1. You can adopt my idea, do something else, or not do anything. Whether you tell them so or not, your listeners always have the option of saying "yes" to you, saying "yes" to someone else, or saying "no" to everyone and maintaining the status quo. By reminding them of their options, you can characterize the benefits and drawbacks of each course of action. Offer support to show them why saying "yes" to you makes the most sense of the three choices.

2. You can act now, wait a while and think it over, or just say no. Again, your listeners can choose any of these options depending on their preferred method of making decisions. You place yourself in the enviable position of helping them assess the pros and cons of saying "yes" immediately, mulling it over, or outright refusal. Your supporting points can induce them to act now, or, if you feel they will respond best if given time to decide, you can invite them to think about it.

3. Let's weigh all the factors and decide. This works well when you are helping someone make a tough decision with lasting consequences. You present yourself as a scorekeeper who tabulates all the reasons for and against taking a certain action. This approach comforts people who must sort through many thoughts and emotions before they are ready to make up their minds. It is particularly useful in helping an individual make a sizable financial commitment.

Prepare to persuade by employing any of these constructs to win over your audience. Most people will respond favorably if you fairly analyze the strengths and weaknesses of your proposal along with other possibilities. Best of all, you leave yourself plenty of room to improvise when, after the rehearsal, real persuasion takes place with all the surprises and distractions that accompany human interaction.

Always watch for opportunities to reinforce someone's existing beliefs. Whenever a speaker reveals an opinion, look for ways to add a relevant point. If you want a reluctant individual to vote for term limits, and you hear him say, "I'm fed up with the City Council," prepare an affirmative response. You might try, "I am, too. Did you know the City Council members enjoy lavish perks at taxpayer expense?"

By using dress rehearsals to master the techniques covered in this chapter, you launch every persuasive salvo with a clear understanding of what you want to say. You are also well equipped to respond to just about anything you hear. You can plan crisp comebacks to objections and leave room for spontaneity. Your evidence, planned in advance, lends weight and credibility to your proposal (whether you use it all or not). Just knowing that you can support what you say breeds confidence.

○ **Now Try This** Make sure your supporting points address unresolved concerns or lingering resistance. Your illustrative facts and experiences should reduce your listeners' defensiveness and strip them of any opportunity to say "no." Use this checklist to help you complete your rehearsal:

_____   You make it easy for the other person to say yes. You invite acceptance by not asking for too much, too soon.

_____   You have plenty of supporting points to strengthen your message.

_____   You give something in exchange for a "yes."

_____   You expect a "yes." Your verbal and nonverbal communication radiate confidence.

_____   You identify your assumptions and ensure they are positive, not negative. Be prepared to voice your assumptions (*I assume you want to lose weight, right?*).

_____   You confirm that acceptance of your idea will not make the other person look weak or beaten. You frame your proposal so that a "yes" is the heroic, triumphant, gutsy, visionary response of a winner.

If you can check each of these elements after completing your rehearsal, you are ready to win over anybody.

QUICK REVIEW

- Talk to yourself to affirm your beliefs and strengthen your will to persuade.
- Tape yourself during rehearsal to clarify your thinking and solve problems.
- Practice speaking in terms of declarations, reasons, promises, questions.
- Always respond to objections with a welcoming verbal embrace.
- Anticipate resistance and disarm the audience with a patient, non-threatening response.
- Anticipate tough questions and prepare an Ideal Response for each one.
- Handle a hostile audience by first demonstrating you understand their hostility.

- Practice the *feel, felt, found* approach as a way to respond to objections.
- Choose a lively mix of supporting material to uphold your main point.
- Categorize your support in terms of facts and experiences.
- Use constructs to structure your remarks and organize your supporting points.

NOTES

1. Wallace C. Fotheringham, *Perspectives on Persuasion,* Allyn & Bacon, Inc., Boston, 1966, p. 110.

CHAPTER 6

Package Your Points Persuasively by Thinking in Threes

I have never known an audience that can grasp more than three ideas.—Michael Harrington

The final stage in preparing to persuade is charting a course to follow so that you know *what* you want to say and *why* you want to say it. Even the most empathetic, flexible, well-rehearsed persuaders need a map that tells them where to go.

This chapter gives you a step-by-step program to create your own map:

1. Devise a goal.
2. Choose the three best points you wish to make in support of your goal.
3. Insert a preview of your ideas.

Let's look at each of these steps in detail.

CRAFTING A GOAL THAT KEEPS YOU ON THE RIGHT TRACK

Whenever you try to persuade, you should have a clear, precise idea of what you want to accomplish. Your goal should answer the question, "What action do I want the listener to take?"

Developing a goal sounds easy. Some participants in my workshops grow restless when I spend what seems like far too long on the techniques to fashion an effective goal. "Sure, sure, we know about goals," they assure me. "Now let's move on."

The urge to press forward despite vague, ambiguous, or unrealistic goals can be overpowering. Many people rush into conversations without knowing where they are heading. You have undoubtedly heard speakers who lacked a goal. You squirmed in your seat, scratched yourself, checked your watch, and finally gave up and ventured into your own private dream land. Without a goal, a speaker will stray from one topic, shift gears abruptly, and indulge in long-winded sentences that say nothing.

Whatever you think of Ronald Reagan's presidency, he had three clear goals when he won the election in 1980: cutting taxes, cutting domestic spending, and spending more on the military. Jimmy Carter, by contrast, could never summarize his goals in such a concise fashion. He shifted his focus from energy to taxes to other issues without setting priorities and following through. Bill Clinton, learning from Reagan, won the 1992 election by promising voters to fix the economy and pass health-care reform.

To take an example closer to home, consider the last time you bought something from a salesperson. Chances are you said "yes" to the sales pitch because you clearly understood what you were buying and why you were buying it. The salesperson did not hem and haw. You *knew* you were being sold something, and you consented to buy because you felt there was some benefit worth the price. The salesperson no doubt had a goal—and communicated it with nonthreatening force and clarity.

The hardest part of goal-setting for some people is choosing only one goal. A trial lawyer in a seminar asked me, "In my job, I'm trying to convince the jury of three or four things at the same time. The jurors need to understand a complicated set of facts, sympathize with my client, have doubts about opposing counsel, see how the evidence relates to the case, and so on. How can I keep my goal simple while encompassing all these elements?"

When you try to bite off more than you can chew, you invite trouble. You will not persuade anyone of anything if you get greedy and set too many goals at once. I suggested that the lawyer select one goal at each stage of the trial. He could concentrate on explaining his version of the facts, and then move on to describing his client's fine character.

"You need to have one clear goal in your mind at all times," I said. "When you have attained the first one, then proceed to the next. Just don't commingle goals or you will confuse your listeners."

Avoid Goal Setting at Your Own Risk

We may grow listless and lethargic without goals. Negative emotions can crush any lingering hope or drive, and we may resort to whatever destructive behavior appeals to us. A dieter without a goal decides to abandon the diet and consume a chocolate cake. A student without a goal decides to ditch class. A salesperson without a goal finds reasons to fail. In the absence of direction or purpose, our activities may turn to burdens that drag us down, down, down.

Even worse, you may have found that when you lack goals, someone comes along and decides for you what your goals should be. A personal example comes to mind. I recall my decision to enroll in law school despite my strong inclination to stay away. The good intentions of others, who believed that life without law school is a life not worth living, led me into the joyless world of torts and contracts. Set your own goals or you may find that outside forces take hold of your life and pummel you into submission.

● **TRAP** Don't assume that you can skip this goal-setting and just start talking your way toward what you want. "My goal is obvious, to increase sales every month," an insurance agent told me. In my opinion, those are the words of a mediocre producer. A proper goal requires more than a vague sense of what you wish to attain. You must clamp down on the actual nature of what you seek, to characterize it accurately and unambiguously. This takes hard work! You will waste words later on if you do not know *exactly* what you hope to achieve before opening your mouth. The process of coming up with your goal is so rewarding because it helps you envision the desired outcome.

How to Reduce Your Goal into One Compelling Sentence

Goals need not be viewed as pie-in-the-sky projections that seem random, artificial, or shoved down your throat. Defining what you want comes from within; no one can do it for you. So grab a pen and paper. Clear your head of distractions so that you can determine *why* you want to persuade. Now compose one sentence that summarizes what you want to achieve.

By focusing on a clear outcome, you can condense your message into a simple, compelling call to action. Examples include *I want to talk Chris into joining me for a weekend getaway* or *I want to invite my neighbors to help me start a neighborhood watch program.*

Now play with your sentence, especially the verb. Strive for lively, high-octane words that drive your thought process. Select a verb that precisely describes your purpose. *Get, find, start, have*—these are flat verbs that will deaden your desire for achieving your goal.

Verbs that Call for Action

conquer	investigate
educate	jolt
excite	marshal
expose	motivate
galvanize	revamp
harness	spark
inspire	unleash

By plugging in an energetic verb, your goal sparkles. *I want to talk Chris into joining me for a weekend getaway* becomes *I want to entice Chris into joining me for a weekend getaway.* And *I want to invite my neighbors to help me start a neighborhood watch program* becomes *I want to invite my neighbors to launch a neighborhood watch program.*

By framing your persuasive goal as a way to *entice* Chris, you go beyond mere *talking* and add a dimension of excitement. One word makes a big difference in the goal: *Starting* a program becomes *launching* a program (we have liftoff!).

A volunteer for a large nonprofit agency asked me to help him craft a goal. I suggested that he write one sentence to explain what he wanted to accomplish as a fund raiser. He wrote, "I want my audience to give as much as they can to my group." We agreed that this statement lacked the precision necessary to inject clarity and force into his message. After some tinkering, he tightened the desired outcome to read, "I want to compel the audience to donate $___." He would insert a specific dollar amount for each presentation. Imagine the difference when he approached prospective donors with this goal driving him forward.

When you have a goal that clearly expresses what you want to achieve, put it through a battery of tests to confirm that you are on the right track:

1. Make sure your goal is stated in positive terms. You will sharpen your persuasiveness if you seek a positive outcome, if you are *moving toward* rather than *moving away from.* For example, *I want to motivate my friends to vote for the challenger* works better than *I want discourage my friends from voting for the incumbent.*

2. Control the outcome.   You must place yourself firmly in charge of achieving your goal. Do not make your success contingent on forces beyond your control. A common trap in a personal relationship or business partnership is for one party to lean too heavily on the other, thus making goal attainment dependent upon the partner's actions. If you are part of a team, then set a goal that defines your own contribution to the team. An effective goal is one that you and you alone can initiate, implement, and steer toward the desired outcome.

3. Measure your progress.   Devise a way to measure the march toward your goal. You need evidence to know when you get there. A goal such as *I want to motivate my friends to vote for Smith* can be strengthened by adding a specific number of votes: *I want to motivate fifty friends to vote for Smith.* Persuade people by informing them of your numerical goal, *You can be the forty-fourth person I have met today who has agreed to support Smith.* Avoid vague aims that do not translate into measurable results.

If your outcome is positive, measurable, and controllable by you and you alone, then you have a winning goal. You may not know it yet, but you have just taken a giant step toward getting what you want. While others may blab their way into a confusing, unconvincing web of words, your message will be wonderfully concise and crystal clear.

Dig Deep Within to Unearth Your True Goal

If you have trouble coming up with a concise goal, then you may want to ask yourself a few questions. Why do you want to achieve this goal? Why do you care? Identify your motivation for seeking to persuade. Be specific. Engage all your senses to see your goal *as already achieved* and describe how you feel. Step into the future and experience how you act now that you have earned what you want. Try to go beyond thinking how happy you would be. Search for the deeper reason or reasons that you want to persuade in the first place. Find the source.

Consider the mother who comes home to an adoring child after a long day at work.

"Mommy, you look so tired," the child observes.

"It was a tough day, honey," she says with a sigh.

"Why?"

"I was kept busy every minute of the day. No time to eat or take a breather."

"Why?"

"Because calls just keep coming in, and I can't ignore the phone."

"Why?"

"Because I want to give you everything I can, and I can't do that unless I work extra hard and talk to people all day long."

"Why?"

The mother smiles. "Enough," she says gently. "Mommy is tired, remember?"

When we are asked why we behave in a certain way, we explore our motives for action. By peeling the onion layer by layer, we identify why we care.

○ **NOW TRY THIS** By adding a dose of urgency or a sense of immediacy to your goal, you will strengthen your persuasiveness. The next time you plan to persuade, try completing this sentence, "This means a lot to me because _____." Make sure your goal reflects your deepest desire to win over your audience.

If our goal revolves around our own narrow needs, then we are already in trouble. If, on the other hand, we realize after some soul-searching that our message is aimed at enhancing the lives of others, then we can persuade far more easily.

MEMORY JOGGER

The best goals are those that you and your audience share. Strive to portray your goal and theirs as the same.

In the business world, salespeople can communicate far more persuasively when they know why they sell. By reminding themselves of their inner belief in their product or service, they bring personal meaning to their goal. They see themselves as educators and trusted advisers rather than mere peddlers hawking their wares. They do not look to silly contests or promotions to prod them to sell. The carrot-and-stick approach is unnecessary when managing professionals who feel their mission is to help others by providing something of value.

Weaving Your Goal into the Conversation

Once you have identified a forceful, captivating one-sentence goal, write it on an index card. If you have more than twenty words, prune the goal down to its essentials. Cut away fluff. Focus on the core action you want.

Use a black or red broad-tip felt marker to emphasize the importance of the message. Write in capital letters.

Keep the written goal prominently visible by taping it to the phone, refrigerator, or mirror. When the time comes to persuade, the goal should be drilled into your mind.

Now that you know why you care so much about achieving your goal, let others know, too. Sincerity, honesty, and enthusiasm help sway even the most resistant audiences. Some examples of how to communicate your goal:

- Let your friend know that the reason you insist he wear his seat belt is that you have heard of far too many severe injuries resulting from gruesome car crashes that could have been prevented with seat belts.
- Let the loan officer know that the reason you want a loan is to finance your dream business, an idea that has percolated in your mind for ten years.
- Let your students know that the reason you teach is because you never had the right kind of teacher when you were in school.
- Let the customer know that the reason you sell life insurance is that your father died and left your family without sufficient financial protection, and you intend to make sure this does not happen to others.

MEMORY JOGGER

People appreciate it when you level with them. They will be more apt to give you what you want if you tell them why you want it.

Negotiators may argue that it is best to keep your motivations to yourself, that you become vulnerable when you reveal why your goal means so much to you. Although this may be true in isolated cases, even the most heated bargaining sessions are usually leavened by a human appeal—a genuine attempt to step back and say why you care about the issue at hand. Negotiators are often taken aback by such an honest, personal approach. When both parties open up, they gain a better understanding of each other's motives and bridge gaps, leading to compromise and agreement.

THE MAGIC OF THREE:
AN ATTRACTIVE WAY TO PACKAGE YOUR IDEAS

If the goal is your destination, then you need a map to show you how to get there.

Think of a time you asked for directions in an unfamiliar town. Without knowledge of the local streets or landmarks, you relied on the kindness of strangers to guide you. You knew where you had to go, but you did not know what roads to take. While a goal defines a desired end point, the process of getting there is where the real fun begins.

Fun? Yes, FUN. You are about to learn a simple, enjoyable strategy to organize your thoughts to maximize your persuasive power. You will soon master a technique, thinking in threes, that transforms preparation from a chore into a pleasure. You think I'm exaggerating? Please, stay skeptical for a few pages. Furrow that brow. I only wish I could watch your brow unfurrow as you read on.

In my workshops, I ask participants how they prepare for a big speech, a job interview, or a heart-to-heart talk with a loved one. They usually respond that they jot down key points, write a "quickie outline," and review the facts so that they are not caught off guard. While each of these steps can strengthen a persuasive appeal, thinking in threes works better.

First, some background on what it means to think of a trio of ideas. The mind readily digests ideas grouped in three. To be persuaded, your listeners need to come away with some specific reasons why they should go along with you. If you just repeat your goal ten times (*I intend to recruit you to join our new volunteer planning committee*) you will probably annoy someone. But if you move beyond the goal and deliver some appealing reasons for the other person to care about your goal (*You bring strong credentials to our committee, you share our concerns for local development; You can make a difference in your community*), then you lure them in.

Effective orators teach us the power of threes. If you listen to politicians who give speeches (but who does?), you will find that they often arouse their audiences by creating a verbal rhythm with a 1-2-3 beat.

Examples of Thinking in Threes:

- William Jennings Bryan's speech against economic protection in 1892 began, "The man who justifies protection as a principle must prove three things: He must prove that the principle is right, that the policy is wise, and that the tax is necessary."

- Franklin D. Roosevelt said, "I see one-third of a nation ill-housed, ill-clad, ill-nourished."

- Douglas Wilder won a 1989 race for governor of Virginia with his "three-for-Virginia" campaign promise: tax relief, jobs for rural Virginians, and a fight against drugs.

- Marian Wright Edelman, president of the Children's Defense Fund, said that depending on how we treat children today, before long they will either be supporting us, depending on us, or shooting at us.

Public figures are not the only ones to talk in threes. When a representative of New York's Department of Transportation was asked to explain why traffic deaths on Manhattan streets ranked far below the national average, he responded proudly, "Accident fatalities are fewer here due to the three Es—improved traffic engineering, enforcement and education."

In addition to the three Es of traffic safety, there are the three Rs of elementary education (reading, writing, arithmetic), the three-beat advertising jingles (*The few, the proud, the Marines; Reduce, reuse, recycle*) and the three-step commands (*Lights! Camera! Action!; Ready! Aim! Fire!; On your mark! Get set! Go!*). *The New York Times* once noted the three As "long considered key to a successful medical practice: ability, affability and availability." During the Vietnam War, a different set of As (amnesty, acid, and abortion) became a popular anti-war rallying cry.

The use of threes crosses cultural lines. In Tokyo, a Japanese diplomat told *The Wall Street Journal* that his country's participation in international meetings is no longer governed by the three S's (smile, sit, silent). During a trip to Indonesia, I picked up a copy of the local newspaper and read President Soeharto's comment that government officials should avoid succumbing to the lure of the "three ta's" (*harta, tahta,* and *wanita*). These traps of *money, power,* and *women,* he argued, could lead to scandals that would tarnish the public's perception of their leaders.

Clustering ideas in three can serve as an effective management tool. Some successful companies create mission statements that reduce their goal into simple, easy-to-remember sets of three. At See's Candies, a store known to Californians for its fine chocolates, workers operate by the three S's of *smiles, service,* and *samples.* Employees of Domino's Pizza know that their jobs revolve around FFF, which means *fast, friendly,* and *free delivery.*

By recognizing the appeal of threes, you can increase your persuasiveness. How many points should you make to convince someone of something without going overboard? The happy medium is three. If you talk too much, you will tax the patience of the listener; if you talk too little, you may not offer enough support to build a strong case. You must navigate between the Scylla of babbling and the Charybdis of brevity.

The tough part of thinking in threes is keeping quiet after stating three concise points. Imagine your head vacuum-packed with data. Someone comes along and removes the lid. Out gushes long lists of reasons, personal experiences, and truckloads of testimonials. Your inclination is to keep talking until you cover every conceivable benefit, even if you drown the poor audience in a sea of words.

MEMORY JOGGER

Your audience need not know every reason why you think you're right. They need to be fed only enough information to strengthen their understanding and lessen their resistance.

Avoid overeducating your listener. You will deaden your message if you give too many justifications or reasons why others should follow your wishes. Too much knowledge, technical expertise, or sermonizing may work against you.

Although your mind may be crammed with solid evidence to uphold your argument, this in itself is not persuasive. If it were, then the person with the longest list of reasons or supporting points would always win. Conversations would turn into boxing matches where the fighters keep swinging until one of them runs out of punches and crumbles to the floor. Unless your goal is to put others to sleep, the scattershot approach (*Tell 'em everything*) will fail.

MEMORY JOGGER

Most listeners are already leaning toward a decision after hearing three points, so there is no need to keep talking. Either they are with you, against you, or undecided. To find the answer, stop talking. If they are with you, they will let you know that they are on your side. If they are against you or undecided, let them raise concerns or objections.

Persuasive Memo Writing: Three Parts Make a Whole

If you have ever taken a business writing course, you have probably heard that an effective memo should be no longer than one page. Most managers agree that this serves as a good rule of thumb. A busy executive will probably not take the time to read more than one page of text, no matter how brilliant! Let me propose an even easier way to write office memos. Structure your memo so that it answers each of these questions:

- What are the relevant facts to help the reader make a decision?
- What do they mean? Why are the facts significant?
- What do we do now? What actions do you recommend?

By guiding the reader in this manner—identifying facts, showing how they relate to the issue at hand, and closing with the suggested course of action—you make it easy for others to agree with you. (In some cases, you may want to both open *and* close your memo with your suggestions. Let the body of the memo treat the facts.)

Here's a sample memo that follows this three-part model:

A Memo Organized in Threes

INTEROFFICE MEMORANDUM

To: Bill Smithers
From: Arlene Aaron
Subject: Lease Administration Policy
Date: April 1, 1994

FACTS:

Leasing costs for our 77 branch offices have increased 16 percent on average over the past year. Prime causes of the increase are:

- inflation in the overall real estate market
- costs for code upgrades that meet new state regulatory requirements
- office sites in high-priced buildings in desirable, "hot" neighborhoods

ANALYSIS:

If the cost of leases continues to increase at this rate in the coming year, it will cut profits and jeopardize the stability of the field operation. After undergoing substantial rebuilding and restructuring over the past five years, our business would be further disrupted if we had to close offices due to unacceptable lease terms.

RECOMMENDED ACTION:

Review all leases with aim of negotiating more favorable terms. Secure lower rents in exchange for commitments to stay longer and fund improvements at key sites.

By composing a memo in three distinct parts, you help clarify your own thinking while making it easier for the readers to follow your recommendations. Select headings for each of your three parts (such as *facts, analysis,* and *recommendations*) to make it even simpler to understand. Everyone wins when you think in threes.

What's Wrong with Two or Four? Why Three Works Best to Sell Ideas

Why is three the magic number, as opposed to two or four? Consider three reasons (See how this works?):

1. Limit yourself to three points and you will reduce the odds of alienating your audience or giving them grounds to object. If you let slip just one weak or objectionable point, listeners may dwell on the sole negative idea and ignore everything else. You may sabotage the effect of, say, forty-nine fabulous points by dropping a fiftieth dud that rubs someone the wrong way. You think you're on a roll, but by piling on the benefits you put yourself in danger of losing it all. You increase the chance of a persuasive mishap by rambling on after expressing your first three points.

MEMORY JOGGER

If your audience finds just one reason to disparage what you say, they may dismiss your whole package of ideas. Three reasons is a good compromise between giving enough evidence without going too far and serving up an idea that's easy to attack.

---

2. Two points may not be enough. A resistant subject will be more tempted to challenge, deny, or rebut two reasons than three. By adding a third benefit, you provide the persuasive push that turns ambivalence into agreement. It is much harder to resist three points than two.

3. Our minds like to unwrap tidy packages of threes. Linguists call this *chunking*: the grouping of ideas into a chunk of digestible data. To force-feed four or more ideas into someone's head will not necessarily produce a well-nourished mind. In fact, listeners will probably tune out if they are expected to absorb too much information.

People may not take the time to patiently concentrate on your remarks, just as newspaper readers may not glance at the portion of the article that "jumps" to an inside page. Americans have notoriously short attention spans. In this age of soundbite elections and snappy video images, it is hardly surprising that so few people make patient readers, viewers, or listeners.

Himan Brown, the producer of such classic radio shows as *Dick Tracy* and *The CBS Radio Mystery Theatre,* said that his new show, *Baker's Dozen,* "will only be three minutes long, because media experts tell me that is the span of attention of today's audiences." Similarly, ad copywriters know that they must quickly offer paybacks to keep a reader's interest. This explains the use of bullet points as a way to break up the copy and make selling points easy to scan.

○   **Now Try This**   Finding it tough to limit yourself to just three points? If so, list *all* of your persuasive reasons or benefits on a legal pad. Do not stop at three; let your mind run wild as you brainstorm for any and all persuasive ideas. Now review your list with your listeners in mind. Ask yourself this key question: If your audience were to take away only three ideas, what should they be?

Choose what's most important and discard the rest. Edit ruthlessly. You may have to cross off some fantastic benefits, but the ultimate test is whether you identify the three most compelling ideas for your particular audience.

USE THE GOAL 1-2-3 FORMAT AS YOUR ROAD MAP TO PERSUADE

Trial lawyers joke that there are two closing arguments: the one you give to the jury and the one you think of on the way home.

Lynn Martin, the labor secretary in the Bush administration, said in reference to the presidential debates, "For the rest of their lives, each will have one line they'll remember, that they know they meant to use but forgot. We've all done it. It's that line you meant to say to the rude guy in the elevator but forgot. You will forget it, so don't worry about it."

Why do we think of great things to say when it's too late? Blame it on the heat of the moment, on what psychologists call *performance anxiety.* Our nerves tend to overpower our cool, clearheaded mind.

Here's where having a goal and thinking in threes saves the day. By structuring your goal and three points in a clear, concise format, you will remember what you want to say and discuss each idea just as you planned. You will no longer forget your punch line or neglect to mention your best point! The Goal 1-2-3 format looks like this:

GOAL: _____

POINTS:

1. _____

2. _____

3. _____

Simple enough, but how is it used?

When William Campbell, president of the California Manufacturers Association, was asked by *The Los Angeles Times* how to rebuild the state's economy, he replied, "There are three essential things California will have to do if we are to expand the economy."[1] He then listed each element: workers' compensation insurance reform, increasing the state's ability to compete, and examining regulatory requirements. His comments may be plugged into the Goal 1-2-3 format as follows:

GOAL: To rebuild California economy.

1. Workers' comp reform.

2. Make California manufacturing more competitive through tax reform.

3. Streamline regulatory requirements to foster competition.

You can use this technique to plan virtually any message. Your job is to develop three ideas that serve as stepping stones for others to reach your goal. By fitting your remarks into the Goal 1-2-3 format, you will enjoy a command over your subject matter that adds to your confidence. Unlike many speakers who "wing it" by talking around their topics and hoping to stumble upon the right words to persuade, you will know exactly what you need to say to win over the audience. And you will not leave out your strongest point!

Label Your Ideas to Make Them Easy to Remember

Another benefit of thinking in threes is that it becomes easy to remember what you want to say. As you sift through your ideas and select the best three for a given audience, try assigning one-word labels to denote each point. This will make preparation far easier—you will have to remember only three words instead of three full sentences. In the above example, *comp-tax-regulatory* could signify of the main points. The Goal 1-2-3 road map can thus be stored comfortably in your head, making index cards or notes unnecessary.

Wean yourself from using scripts or extensive notes when attempting to persuade. Instead, know your goal, and prepare three one-word labels to represent your main points. You will read in Chapter 9 how one-word tags can help you listen better, too.

Past-Present-Future—and Other Ways to Apply the Goal 1-2-3 Format

The nature of your topic influences the Goal 1-2-3 format. If you are giving advice, choose a tripartite structure such as *problem-cause-solution, past-present-future, or example-point-reason*. Examples:

- When my friend wanted to persuade her brother to seek counseling, she began, "Let's look at the problem, the cause, and the solution." This immediately set her brother at ease and promised an upbeat outcome (a solution) to the conversation.

- A high school teacher met with Tommy's parents to discuss his grade. He said, "Tommy and I have spoken often in the last two months about what he must do to earn an A. *[past]* Now, he's halfway there. *[present]* By the end of the semester, with your help, he may get there. *[future]*"

- A police officer, waving off a driver's desperate protestations, issues a speeding ticket while saying, "Let me give you an *example* of why we ticket drivers like you for going too fast. Then you'll see my *point* and you'll understand the *reason* for all this."

Armed with your finely tuned goal, you can select a 1-2-3 format that captivates your audience (*and* helps you stay on track to persuade!). When you discuss a complex or technical topic, you may want to reduce the material into steps or stages. Here are some ways to classify your information in threes so that you march steadily toward your goal:

- three keys of winning
- three steps to maximize profit
- three ways to create a chain reaction
- three secrets of baking good cookies
- three main risk factors for contracting the disease

Effective speech titles often revolve around threes:

- Three Life Lessons
- The Three Best Excuses
- Africa's Future: Three Views
- Three Sales Techniques That Will Earn You $10,000

○ **Now Try This**   Think of someone you need to persuade. Now's the time to plan your remarks using the Goal 1-2-3 format:

GOAL: _____
　　　　　[no longer than one sentence]

POINTS:

1. _____

2. _____

3. _____
　　　[select a one-word label for each of your three points]

Here are some things to keep in mind when using the Goal 1-2-3 format:

- Keep your goal short, simple, and powerful.
- Select the three most appealing ideas for your particular audience. Empathize carefully so that you choose the best points for whomever you seek to win over.
- Do not memorize each point in its entirety. Instead, choose one-word labels for easy recall.

Lining Up Your Three Best Points in the Right Order

No matter how great your three supporting points, your listeners will inevitably find some of your arguments more persuasive than others. You need to pick which of your ideas are the most attractive ones, and then line them up in the correct order to strengthen your persuasiveness.

So how should you order your three ideas? Do you put the best one first, last, or in the middle?

When I pose this question to my classes, most participants vote to insert the best point first because it captures attention and builds momentum. "You might as well start with your best foot forward," is a typical response.

This approach also ensures that you will get your strongest point across, which may prove harder than you might expect. In the United States Supreme Court, for instance, a lawyer usually has a limited time to present arguments. Supreme Court Justices are free to interrupt as they please with questions or comments, thus cutting into a lawyer's allotted time. Saving the best for last can backfire when time runs out.

Although anticlimax order (best point first) may attract your listeners' attention and help you gather steam, especially when you face strict time limitations, climax order (best point last) usually works best. This way, you can push fence sitters over to your side by saving your strongest argument for last. You can also end with a burst of passion and dramatic finality.

For example, an official argues for strengthening environmental regulations with three points: cleaner air, future cost savings from improved public health, and preservation of scenic beauty. The speaker decides that the audience, a group of concerned parents, will be most drawn to the lasting treasure of scenic beauty. The presentation thus ends with, "A final benefit of stronger regulation, even more crucial than cleaner air and the cost savings from improved public health, is the preservation of natural beauty not only for *our* enjoyment but for our *children*."

An added benefit of putting your best point last is that you can fall back on the phrase, *Third, and most important* as a transition to your heavyweight finale.

After you finish speaking, listeners will be most swayed by what you said last. These are the comments that are freshest in their minds, so you had better make them count.

HOW A PREVIEW OF IDEAS WHETS YOUR AUDIENCE'S APPETITE FOR MORE

Now that you know how to think in threes, add a *preview of ideas* early in the conversation. A preview of ideas is an overview of the points that you intend to cover, stated in a simple sentence. Examples:

A teacher begins the lecture by explaining, "*today we will discuss the social, political, and economic factors that led to war.*"

A friend asks for a favor, "*I need your help. It won't take long, you're the perfect person to help me, and I'll owe you a big one in return.*"

A salesperson promises a client that the product will *"save you money, reduce your overhead, and increase your visibility."*

A job recruiter asks a candidate, *"Why should I hire you over other qualified applicants?"* The candidate responds, *"I bring a wealth of hands-on experience, a strong results-oriented track record, and a love of this business."*

A couple is arguing. One of them says, *"Rather than fight, let's take a time-out. We both can rest, reflect, and maybe come up with some answers."*

MEMORY JOGGER

Use parallel verbs (*strengthen* efficiency, *spark* creativity, and *increase* membership) in your preview of ideas. The ideas flow more smoothly when they build upon each other.

A preview of ideas gives listeners a glimpse of what follows. Like the "coming attraction" screened prior to a feature movie, a preview of ideas whets a listener's appetite to hear more. It also shows that you have taken the time to plan your remarks, which reflects positively on how you organize information and express your ideas.

I once helped a congressman prepare for a speech to a group of influential import-export executives. Together we drafted a tight goal (*I want to condemn high tariffs and champion free-market principles to guide our trade policy*), three key arguments (*strengthen alliances, advance our shared economic interests, and provide economic opportunities to developing nations*), and a preview of ideas (*A free market strengthens our alliances, advances our economic interests, and provides economic opportunities for developing nations*).

Another example comes from that great orator Franklin D. Roosevelt, who began his first Fireside Chat in 1933 with an excellent preview of ideas:

> I want to talk for a few minutes with the people of the United States about banking—with the comparatively few who understand the mechanics of banking but more particularly with the overwhelming majority who use banks for the making of deposits and the drawing of checks.

> I want to tell you what has been done in the last few days, why it was done, and what the next steps are going to be.[2]

Roosevelt's ability to level with his listeners helped reduce the financial panic and restored public faith in the banking system.

In a heated exchange, your ability to deliver a concise preview of tightly packaged ideas can, in itself, persuade. Say one half of a bickering couple suggests, "Let's take a time-out. We both can rest, reflect, and maybe come up with some answers." The other half may welcome the opportunity to (1) rest, (2) reflect, and (3) offer solutions. There is no need to elaborate on the three points, because the preview of ideas sounds appealing on its own.

How to Persuade Using a Preview of Ideas

In one of my sessions, Tim, a young executive, asked me how he could "keep the offensive" during an upcoming presentation to senior management. He shook his head in frustration and said, "I carefully plan what I want to say at our Monday meeting with the head honchos. I make nifty slides and prepare dynamite handouts. I list all the reasons why my proposal makes sense. But when I start to speak, all my planning goes down the drain. These guys start interrupting me and going off on all these tangents. Then they interrupt each other, the meeting ends, and no one even remembers or cares about what I was trying to say."

As the class nodded, clearly identifying with Tim's situation, all heads turned to me for an answer. These are the moments that make teaching such a joy (the next learning tool I wanted to cover was the preview of ideas, and Tim's question provided a perfect lead-in).

"Tim, if you were to state your goal in one sentence, what would it be?"

"I want to make them see the need for an overhaul of our compensation structure. We need to institute pay-for-performance incentives and align our salary ranges and job grades more closely with the competition."

"Good. Now condense that into one powerful sentence, and pick a lively verb."

"I want to *enlighten* them on the benefits of pay-for-performance as an effective way to upgrade our compensation policy."

"All right. You've got a goal. That's step one. Now, stepping into their shoes, what are the three most important, compelling reasons why these senior executives should adopt your plan?"

"That's easy," he said with bravado. The class laughed. "I've given this plenty of thought, and I am convinced that my idea will result in *more motivated employees, lower turnover,* and *a more efficient operation.*"

"Great," I responded. Tim gave the class a shining example of a preview of ideas. "What you've just said is your opening. You will increase your chances of riveting your audience's attention if you state that preview at the start. They will want to hear more."

Tim called a few weeks later to tell me that pay-for-performance was now in place at his company, and he was put in charge of implementation.

"Let me tell you what happened," he said excitedly. "I waited for my turn to speak, and then I waited an extra few seconds to build suspense and make sure I had everyone's attention. Then I said, 'We repeatedly discuss the need to revisit our compensation policy and assess different plans. After months of research, including surveying our competitors, I propose that we adopt a plan that will result in more motivated employees, a dramatic drop in turnover, and a more efficient, productive operation.' They were quiet, real quiet. They actually invited me to continue. I got to expand on each of my points: morale, turnover, and efficiency."

The beauty of a preview of ideas is its simplicity. Like a goal, a preview consists of just one sentence. By providing a concise overview of what follows, you can carry your audience along for a smooth ride by letting them know where you're heading, and how you plan to get there.

QUICK REVIEW

- Devise a simple, one-sentence statement of your goal.
- Choose a lively action verb.
- Know why you want to accomplish your goal—explore your motives.
- Think of the three best points you wish to make.
- Use the Goal 1-2-3 format to outline your persuasive ideas.
- Select one-word labels to represent each of your three points.
- Rank the relative strength of your three points based on your audience.
- Use climax order (best point last) and end with your strongest benefit.
- Consider anticlimax order (best point first) if you face time restrictions.
- Prepare a one-sentence window overview of your three points.
- State the preview before you start to cover each of your three points.

NOTES

1. *The Los Angeles Times,* 11-29-92, p. D3.
2. *Vital Speeches of the Day,* 3-1-88, p. 313.

STEP TWO

Listen to Learn

CHAPTER 7

How Listening Makes You a More Compelling Communicator

Nature has given to man one tongue, but two ears that we may hear from others twice as much as we speak.—Epictetus, a Greek Stoic philosopher

Almost every self-help book, with topics ranging from codependency to one-minute managing, devotes a few pages to what Mortimer Adler has called "the untaught skill" of listening. The authors repeatedly berate us: we do not listen enough, failure to listen ruptures relationships, listening is difficult, and listening is far harder than speaking.

This list summarizes the tips typically found in self-help books:

1. Listening is not the same as hearing.
2. You must sit still and be quiet to listen.
3. We tend to listen better when we are interested in the topic.
4. We tend not to listen to what we do not want to hear.
5. Our moods can block our willingness to listen.
6. Listening is easier when we like the speaker or we find the speaker attractive.

7. Listening is absolutely necessary for true human communication; there is no substitute.

8. You cannot listen if you are talking.

9. Listening is easy to fake with canned nods and smiles.

10. Active listening is the key.

Okay. Thank me. You do not need to trudge through piles of books to find out how to listen. Everything you need to know (or at least virtually everything these books will tell you) appears above.

Listening is one of those things that everyone loves to talk about. That's just the problem. People spend their lives being disgusted at how poorly they listen—and they do it so loudly. Management consultants, marriage counselors, and social workers blame faulty listening for any and all dysfunctions.

This has been going on for a long time. *Personnel* magazine, in its July 1955 issue, appealed to readers to sharpen their attentiveness:

> Listening is part of the job of every executive; studies show that it enters into almost everything he does, and that he spends several hours a day listening. One would expect business to try harder to get its money's worth from these high-paid hours. In a poll by the Bureau of National Affairs a few years ago, the overwhelming majority of top executives agreed that listening remains one of the most overlooked tools of management.

The best communicators know that they need to listen first to persuade later. They do not request things or plead their case until they have paid attention to others. Sometimes called *pregiving,* this means you must reward others by listening to them before asking for their cooperation or compliance.

The three-step persuasive program presented in this book—prepare, listen, speak—requires that you resist the urge to talk too soon. The single biggest mistake made by poor persuaders is their tendency to rush ahead of themselves and start blabbing before making an effort to understand their audience. If you want to sell more of your ideas or assert yourself more forcefully in your personal relationships, then make a commitment never to speak up *unless and until you have prepared and listened first.*

○ **Now Try This**   Make tomorrow your Day to Listen. Decide right now that you will follow each of these rules from the moment you get out of bed in the morning to the moment you collapse back to bed at night:

1. I will allow speakers to complete their points and count at least two seconds of silence before I respond. No interruptions.
2. I will listen in the here-and-now, keeping pace with the speaker. No jumping to conclusions.
3. I will focus on the speaker and harness my mental energy to understand the message. No daydreaming.
4. I will paraphrase a speaker's remarks at least once during the day to demonstrate my understanding. No abrupt redirecting of the conversation.

At the end of your Day to Listen, assess your performance. Did you follow each of these rules? Was it hard to resist interrupting, daydreaming, jumping to conclusions, and changing the topic abruptly?

Although these four rules are by no means an exhaustive list of what makes a good listener, they are accurate indicators of your discipline and concentration. Your findings serve as a baseline as you plunge into the following chapters and gain a toolbox full of skills.

Most people spend about 80 percent of their work day communicating. Listening occupies about half of that time; the other half is devoted to speaking, reading, and writing. Even though we do more listening than speaking, listening is rarely viewed as a top priority.

Face it—there is no glamour in keeping quiet. A common, albeit mistaken, perception is that silence equals passivity. Many people falsely believe that conversational control comes from talking louder than everyone else in the room—that speaking signals authority and listening signals subservience. By letting others do most of the talking, however, we will have more opportunities to gain knowledge about them. This insight pays off when the time comes for us to persuade.

MEMORY JOGGER

When it comes to listening, we can best establish control when we risk giving it up by keeping quiet.

It all boils down to your attitude and expectation whenever you approach a conversation. If you think, *When I talk, people listen,* you will plow forward with little regard for your audience. If you condition yourself by thinking, *When I listen, people talk,* you set the stage for true communication.

WHY LISTENING IS SUCH A PROBLEM
AND WHAT YOU CAN DO TO SOLVE IT

Feeble listening is so prevalent in our daily encounters that we may no longer expect to be heard. I met someone who told me that he intentionally makes outrageous comments at work to see whether anyone is listening. He said that no one reacted when he announced that the roof was collapsing or that major league baseball had disbanded. His next big experiment: insult people to their face and see what happens.

Why do we resist paying attention when someone speaks to us? There are many reasons, beginning with the fact that *we can get away with it.* In a world where so few people truly listen, everyone's skill level drops. We may hold each other to high standards of behavior in other areas, but when it comes to listening, all bets are off.

Here are some specific causes of poor listening:

- You are immersed in thought (*How will I pay next month's rent?*) or action (*doing a crossword puzzle*) at the same time someone addresses you. Rather than stop whatever you are thinking or doing in order to listen to the speaker, you remain preoccupied.

- You do not like the speaker or the speaker's topic, so you tune out. In Chapter 10, I discuss how some people "erase" what others say because they just don't like something about the conversation.

- Your apathy gets the best of you. If you simply do not care about the speaker's remarks, then listening becomes an awful chore.

- If you care *too much* about the topic, you may be so eager to jump in with your own comments that you barely listen to the other person. Sometimes, we think about what we want to say next while the speaker continues to supply new information (that, to our embarrassment, we fail to pick up).

Think about what happens when you eavesdrop. You exert energy to pick up on what you overhear because your curiosity is aroused. You go beyond hearing to *interpret, evaluate,* and *respond.* Interpreting meanings of words, evaluating information, and responding either verbally or nonverbally all comprise the listening process.

If we were always curious, then we would happily listen all the time. Tuning out would never pose a problem. We would listen because we had a reason to care or an opportunity to gain something.

Most successful communicators know that the best way to make people listen is to appeal to their self-interest. A kindergarten teacher knows all about arousing curiosity to keep thirty unruly youngsters from tearing up the classroom. A top salesperson offers to fill a prospect's needs by supplying a desirable, reasonably priced product. A riveting public speaker captures an audience's attention so that they want to listen.

Unfortunately, speakers do not always make listening easy for us. Many times we are stuck in boring conversations or tranquilized by dull lectures. In law school, I was literally put to sleep by the Contracts professor, who rambled on about *consideration, offer*, and *acceptance*. A few budding lawyers in class found this stuff fascinating; I headed for the sink to splash water on my face.

HOW TO OVERCOME THE FACT/OPINION BLUR SO THAT YOU LISTEN ACCURATELY

Have you ever asked two people who have been in a fight to describe what happened? Chances are you received two different answers.

Beat cops and baseball umpires know all about breaking up fights. Whenever they ask the battling parties to explain what happened, they know they will hear two versions of what occurred. They will usually get opinions rather than facts.

If you are faced with the task of mediating an argument, you must listen carefully to separate fact from opinion. Your willingness to let both parties talk and the way you ask questions can help you unravel what actually happened so that you can propose a fair solution.

If you ask, *What did you do?* then you are off to the right start. This type of action-based question invites more facts and less opinion. Respondents must think through their behavior and report what they *did* rather than what they *thought* or *felt*. Getting antagonists to focus on their outward actions helps them resolve their conflict. There is a time and a place for touchy-feely sharing, of course, but the first order of business when bringing adversaries together is to get at the truth of who did what and why.

Two Ways to Mediate a Conflict

The situation: You come home from work to find your two children arguing and crying.

The response: You look at your spouse, who reminds you it's your turn to play the disciplinarian. Your goal is to find out what happened and get the kids to "kiss and make up." You can go about this task one of two ways:

SCRIPT 1:

Parent:	Okay, you two. Break it up. What's going on here?
Chris:	He hit me!
John:	He stole my book!
Chris:	Look, it hurts right here where he hit me. He hit me so hard! [He begins to cry.]
John:	He took my book and ruined it! He did it before and you punished him. But he did it again. I'm sick of him taking my stuff. I thought you said that wasn't allowed.
Parent:	Let me take a look at that bruise. [examines Chris]
John:	Why don't you punish him?! I barely touched him. I didn't *hit* him.
Parent:	Chris, does it hurt now?
Chris:	Yes, yes. [He shrieks in pain, although it's unclear how much he is exaggerating.]

SCRIPT 2:

Parent:	Okay, you two. Break it up. Chris, you wait in your room a minute. I want to talk to John alone. [Chris leaves.] Now John, what did you do while I was away today?
John:	I was reading my new book, you know, the one I got from Grandpa.
Parent:	Where were you reading?
John:	In my room.
Parent:	And what else did you do?
John:	Well, I got some cookies from the kitchen. Chris wanted the cookies, too. And, well, we, we...got in a fight over the cookies.
Parent:	And what happened?
John:	Um, we shoved a little.
Parent:	And?
John:	I guess I shoved him too hard, because he got upset and stole my book.
Parent:	What happened next?
John:	I got angry that he stole my book. Maybe I hit him again.
Parent:	Well, did you hit your brother or not?
John:	Yes, but he deserved it!

In Script 2, the parent wisely separates the two children and hears their stories, one at a time. Also note how the parent in Script 2 leads off with, "What did you do?" rather than the vague, "What's going on here?"

You can bet that harmony in the household is reestablished more quickly in Script 2, where the parent interviews the kids separately and knows how to listen attentively for both fact and opinion.

The Best Listeners Do Not Mistake a Speaker's Opinions for Facts

Effective persuaders continually listen for both facts and opinions. They can thus clarify how others process information and perceive the world, and this knowledge pays off when the time comes to persuade.

Pay close attention to how a speaker blurs fact and opinion. Some people will dogmatically assert their views as well-established, "obviously" true facts. Examples:

The liberals clearly lack an agenda for the country.

There is no way the team can win with that starting lineup.

No three-hour movie will ever earn $200 million at the box office.

Sharp listeners realize that such statements are actually opinions presented as undeniable, unconditional truths. How can you tell the difference? *A fact can be independently verified, while an opinion cannot.*

Memory Jogger

When someone asserts an opinion as fact, ask, *What makes you say that?*

Listen for speakers who make subtle attempts to transform dogma into empirical fact. For instance, I recall a friend who insisted that his writing lacked grace. "I'll never make it as a writer because I don't have any artistic sense," he explained. "Anyone can see that."

He kept repeating this "fact" as if it were a self-evident truth. I told him he was entitled to his opinion, but he should let others draw their own conclusions from his submissions. Only after acknowledging that his displeasure with his writing represented a belief, not a verifiable fact, did he start sending his writing to editors. He now enjoys a successful career, although to this day he almost always doubts his writing skills.

When you listen closely for facts and opinions, you realize how speakers routinely mix the two. They will express biases or preferences as well-established facts (instead of admitting they like sweets, they rationalize their eating habits by telling you that "these snacks are actually good for you" or that "candy makes you more alert"). They will fudge data to prove their points (*studies show...; I heard an expert on television say that...*). Listening will help you detect these fact/opinion blurs so that you are not misled or frustrated when you try to persuade.

○ **Now Try This**   Looking for a way to distinguish between fact and opinion? Put others' comments through the Verify Test. Ask them how you can verify what they just said. Can the "fact" be supported by primary or secondary sources, observation, or experimentation? If not, then you know you've got an opinion and not a fact.

LEARN WHILE YOU LISTEN WITH THE "TEACH ME, TEACH ME" TECHNIQUE

Mentally repeat *teach me, teach me* whenever you listen. Make this your mantra—a message to remind yourself that the whole point of listening is to learn something.

One reason listening poses such a challenge is that we spend much of the time evaluating the speaker rather than paying attention to what's said. Pushing aside our judgments (*He's such a loudmouth; Her dress is so out-of-style; I can't take that grating voice for another second*) takes discipline. Concentrating on what people say requires more work than noticing their clothing or dwelling on what you want to say next. Judging, rather than listening, offers an easy way out.

Listening is a breeze when we like the speaker. The tough part comes when we interact with those who do not meet our "most favored" status. In the absence of personal chemistry, listening turns to labor. If only all of the people we spoke with every day were wonderfully compatible...but then listening would be too easy and authors of how-to books on effective communication would be out of a job.

When people ask me what makes listening so difficult, I say that it is easier to judge than to listen. Focusing on the message requires far more effort than judging the messenger (*He's gaining weight; Her dress looks wrinkled; What a snob*). Taking mental pot shots instead of paying attention is a popular way to kill time during an unsatisfying conversation.

You may think you are immune to this disease. A few participants in every class say, "I would never let my judgments about someone stop me from listening."

A good way to test whether you judge rather than listen is to think of three unflattering adjectives that you commonly use to describe people. Examples are:

dull	opinionated
loud	ignorant
pathetic	hypocritical
arrogant	insensitive
nasty	annoying

Now consider how often you find yourself chatting with such people. If you frequently find others *dumb, lazy,* and *boring,* then you will apply these words more readily as an escape from listening. The more people you deem *naive,* for instance, the more likely you will look for and find naivete in those you meet.

Know your biases. Identify those adjectives that color your impression of others. Try not to deny the legitimacy of a speaker and give yourself a reason not to listen.

A few years ago, a financial services company asked me to help them find a manager to head a new department. I recall a job applicant whose unruly hair, sickly complexion, and flashy bow ties hardly fit the typical corporate image. Yet this guy demonstrated a technical mastery required for the position, and I encouraged the firm to consider him. The first few interviewers rejected him as eccentric and ill-suited to work at the company. Luckily, a top executive actually listened to the candidate and found him well qualified for the job. The executive refused to judge on appearance; instead, he asked challenging questions and focused on the quality of the answers. Later, when this fellow was hired, he earned the respect of his co-workers despite their initial amusement at his funny ties and "mad genius" hair.

True listening consists of the ability to extract a speaker's main points and absorb the message without adding opinions or commentary. This way, ideas are exchanged and learning takes place. Persuasive speakers lay the groundwork for their ultimate success by listening with patience, clarity, and focus.

You listen receptively when you thirst for knowledge, when you enter into dialogues expecting to learn and excited about the opportunity to gain insight. Your genuine interest in learning something new or just getting to know someone better turns listening into a stimulating activity, not a chore requiring fake nods and smiles.

This attitude of positive expectation not only enhances your willingness to listen, but it also makes you more persuasive. After listening to learn what makes others tick, you are well equipped to stir their self-interest and win them over.

Expect to gain at least one fact or opinion from every conversation.

Let your curiosity roam free. The best listeners are filled with "dumb questions," and they know that most people will happily provide helpful answers.

○ **NOW TRY THIS**   Try to identify the speaker's main point and conclusion when you listen. If you are unsure of what's being said, ask, "If I understand you correctly, are you saying...?" If you understand the main point but are unsure of its significance, ask, "What do you conclude from that?" By confirming the speaker's main point and the conclusion, you can design your persuasive appeal so that it plugs right in to match the subject's belief system.

The Teach Me, Teach Me approach is especially useful when you must converse with someone whom you do not like or respect. A participant in one of my workshops disliked her new boss to the point where she avoided seeing him. "I find him pompous, which would be okay if he could back it up with some smidgeon of intelligence," she said as her classmates chuckled. She agreed to repeat *teach me, teach me* the next time they spoke.

The result? She reported a week later that "I kept reciting this *teach me* thing over in my head. The more he talked, the more I began craving some knowledge. And you know what? He became more interesting. I noticed that he kept using sports metaphors, and that helped me communicate with him on his level."

Even when bored or frustrated, you can collect useful information as long as you resist the urge to tune out. Your determination to learn something will make it easier to sell yourself later. The more advance knowledge you bring to any persuasive encounter, the more likely you will reach a mutually satisfying accord. Listening can help you successfully frame an idea in terms most appealing to the other person.

HOW TO LISTEN WHEN THE SPEAKER
IS BORING

Many frustrated persuaders, such as hard-working but low-producing salespeople or disgruntled technicians who never seem to advance into people-management positions, may bring on the frustration themselves. Poor listening habits may be to blame. They may fail to pick up on the feelings, preferences, and opinions of others. Many people do not realize that entry into the inner sanctum of the human mind is a giant step toward establishing honest, win-win communication. Lazy listeners do not take advantage of this access and choose to sink in the mud of their own ignorance.

I know. One of the ongoing projects of my adult life is to overcome my impatience with boring, windy speakers. At professional seminars, I often sit and listen to "experts" expound on their academic findings. After a few minutes, I am already yawning and noticing just how uncomfortable I feel (*It's so hot/cold in here; I'm hungry; My nose itches*). Then I plot an escape, usually by checking the time, the nearest exit, and the number of people who will see me leave. I am usually seated in the middle of a long row near the front of the room, making my premature departure all the more embarrassing to me and distracting to others.

Why do I sit in the front middle instead of in the back near the door? Call it a self-discipline test: If I plant myself in a conspicuous place, I hope to force myself to pay closer attention to the speakers and fight the urge to dart out early. Yet this strategy rarely works. I repeatedly flunk the test by leaving well before the end of the presentation.

In recent years, however, I have grown more patient by attempting to dig deeper into a speaker's message. I try not to tell myself *this is getting boring.* Instead, I concentrate on the substance of the lecture. After identifying the main point, I will try to outline the organizational structure or analyze the strength of the speaker's evidence. I pay particular attention to any personal asides or other moments when the speaker's authentic personality shines through (sadly, such moments of humanness come far too infrequently). I get excited, for example, when speakers lift their eyes from the prepared text and make a spontaneous comment such as *this just happened to me last night* or *my children often remind me of that.* A speaker's personal observations lighten the load of a heavy, dry topic and make it easier for me to focus on the message.

THREE STEPS TO SHARPEN YOUR LISTENING SKILLS

How can we do a better job of learning from what others say? Aside from reciting Teach Me, Teach Me as your mantra, pick and choose among these three strategies for good listening:

   1. Do not dwell on whether you agree or disagree.   You do not need to jump in with opinions or feedback every few seconds while someone speaks with you. Listening does not oblige you to pick a side. Keep your mind focused on the message itself, not on judgments of right-wrong or good-bad. Free yourself of the pressure of having to *do something* with what someone says; rather than talk back, assess the speaker's ideas and viewpoints in your most clearheaded, unbiased frame of mind. Let the message hang out there, in beautiful silence, without the static that so often turns a conversation into a contest.

   2. Pay special attention when the topic is unfamiliar to you. Information that does not overlap with what you already know goes down slowly. It's like sampling a new dish at a foreign restaurant: You don't really know what you are ingesting, so you nibble at it bit by bit. As you listen to learn, let the speaker know that the subject matter is new to you and that you want to absorb it one step at a time. Do not let a fast talker race ahead unless you have caught up. Most speakers will appreciate your eagerness to learn and will be flattered by your strong desire to comprehend what they say. They will probably go out of their way to ensure that they express themselves clearly and concisely for your benefit.

   3. Integrate fresh information with what you already know.   As you learn from what others say, mentally link new data to familiar ideas. If a dealer describes a new car, compare it to cars you have seen or driven. If a friend raves about a recent vacation, conjure up all you have experienced or read about that destination. If a manager explains a procedure, associate it with other procedures. Imagine a notepad in your mind jotting down what someone says under broad categories such as Career Issues, How Things Work, Where To Shop. Classify what others say so that you neatly compile data in your head. Continually strive to compare and contrast groups of ideas. This process of mental linkage will not only make you a better listener, but will help you retain more of what others say.

●   **TRAP**   You judge a speaker as slow, silly, or stupid: that's your excuse to shut your ears off. You assume that you couldn't possibly learn anything from such a person. A colleague told me about a teenager who suffered from attention-deficit disorder (ADD), making it hard for him to remember things. While some teachers and classmates assumed he was high on drugs, it turns out his forgetfulness was apparently caused by a medical problem—a lack of neurotransmitters relaying electrical impulses in his brain. If someone has a poor delivery or strikes you as dim-witted, beware of letting your judgments interfere with your efforts to listen and learn.

WARNING: IF YOU JUDGE SPEAKERS, YOU WILL NOT LISTEN TO THEM

You've heard the "don't judge a book by its cover" lecture, so I'll spare you. Instead, consider how we arrive at first impressions.

Dr. George Kelly found in 1955 that people develop constructs to interpret others, that we are in the "business of prediction" when we meet someone for the first time. Each construct comes with a list of adjectives that we immediately attach to others when we are introduced to them. For example, our first impressions may be influenced by such constructs as *short-tall, blue eyes-brown eyes, man-woman, foreign accent-familiar accent.*

Kelly concluded that we make snap judgments when we meet people. A tall, blue-eyed man who speaks with a foreign accent may trigger a flood of adjectives in our mind (such as suave, adventurous, mysterious, dishonest, arrogant) that produce an instant impression. A short, brown-eyed woman who speaks in a familiar accent may trigger an opposing set of adjectives. Our judgments may make it harder to listen with an open mind, which diminishes our ability to overcome barriers and mend differences.

By realizing that first impressions can lead to rash judgments (and that discounting others can waste opportunities to learn), we can accept all speakers at face value.

MEMORY JOGGER

Listening is receptivity. The deeper you can listen without judgment, the better you can persuade.

Receptivity sounds nice, but we all know there are times when listening seems futile. Admit it: Sometimes speakers say things that strike you as so obviously wrong that you interrupt to correct them. Why listen to people who do not seem to know what they are talking about? Why remain receptive only to "learn" stuff that makes no sense?

Power influences how well we listen and learn. Politicians, like chief executives, tend to contradict those perceived as having less power (that covers just about everyone they interact with every day!). While a manager can say *you're wrong* to an underling, the same message rarely travels quite so bluntly in the opposite direction.

When the press describes a public figure as "combative," this means the subject prefers to argue rather than listen. The epitome of combativeness is former New York mayor Ed Koch.

Koch, a world-class talker but not much of a listener, resorted to interruption in many of his public appearances. In May of 1988, just prior to launching his unsuccessful reelection campaign, Koch held a question-and-answer session for 300 people at St. Vartan's Armenian Church on Manhattan's East Side. During the 90-minute discussion, Koch repeatedly interrupted constituents before they could complete their questions. His confrontational know-it-all style antagonized the group, and he seemed to delight in telling people they were wrong.

During the course of the session, participants began grumbling, "He works for us! Answer the questions!" The evening ended with someone shouting, "Why don't you listen?" Koch later told a reporter that he should have tried to "cultivate a bedside manner" when dealing with the public, to listen rather than to talk over his constituents.[1]

As Koch shows us, listening can prove particularly tough if you think you know more than those around you. You will not bother with Teach Me, Teach Me if you are convinced you have nothing left to learn.

There must be an unwritten rule somewhere that allows self-proclaimed *smart* people to cut off *dumb* people at will. "I always find myself correcting students who don't have a handle on the assignment," a professor told me. "I always thought of myself as a good listener, but that doesn't mean I sit still and pretend to listen when someone is just plain wrong." No wonder this professor complained that "students give me low marks on listening."

Diagnostic Self-Test: What You Do When Speakers Upset You

Answer the following questions regarding how you listen under duress. After reading each question, your first reaction might be, "That depends." Although every situation is different, choose the answer that comes closest to describing how you would act *most* of the time.

___ 1. If, while having a one-on-one conversation, you are certain that a speaker is wrong (or doesn't know the subject matter), how will you respond?

A. Let the speaker finish and then offer corrections.

B. Let the speaker finish and move on to another topic.

C. Interrupt to ask the speaker, "Are you sure about that?"

D. Interrupt the speaker to offer corrections.

___ 2. If your boss makes a snide comment that causes you to take offense, how will you usually respond?

A. Let it pass without comment.

B. Let it pass for now, but express your disapproval if it happens a second time.

C. Interrupt to express your disapproval and disappointment with your boss.

D. Let the speaker finish and ask, "What makes you say that?"

___ 3. If a speaker shows no interest in what you have to say and simply rambles on, what will you usually do?

A. Find the first chance to gracefully end the conversation.

B. Keep nodding and prompting the speaker to continue, while you daydream.

C. Disagree with the speaker, if for no other reason than to enliven the dialogue and stay engaged in the conversation.

D. Interrupt repeatedly, even to agree or support the speaker's points.

___ 4. If you are preoccupied with a serious matter, and this prevents you from listening to a speaker, will you:

A. Let the speaker finish expressing a point and then ask, "Can we discuss this later? I've got a pressing matter to attend to now."

B. Keep nodding to give the outward appearance that you're listening, while you inwardly ponder what's actually weighing on your mind.

C. Rush the speaker to finish so that you can pry yourself away from the conversation.

D. Interrupt immediately to tell the speaker that you have to go.

___ 5. How do you react when a speaker tells you that you behaved badly or that you were wrong about something?

    A. Let the speaker finish and not say anything in your defense.

    B. Let the speaker finish and ask a follow-up question (such as, "Have you ever seen me do that before?" or "Do you have any ideas how I can improve?")

    C. Interrupt to defend your behavior.

    D. Interrupt to criticize *the speaker's* behavior.

While there are no right or wrong answers in this exercise, you should review how many answers involve interrupting versus allowing the speaker to finish. Resorting to interruption may occasionally be justified (especially, as in question number 4, if you have a serious matter that requires your prompt attention). But if you fall into the habit of cutting speakers off who upset or annoy you, then you reduce your capacity to listen and persuade.

Also note whether you selected any responses that involve questions. This gives you a sense of your comfort level asking questions in difficult situations. As you will learn in Chapter 12, questioning can be a powerful tool in your persuasive arsenal.

Freeing Yourself to Listen with an Open Mind

Why take the trouble to pay attention when it appears there is nothing to gain, you are bored, or you are convinced the speaker is a misguided, misinformed fool? Answer: You never know when you will learn something.

Learning and listening go together. You will find that the more information you capture and retain, the more you will want to listen. The motivation to learn will feed your desire to listen better. "It's as if I'm making up for lost time," said one workshop participant at our monthly follow-up session. "These last few weeks have been great, because I feel so much more engaged in what people say. I used to judge a conversation a waste and not pay attention. Now I try to treat every conversation as a chance to learn something. It really works."

Persuasive speakers like people. They do not dwell on the perceived failings of others. They have wide arms for accepting those around them. They do not make snap judgments. The lens through which they view the world is not tinted with negativity or cynicism. By contrast, less persuasive individuals complain about how others "let me down" or how "those idiots have no idea what they're talking about."

MEMORY JOGGER

Those who see the good in people persuade more readily than those who assume everyone else is up to no good.

○ **NOW TRY THIS** Need a handy test to gauge someone's persuasiveness? Do you want to check whether your conversational partner sees the good (or bad) in people? I developed this technique for a sales manager who spent much of his day interviewing candidates to join his sales force.

1. During a casual conversation or formal interview, pose a question or observation, phrased neutrally, about why people behave in a certain way. Examples:

I wonder why so many people watch that show. I can't understand how it gets such high ratings.

I'm amazed at how many drivers go beyond the speed limit on the highway.

Why do so many registered voters fail to vote on Election Day?

2. Persuasive speakers will respond to you in an analytical, nonjudgmental way (or simply say "I don't know"). Others, dripping with negativity, may launch a diatribe attacking the foolishness of viewers who watch such garbage on television or the recklessness of "those fools who drive too fast." You can spot a poor persuader a mile away—he or she is the one spewing bile, shaking off the disgust of having to "deal with all this incompetence," disdainful of everyone, and unwilling to give anyone a second chance.

At the risk of sounding like your grandmother dispensing advice, it helps to look for the good in people. Instead of threats or ultimatums, persuaders adopt a more supportive tone and appeal to the finer aspects of the human spirit. They tend to make positive assumptions about others' character and motivation. Examples:

- A salesperson who spots a browser in the shoe department sees a potential buyer, not a nuisance who messes up the displays.
- A teacher who advises a struggling student strives to offer gentle guidance and encouragement, not issue punishment.
- A detective trying to elicit information from a witness assumes the subject wants to help, not hinder, the investigation.

- A negotiator seeking to close a deal might say, "As you seem driven by a sense of justice, I think you will find this settlement fair."

- A manager encouraging an employee to quit and accept a severance package might say, "You've told me you want to make progress in advancing your career, and you know how few opportunities exist here, so this offer gives you a running start with our resources behind you every step of the way."

When you approach people in a positive frame of mind, you steer clear of judgments and give them the benefit of the doubt. You also become a stronger, more influential communicator.

LISTEN IN THE HERE AND NOW SO THAT YOU DON'T MISS ANYTHING THAT MIGHT HELP YOU LATER

You may think no one will notice if you mentally race ahead of a speaker to plan your response. After all, people cannot read your mind. If you maintain eye contact and appear to listen, what's the harm in allowing your mind to wander?

Most people talk at a pace of 150 to 200 words per minute. That may sound like plenty of words pouring out of our mouths. But we think even faster. Our ears and brain can process words about four times as fast as the rate of speech, leaving lots of spare time to pick apart a speaker's argument, develop a counterattack, rehearse what we are about to say, or simply ignore the speaker's conclusions if they rub us the wrong way. With so much extra room for our minds to wander, it is easy to see why we have so much trouble listening.

Listen in the present moment. Sounds easy, but watch out! With all that mental room to roam, it takes concentration to stay put and not allow your mind to break free from the demands of listening. When a speaker is less than enthralling, of course, it becomes even harder to pay attention.

To make matters worse, we sometimes carry stress or other mental baggage into our conversations. Past events or future worries may seem more pressing than whatever someone says at the present moment. Your anxiety may overpower your efforts to listen and learn.

MEMORY JOGGER

Block out all thoughts of the past and future when another human being is talking with you.

Your ability to persuade can erode when you miss a comment because you assumed you knew what the speaker was saying or you allowed some preoccupation to reduce your attentiveness. Once you think you've captured the gist of the message, mental distractions can multiply. Don't give yourself permission to tune out.

Listening in the here and now can prove particularly tough on the phone. During a phone conversation, you may find yourself engaging in five separate activities at once: watching television, thinking about a previous call, worrying about an upcoming date, writing a note to remind yourself to run an errand, and listening to the voice on the other end of the line.

If you harness *all* of your mental energy to capture what a speaker says at the present moment, you gain an edge that will help you persuade that person. Devote your mental energy *not* to dwelling on the past or dreading the future, but to summarizing the speaker's ideas, assessing the soundness of the speaker's arguments, and cutting through all the chatter and identifying the main points.

MEMORY JOGGER

Most people devote only 20 percent of their attention to the here and now, leaving 80 percent of their mind to worry or wander off.

Diagnostic Self-Test: Do You Listen in the Here and Now?

The following questions help you assess whether you allow past or future anxieties to cloud your ability to concentrate in the here-and-now:

_____ Do you find it hard to listen when you have just come from a stormy meeting?

_____ On a "bad day," do you give up listening and just go through the motions?

_____ Do you let "little things" bother you (getting a parking ticket, having a lunch date cancelled) for many hours after they happen?

_____ Do you start dreading an undesirable event (a big speech, root canal surgery) days before it is scheduled?

_____ Do you frequently daydream about the same thing (weekend plans, stock picks, a perfect romance) instead of listening?

_____ Are you easily distracted by time pressures such as racing to appointments? Do you find yourself running late often? Are you frequently checking the time while listening?

If you answered yes to any of these questions, these are your warning signs. Strive to listen at the same moment someone speaks with you, and banish nagging distractions from your mind. As Adlai Stevenson once said when opening a speech, "My job is to speak. Your job is to listen. Let's hope we finish our jobs at the same time."

ALARM BELLS THAT REMIND YOU TO LISTEN: OPINION AND DECISION PHRASES

When I started teaching communication skills workshops in 1985, I wanted to earn some extra money to fund my hefty college tuition. I figured that, as a student with a heavy course load, I could devote a few hours each week to lead adult education programs while still meeting my academic requirements.

In developing my material on listening skills, I designed checklists, case studies, and clever reminders, thinking that participants would simply go out and apply whatever I taught them. As enrollments grew, I became convinced I hit upon a formula for success.

Then unpleasant reality struck like a bolt of lightning. I invited participants to join me for informal follow-up meetings to review their progress. When I asked the group to discuss their success stories, they kept telling me they were "too busy" to practice the listening skills we covered in the course. "My days get so hectic, I just don't have time to think about how I listen or all the other stuff from your course," was a typical response.

Discouraged, I fled to the proverbial drawing board to reassess my methods. What could I do to encourage participants to follow through? Beyond motivating them, how could I get them to *apply* the learning points from the course? How could I prevent the ideas from fading over time? Although the participants seemed pleased with my programs and eagerly referred others to enroll, I still worried that the effects of the workshop were short-lived. If the program failed to produce any lasting improvement, then why bother?

Troubled by these issues, I decided one day to take a long walk. Strolling along the cobblestone streets of Providence, Rhode Island, as if in a trance, I groped for solutions. Suddenly, I heard bells—not in my head, thankfully—as I spotted the Baptist church with its bell tower. *Three bells,* I thought, *must be three o'clock. Better get back to campus for class.*

Then it hit me. The sound of the bells reminded me of the time of day (a good thing, too, since I never wear a watch). Even though my mind was far away from thoughts of my 3 P.M. medieval history course, the bells served as an alarm to send me scurrying back to campus. As I raced to class, I wondered whether I could produce the same effect in my workshops by introducing "bells" as a signal for participants to listen.

I realized that in place of bells, certain phrases could trigger an alarm in a listener's head. Specifically, phrases that reveal a speaker's *opinions* or *decisions* can be wonderfully revealing in helping listeners to learn. Why? Because attentive persuaders need to understand how others arrive at an opinion or render a decision. This understanding does not come by speculation or guesswork; rather, effective persuaders listen carefully to a speaker's opinions or decisions.

As you mentally recite Teach Me, Teach Me, pay special attention to comments that state a preference or trace a decision-making process.

Examples of Opinion Phrases:	Examples of Decision Phrases:
I like...	*I've decided to...*
I can't believe that...	*It makes sense to...*
That makes me so...	*That leads me to...*
My favorite...	*It's clear that I need to...*

Every time you hear these phrases, imagine a bell clanging in your head. Condition yourself to respond. Think of the dog who salivates when the dinner bell rings. Or if you prefer a human example, consider how well you listen when someone says *I've been meaning to tell you how great/wonderful/thoughtful you are...*

Opinion and decision phrases can serve as your own private reminders to listen. No matter how busy or preoccupied you are, these phrases should sound an alarm in your mind: TIME TO LISTEN.

As you practice detecting opinion and decision phrases, you will spend less time dwelling on distractions (whether your fly is open or whether to pick up the dinner tab) and more time concentrating on what is said. By knowing what to listen for, you can operate in the here and now and gain information to help you persuade. By understanding how a speaker arrives at a decision or forms an opinion, you can frame your persuasive appeal accordingly.

○ **NOW TRY THIS**   Check the boxes that accurately describe you:

[   ]   I listen for the main point of what someone tells me.

[   ]   My willingness to listen depends on my mood.

154   *Chapter 7*

[   ]   I constantly must resist the temptation to interrupt slow speakers.

If you checked any of the boxes, this does not make you a terrible listener. Many people listen selectively to catch the main point. They also undergo mood swings that affect their willingness to listen. Still others lack the patience to keep quiet while slow talkers crawl toward a point. Given these obstacles to listening, opinion and decision phrases can help. These phrases work the same way as an emergency break-in on a phone line: You stop whatever you were doing and pay attention to what comes next.

QUICK REVIEW

- Never attempt to persuade people until you have listened to them first.
- Adopt the attitude *when I listen, people talk.*
- To listen properly, you need to interpret, evaluate, and respond.
- Listen for both facts and opinions. Beware of speakers who blur the two.
- Mentally repeat *teach me, teach me* whenever you listen so that you thirst to learn.
- Identify the speaker's main point and conclusion whenever you listen.
- Listen for understanding, not agreement.
- When you listen, integrate new information with what you already know.
- Listen without judging the speaker, especially if you think you know more.
- Block out all thoughts of the past and future when listening at any given moment.
- When you hear opinion or decision phrases, activate all your listening skills.

NOTES

1. Gary Woodward, *Persuasive Encounters,* Praeger, New York, 1990, p. 180.

8

How to Be More Persuasive by Showing Everyone How Well You Listen

There is a powerful impression that [President] Clinton listens to people. It is perhaps the strongest element of his character at the moment. It's seen to be his geniune character.—Stanley Greenberg, Democratic pollster[1]

This comment by one of Clinton's top political advisers sounds like a compliment. But read between the lines and you uncover something more revealing. Note that Greenberg does not praise Clinton's listening skills or actually say that his boss knows how to listen. Instead, he focuses on the public's *perception* that their president knows how to listen.

What's the difference?

Great listening is not enough. You also have to create the "powerful impression" that you listen. This way, people appreciate your sensitivity and feel closer to you. If you want to win over others, you better let them know you listen.

Your determination to learn something (Teach Me, Teach Me) will help you concentrate. But you also need to show outward signs of attentiveness so that the speaker cannot help but notice your superb listening skills.

155

When others see how much you care about what they say, they will look more favorably upon you. When it's your turn to speak, they will return the courtesy and listen better. They will trust you and confide in you. There is no better way to make friends and gain respect than to show others that you intend to listen to them.

Here's where some of us slip. We want to talk people into something, and we realize they must feel comfortable with us first before we start selling ourselves. So we listen to learn. *The problem is we do not show that we listen.* We fiddle with a rubber band or paper clip while we speak. We take phone calls in the middle of the interview. Our eyes wander all over the place instead of focusing on the speaker. In short, we seem distracted and disinterested—hardly the kind of nonverbal stance that signals curiosity and receptivity.

Inwardly, we might truly listen. Outwardly, it appears we could not care less.

We form impressions of people based on their behavior. If we talk to someone who does not appear attentive, we may feel hurt or simply give up trying to communicate to that person. It's like getting a bad feeling about an airplane's engine maintenance when you notice crumbs on the flip-down tray. By not demonstrating that you listen, you invite others to form sweeping negative impressions of you.

This chapter explores the perception of listening—how to let someone know through verbal and nonverbal cues that you intend to sit still and listen. Sending a message of support or concern by keeping quiet while someone speaks makes persuading them far easier, because you are viewed as a wise, sensitive "sounding board." People say yes to those who seem genuinely attuned to them.

DIAGNOSTIC SELF-TEST: YOUR NONVERBAL COMMUNICATION HABITS

Sometimes, an excellent listener still has trouble with the art of persuasion. The reason often involves nonverbal communication. Even the best listeners need to control their nonverbal communication so that the speaker feels listened to. In the following exercise, rate yourself as a nonverbal communicator.

KEY: 4-Always 3-Usually 2-Sometimes 1-Never

_____ I keep still when I'm listening to a speaker. I do not shift around, shake my foot, or fidget.

_____ I look a speaker in the eyes. I am comfortable maintaining eye contact.

_____ I think about what the speaker says, rather than worrying about how I look or feeling self-conscious in any way.

_____ I smile easily and show animated facial expressions when appropriate.

_____ I feel in control of my body while I listen.

_____ I encourage speakers to "talk away" by nodding or otherwise acknowledging their remarks in a supportive, friendly way.

Add up the total of your responses. If the sum is greater than 15, your nonverbal skills are fine. If your score is 10–14, you are in the middle range and can stand some improvement. If your total falls below 10, read on: This chapter can work wonders for you.

Beyond the benefits of learning, listening lets you shower someone with the exhilarating splash of affirmation. It makes a speaker feel wanted, acknowledged, heard. By appearing intent and interested in what's said, indicating that you understand, and asking follow-up questions, you let people know that you actually *want* them to speak. There is no better way to establish rapport and lay the groundwork for persuasion.

THE RIGHT WAY FOR PARENTS TO LISTEN TO THEIR CHILDREN

Do you recall a time when you were fooled into thinking that someone was paying attention, only to find you were mistaken? We all know the feeling. You keep talking, all the while appreciating the fact that the other party does not interrupt or look away as if to escape. You feel so lucky that someone listens so patiently!

But you set yourself up for a fall. When you stop speaking, you realize that you have been talking to a mannequin, a shell of a person. Instead of responding, the mannequin remains expressionless. No follow-up question. No paraphrasing of what you just said. No overlapping comments or criticisms. Nothing. It's as if one of the pod people from *Invasion of the Body Snatchers* has landed next to you in conversation.

Relationships sour when individuals feel they are "talking to a wall." In the business world, employees may feel less involved in their work when supervisors do not attempt to solicit their ideas or ask how they are doing. Persuading the troops to adopt a new procedure usually requires "buy in" that results from a show of concern for their welfare.

Similarly, children may grow distant from families who do not listen. Well-meaning parents sometimes respond to their kids' feelings by telling them not to trust their perceptions. A child says, "I'm hungry," and Mom replies, "You can't be hungry because you just ate." The mother replaces listening with a comment that contradicts the child's observations and denies the child's right to experience distress or discomfort.

A parent's instinctive desire to play the role of fixer can also pose problems. *Working Mother* magazine writes about a mother who tries to stop her three-year-old child from crying by using Scotch tape to repair a broken pretzel. The mother's sweet but desperate act sends the message, "Don't cry. I'll fix everything." Even worse is the mother who says, "Why are you crying? It's only a pretzel. I'll get you another one."[2]

In both cases, the parent's urge to instantly solve the problem severs an opportunity for the child to freely express feelings that may otherwise go unspoken. As the toddler grows into a teenager, parents may be left wondering, "There are times when my child is unhappy, but when I ask what's wrong the answer is always 'nothing.'"

The solution is to show children that you listen. Acknowledge their feelings and give them room to work through their tears or anger so that they can open up to you. If a youngster complains about the weather (*It's so cloudy outside*) or house guests (*I don't like them*), resist the temptation to replace their negative feelings with positive ones. Instead, accept their comments and help them work through the negativity without letting your interpretations get in the way. Listen carefully and ask follow-up questions:

How do the clouds make you feel?

What don't you like about the guests?

so that they grow comfortable expressing themselves honestly to you.

● **TRAP**   A pitfall that ensnares many communicators is offering unwelcome opinions. Try not to give advice unless you are invited to do so. Suppose Greg says, "I played a terrible game today, and I wish you hadn't been there to watch it." You respond, "Oh, you played fine. Don't worry." Greg disagrees, insisting he played poorly. You insist with equal firmness that it is "no big deal." Denying Greg's dejection will hardly prove persuasive; rather, Greg may learn to simply keep his thoughts to himself. Rather than contradicting a speaker's feelings, draw out the underlying emotions by listening.

SEVEN WAYS TO SEND A MESSAGE OF CONCERN WITHOUT SAYING A WORD

Once you decide to listen, you might as well make it obvious. Send a non-verbal message of support by remaining attentive and giving the impression that you are interested in hearing more. Strike a posture of involvement by maintaining outward signs of responsive listening.

How do you show people that you listen? Use the following techniques:

1. Align yourself physically with the speaker.   Although you do not have to copy every move the speaker makes (no need to pick at your eyebrow hairs just because the speaker does), carry yourself (head, shoulders, legs) in a like manner. Make sure your head is perpendicular to your shoulders and not tilted to one side. Speakers rarely tilt *their* heads, so neither should you. Try to align your shoulders with the speaker's. Observe whether the speaker leans toward you or slouches. If you stand ramrod straight while a speaker prefers a less imposing posture, then you introduce a dimension of discontinuity into the conversation. You need to make speakers feel comfortable so that they open up to you.

MEMORY JOGGER

Stand when a speaker stands; sit when a speaker sits.

---

2. Acknowledge comments with occasional listening sounds such as mmm hmm and uh-huh.   These cues work particularly well over the telephone. In the absence of face-to-face communication, demonstrating your listening skills requires greater emphasis on periodic feedback in the form of monosyllabic grunts of understanding. Limit these acknowledgments to brief sounds every fifteen seconds or so. Do not feel obliged to punctuate the end of every sentence you hear with another *yes* or *sure*. Beware of overdoing it. If you condition speakers to expect you to "sound off" whenever they pause during their remarks, then you run the risk of distracting them. They may also wonder what went wrong the one time they do not hear you grunt after they say something!

3. Maintain eye contact.   On a first date with a captivating new friend, you will have little trouble keeping your eyes from darting away.

Yet when distractions swirl around you, eye contact demonstrates your ability to stay focused on the speaker. Train yourself to ignore traffic noise, background music, and nearby whispering.

New Yorkers know all about communicating under duress, where the surrounding din of sirens, honking, and yelling replays itself day and night. The temptation to look away from a speaker and see what's going on outside or what all the commotion is about across the street can prove overpowering, especially if you are not in the mood to listen.

Soon after arriving in Manhattan, I bumped into an old high school friend on the corner of Fifth Avenue and 57th Street. We started to update each other on our lives, and the discussion turned to job opportunities. As this was the number one issue on both our minds, we listened carefully and easily maintained eye contact despite the considerable hubbub around us. Ten minutes later, a police officer approached us and asked, "Well, what did you two see?" It turns out a mugging had occurred right near us on the sidewalk, but we were too engrossed in conversation to notice.

● **TRAP** Avoid Cocktail Party Eyes, where you people-watch instead of looking at the person speaking to you. Politicians often do this as they work a room in search of rich campaign donors. They may find themselves shaking hands with robotic insincerity, all the while peeking out from the corner of their eyes to see who else lurks nearby. Individuals go away thinking, "What a phony. I felt as if I was invisible." High-ego types wrapped in their own self-importance are particularly susceptible to looking away when someone speaks to them. Failing to maintain eye contact is a dead giveaway that you do not want to listen, and this will surely diminish your chances to persuade.

4. Move closer to a speaker. Depending on the situation, you can take a step toward the speaker or lean forward in your chair to show that you want to hear each and every word. Some salespeople deliberately start an interview by remaining an extra few feet apart from the prospect and then subtly draw closer as the conversation proceeds. This makes the prospect think, "Wow, this guy is really trying to hear me out."

5. Use a range of nonverbal cues. There are many ways to let a speaker know that you are a responsive listener, from nodding your head to smiling to adopting animated facial expressions (such as concern, curiosity, skepticism, anticipation). A sprinkling of genuine laughter, for example, acknowledges what's just been said or what's about to be said and encourages a speaker to continue. Do not rely too much on any one cue or you will leave the speaker wondering whether you really care or just operate on autopilot. You can probably recall a conversation with someone whose head kept bobbing up and down like a yo-yo, or whose ceaseless smile seemed frozen and strangely false. To expand your repertoire of nonverbal behavior, observe how others respond while you speak. What cues encourage you to continue? How can you tell when someone listens to you? Recall from Chapter 4 that persuasive people know how to adjust themselves to appeal to a wide range of audiences. You can practice flexing your personality muscles by continually experimenting with new ways to show others that you are listening.

MEMORY JOGGER

The muscles in your face can make over 5,000 different facial expressions. Start exercising them now!

---

6. Keep your hands away from your face.   Impatient listeners tend to rub their eyes, scratch their cheeks, stroke their hair, and bury their chin in their hands. The more they rub and scratch, the more it becomes an ingrained habit. Like the sparkling facade of a new home, you want your face to be unblemished by signs of wear and tear. You will be more relaxed if your hands rest comfortably at your sides. Do not cross your arms or otherwise shield yourself from the speaker. Send a signal of openness that tells a speaker, "Please continue." If you are seated, keep your back straight, and do not curl your body into the chair as if you want to escape. Stretch your arms along the armrest and leave them there.

7. Make sure you can hear everything.   If you have any trouble hearing what's said, stop and ask for clarification. Speak up—don't sit there like a stone if you need help. Do not be hesitant about asking, *Can you repeat that?* or *I'm having trouble hearing you, can you speak up?* If a speaker swallows a phrase or uses an unfamiliar word, ask about it. In Manhattan, where restaurants are cramped and noisy and sirens seem to fill the background of every phone call, distractions can make hearing even more challenging. Do not assume that you will "make up" for a lost word or phrase by simply letting the speaker continue. It is usually better to let the speaker know you care about the message and you want to confirm the meaning of what's said to ensure your full understanding.

RETAIN PERSONAL FACTS ABOUT OTHERS, AND DELIGHT THEM BY SHOWING THAT YOU REMEMBER

It's tough to generalize about human beings, even those who share the same culture and uphold the same principles. Each of us has a unique personality shaped by attitudes and values. We come from different backgrounds and form our own belief systems based on experience and upbringing. We develop our own distinct taste in food, fashion, and people. But there is something we share in common, one simple rule that applies to almost everyone: We love when someone remembers our birthday!

Wish someone a happy birthday, and they will feel closer to you. They will appreciate that you care enough to recognize them on their own personal holiday, that you make the effort to remember what is surely a noteworthy day out of the 365 that come along each year.

What does this have to do with building your persuasive power? When you recall someone's birthday or some other tidbit of biographical information, you show that you listen. You demonstrate that the other person counts in your eyes. It is hard to resist the persuasive pull of someone who successfully steps into our world and understands how we think and feel. Remember from Chapter 3 that one way to empathize is to take mental notes of what others say. Another benefit of retaining what others say is that you prove yourself an excellent listener.

People will be impressed and perhaps deeply moved by your ability to remember their birthday months after they casually mentioned it in conversation. They will ask in amazement, "How did you know today was my birthday?" You will remind them that they told you "a few months ago when you were telling me about last year's surprise party" or "we discussed back in January that you would qualify for a lower insurance premium after your next birthday."

How do you retain key biographical facts?

When speakers mention anything related to their birthday, ask for a date. A colleague told me how he found out a friend's birthday:

> Mary and I were dining at an Italian restaurant when the waiters started singing "Happy Birthday" to someone at another table. So I casually asked her, "So when's *your* birthday?" And when she said "June 2," you can bet I never had to be told again. She was floored when, four months later, I remembered.

Bells should clang in your head whenever a speaker mentions such personal facts as a favorite movie, vacation plans, or the name of a family member. When a colleague mentions her upcoming time off, ask where she plans to go. Dig for facts within the context of the conversation. Always keep a notepad by the phone to record such useful data.

In a face-to-face conversation (where note taking is inappropriate), store any facts in your head until you can slip away to write them down. If you have trouble remembering these kinds of facts and figures even for a few minutes, then use memory games to retain what you hear.

○ **NOW TRY THIS** Do you find it tough to remember someone's name? The next time you meet someone, listen carefully to the name. Repeat it out loud. If it's an unusual name, ask how to spell it. Then imagine drawing the name across the speaker's forehead. Really. If you meet a female wearing lipstick, visualize taking her lipstick and writing her name in a semicircle above her eyes. For the rest of the conversation, "see" the name on the person's face. This will create a visual imprint in your mind. When you run into this individual again, you will surely recall the name.

Get in the habit of repeating any biographical facts you hear. Even better, move beyond mere repetition and weave your response into the conversation. This helps you ensure that you get the facts right while reinforcing the information in your head. The act of repeating facts aloud can, in itself, mentally embed the data more firmly so you do not forget it later. Examples:

- When someone lists the names and ages of their children, say:

  With Steve seven and Jeannie four, you must be wondering whether that local school bond measure will pass.

  So your oldest, Robert, is fourteen. Does that mean he gets to babysit Rachel and Chris?

  Roger is five. I also have a five-year-old. Where does Roger go to school?

- When someone mentions his birthday, repeat the date. If it comes near any holidays or other special days (such as tax day, the first day of a month, or a new season) associate the date with anything that falls close:

  December 17. Another reason to celebrate during the holiday season.

  June 21. What a great way to kick off summer.

  April 9. I'll be rushing to file my taxes by then, no doubt.

- When people tell you where they intend to vacation this year, where their son or daughter is getting married, or where their parents or grandparents live, ask what made them choose that place.

Aside from listening for biographical facts and figures, capture any comments that reveal a speaker's deeply held beliefs. Some people are fond of repeating such statements as:

You know my philosophy: brutal honesty at all times.

I've always believed in numbers, that the truth is in the bottom line.

If you do a job, give it the best you've got. Don't give a half-assed effort.

These remarks reveal the guiding principles that shape how people make decisions and how they view the world. Retain these types of statements and refer to them later so that you can show how well you listen. Even better, tie a speaker's beliefs to your persuasive message. Use this format:

You've told me before about [deeply held belief]. That's why I'm proposing [idea].

When you want to persuade someone, think back to past conversations with that person. What beliefs has he shared with you? By matching your persuasive goal with his personal philosophy, you can make your listening pay off by winning him over. Examples:

You've told me before that you believe in brutal honesty at all times. That's why I want to come right out and say that my idea entails some risk but will result in an enormous reward if we go forward.

You've told me many times that you look to the numbers for the bottom line. That's why I'm proposing a way to directly and positively impact those numbers by investing in expert systems technology.

By retaining what others tell you, you reap all kinds of rewards. You will earn trust, gain respect, and develop the inside track on understanding how they think. With listening in such short supply, you stand out even more. Many individuals do not even try to retain biographical facts. They repeatedly squander opportunities to make others feel special. They listen half-heartedly at best. And then they wonder why it is so hard to persuade.

Let speakers know that what they say matters to you.

HOW FOLLOW-UP QUESTIONS LET OTHERS KNOW YOU'RE LISTENING

Sending nonverbal signals and retaining personal facts about speakers are two steps to show that you listen. Here's one more technique: Ask follow-up questions.

This simple but often overlooked tool works for almost any type of conversation. And it is easy. When someone finishes speaking, ask a question that invites the speaker to continue or elaborate. That's it.

Many people fail to ask questions when someone stops speaking. Instead, they yank the conversation back to themselves at the earliest opportunity. They show minimal interest in what the other person has to say. This approach hardly lends itself to the kind of healthy two-way exchange that promotes persuasion.

If you teach groups of children or adults, you probably look to the students' questions as an indicator of how well they listen to you. Questions demonstrate that your comments make people think by provoking a need to know more. A question-and-answer exchange also breaks down the barrier between teacher and student and creates a more vibrant atmosphere for learning. College professors may find that after an hour of lecturing, it can be demoralizing if no one in the classroom has anything to ask.

In my corporate training sessions, the participants who make the most progress in advancing their communication skills are generally the ones who ask the most questions. They often want clarification of a certain point or request more facts. Their queries almost always lead others to pose questions, and the level of give-and-take in the room contributes to a lively, entertaining learning experience.

Doctors can use follow-up questions to show patients that they want to listen. In fact, some medical schools and residency programs teach students how to interview patients without interrupting them. A sociologist describes one of these training sessions:

> In the area of interruptions, we encourage our physicians to do two things. The first is to shut up during the first part of the interview

and the second is to solicit additional concerns from the patient—and to keep asking until they're sure the patient has told them everything they need to know. We've found that in all cases, the effect has been positive. Physicians were more satisfied. They found their visits more organized. The patients were also more satisfied and got better and more comprehensive care.[3]

What's the best way to ask follow-up questions? First, wait for speakers to complete their point. Pause an extra few seconds to make sure they have nothing further to add. Then prompt them to continue talking.

You can accomplish this by either seeking additional information or "playing back" what they just said in the form of a question. Note how each of these approaches works in a conversation between two old friends.

Script 1: Seeking More Information

Bret: I'm thinking of moving to New England to retire. I've visited a few times and loved it. Living here in the big city gets to me sometimes, and I'm just looking for some peace and quiet.

Charles: Where in New England are you thinking of moving?

Script 2: Playing Back the Speaker's Comments

Bret: I'm thinking of moving to New England to retire. I've visited a few times and loved it. Living here in the big city gets to me sometimes, and I'm just looking for some peace and quiet.

Charles: You're looking for peace and quiet?

In Script 1, Charles shows he listens by digging deeper to gather information from Bret about his future plans. Bret has probably asked himself the same question, so it makes sense that Charles would want to learn more.

In Script 2, Charles allows Bret to add whatever he wants by repeating Bret's comment as a question. Many therapists use this type of non-threatening follow-up question to encourage a soft-spoken communicator to open up. Dr. Carl Rogers popularized this approach in the 1960s with his "encounter groups."

● **TRAP**   Never pose a question unless you have listened closely to everything that the speaker has said. It can be embarrassing to ask what you think is a sensible, fact-finding question only to hear the words, "If you had been listening, you would have heard me answer that question."

The act of questioning is in itself a wonderful way to affirm the speaker. Simply by asking an intelligent follow-up question or framing an inquiry using the speaker's own words, you send a clear message that you care about what that person has to say.

PARAPHRASING: THE ULTIMATE LISTENING TOOL

Aside from follow-up questions, you can demonstrate your listening skills by summarizing what's just been said. Paraphrasing, or restating to clarify meaning, helps you keep pace with the speaker and prevents misunderstanding.

Think of the last time someone paraphrased what you just said. How did it make you feel? Chances are you felt closer to the other person. You probably thought, "I'm getting through. I'm making sense. I'm being understood."

You can paraphrase in almost any situation—whether personal or business, among friends or strangers, with serious or light topics. It is an easy way to show you understood the speaker while striking an attentive listening pose in the conversation.

Here are three examples of how you can use paraphrasing to send a powerful message to others that you truly listen:

Listening to the Customer

Susan, the owner of Acme Messenger Service, visits Craig, a potential client, on a sales call.

Craig:	What we really need is a dependable messenger service that does what it says so we never have to worry about a late delivery. We're willing to pay what it takes, as long as it's a fair price and the service is there. Our facility is different from our competitors because of our high volume, so we need someone who can deal with a lot of activity at once.
Susan:	So what you need is dependability.
Craig:	Yes, yes. [He goes on to reveal more.]

Susan's paraphrase invites Craig to continue by showing him that she understands his point. He views her as an excellent listener and is inclined to do business with her.

Listening to Your Boss

Jane, a buyer, works for Don in a large toy store chain. He asks her to come into his office, where he explains his ideas to change the stores' focus.

Don:	I've decided to shift our focus away from kid's toys and more toward adult games. The kiddie stuff just sits on the shelf too long.
Jane:	You want us to carry more adult games.
Don:	Yes. Our profits are down, and I think we'd do better meeting the needs of a less fickle shopper. It's so hard to predict what kids will like, and their attention span is so short.
Jane:	Yeah, kids are unpredictable! You never know from week to week what they want their parents to buy for them.
Don:	Now I'm not saying we should get out of the kiddie toy business for good. I mean, we still need to bring kids into the stores. I just think we could do a better job attracting adults as well.
Jane:	You would like to have adults in the stores buying our merchandise not only for kids, but for themselves.
Don:	Yes. Exactly. You got the picture, Jane.

Jane's ability to paraphrase her boss lets Don know without a doubt that she understands him. He need not wonder whether Jane was listening or whether she grasped what he was trying to say. When buying season heats up and Jane wants to persuade him what kind of products to carry, he will be more apt to approve her suggestions because she shows that she listens to him and complies with his wishes.

Listening to Children

Parents persuade their children to confide in them by paraphrasing in a nonjudgmental manner. If a child says, "The kids made fun of me at school today because of my hair," a parent should respond with a neutral question or comment free of interpretation:

How did that make you feel?

They made fun of you?

They talked to you about your haircut?

As long as the parent follows the paraphrase by pausing, the child will probably open up, perhaps moving on to reveal more important matters (dislike of her overall appearance, lack of friends at school). The key is for the parent to verify the child's feelings rather than instantly trying to contradict those feelings. A well-meaning but potentially damaging response (*Why, your haircut makes you look adorable.*) shuts down the dialogue without giving the child's feelings a chance to surface.

MEMORY JOGGER

Paraphrase what speakers say and you will grow closer to them.

○ **NOW TRY THIS**   Almost everyone knows a repetitive speaker. The next time you come face to face with someone who talks like a broken record—rehashing the same point endlessly—remember the art of paraphrasing.

Repetitive speakers want to make sure their points are understood, so they speak in loops to convince themselves their message is clear.

Paraphrasing assures them that you follow their points. You can prompt a repetitive speaker to move on with a remark such as "That makes sense, go on," or attaching a forward-looking question such as "What do you conclude from that?" or "What do we do next?"

Restate what they say, and then use your listening skills to push the conversation forward.

THE ULTIMATE TEST: REMAINING ATTENTIVE WHEN YOU HEAR WHAT YOU DON'T WANT TO HEAR

Okay, now comes the hard part. Follow-up questions and paraphrasing are a piece of cake compared to having to listen when hearing what you don't want to hear.

President Clinton gives the impression he listens by nodding sympathetically and tearing up when he hears a sad story from an unemployed worker or a single mother without health insurance. Like all presidents, he usually interacts with prescreened "real people" as selected by his advisers, not a random crowd of strangers. This way, he avoids facing angry citizens who may scream in his face (and if a malcontent accosts him, his ever-present aides will whisk him away).

The rest of us are not so lucky. We never know when someone will say something awful that rocks our emotional boat. Listening to what we don't want to hear can hurt. It is easier to tune out, lose our temper, or distort the message to make it more palatable. This is particularly true when we discuss sensitive or controversial topics such as family, politics, or religion with someone who harbors opposing views.

○ **NOW TRY THIS**   To learn how to listen without emotional blocks, seek out someone with different beliefs and launch a discussion. To maximize the value of this exercise, think of an individual whose extremist views disgust you. Select a controversial topic that you feel strongly about (the death penalty, taxes, guns) and just let the conversation flow. Argue at will. This may sound like pouring lighter fluid on a flame, but treat it as an experiment to upgrade your listening skills. Strive to understand the opposing point of view. Make room for differences in outlook; do not ignore them. Check whether you listen fairly and accurately by restating what you hear. Although you may not necessarily enjoy this encounter, you will sharpen your communication skills by showing that you listen to even the most difficult, objectionable remarks. This will make you a stronger, more resilient persuader.

There is a moment early in a verbal confrontation when you make a choice to act as speaker or listener. Do not lock yourself into the role of speaker where you wind up interrupting, defending, and yelling. Speakers lose their temper and let slip comments they regret later. Listeners, by contrast, maintain a sense of inner control. Just hearing the other person out (wicked taunts and all) dissipates most of the negative emotional energy that would otherwise go toward flinging insults or intensifying the argument.

How to Control Your Emotions When You Listen So That You Do Not Say Something You Regret Later

It is tough enough to hear the rantings of a strident ideologue. Even tougher, of course, is listening to emotionally jarring news. We do not want to hear why we have just been fired or why "this relationship just won't work." Our minds may go haywire when we hear the terrible truth.

When you hear unpleasant news, your first thought should be *why* you do not like what's said. Does the message unleash feelings of fear, anger, or confusion? Does it pack an unwelcome or insensitive punch of personal criticism? Or how about if, after an awful week of tragedy, you hear one more upsetting story that tips your emotional scale? By understanding why a comment strikes a negative chord, you can let the speaker know how you feel and perhaps postpone the discussion to another time.

If you have no choice but to hear the nasty news, then try to detach yourself from the message. Hear the words, listen for their actual meaning, and then, like a reporter covering a story, double-check the facts so that you objectively and accurately digest the points. Go slowly, and listen in steps. Focus on understanding the message first—assess its ramifications later.

MEMORY JOGGER

Listening does not oblige you to *do* anything except understand what's said.

Allowing emotions to take hold can block understanding. I have watched in amazement as listeners erupt in anger the moment a speaker utters a single word (*fundamentalists, homeless*). Introducing a panel discussion on School Prayer and the Role of Religion, for instance, can lead to a verbal free-for-all. You can probably recall a time when your emotions made listening seem impossible.

A potentially destructive phenomenon occurs during *emotional runaway*, when there's just no controlling all those intense feelings that engulf you. Instead of concentrating on the topic itself, we suddenly shift our attention and anxiety to the speaker. Anger triggered by the red-hot subject matter is transferred to the messenger. We start thinking:

How dare they!

I've heard this all before.

They better shut up soon or I'm going to…

Such thoughts stoke the fire and breed antagonism. I know the feeling: when some abortion protestors marched down my block when I lived in Manhattan, I mistakenly tried to reason with them. Hearing their views only fanned my anger. Those ten minutes of heated debate made me furious for days.

You may be thinking, *It's only human to occasionally let your emotions get the best of you. That's life. It's healthier to release pent-up feelings rather than bottle them up and bring on ulcers.* You're partially right. There's nothing wrong with expressing deeply held beliefs or passionate feelings. But beware of using the *I'm angry* attitude as a reason not to listen.

One way to contain the spread of emotional fallout is to stop the mental meltdown before it reaches its final, uncontrollable phase. This requires visualization. When you find negative emotions enveloping you, imagine various levels of alert like DEFCON 5 through 1 (a code used by the American military to prepare troops as hostilities escalate). Tell yourself, *I'm getting so mad I need to move to DEFCON 4* or *That's it, I'm shifting to DEFCON 3.* Sounds silly perhaps, but it works. Why? Because it forces us to put our emotions in perspective. Such a measured response not only adds a dose of rationality to an irrational impulse, but it also provides a momentary reminder that we choose how much or how little emotion to bring to the party of everyday life.

How Listening and Paraphrasing Can Prevent an Argument

When we let our emotions take over, we tend to bicker rather than maintain a steady determination to listen. The last thing on an angry person's mind is creating the impression of being a rapt listener!

In the following script, we see how a potentially heated debate stays cool, thanks in large part to the ability of the boss to continually exhibit her listening skills. Count how many times she paraphrases what her employee says.

Mitch, a computer programmer, argues with his manager Harriet, the vice-president of a large software firm, over the deadline for delivering a new product:

Harriet:	We must have all the bugs worked out by Friday. That's it. We're under contract to deliver the goods by then.
Mitch:	It's just not possible. We're too burned out already after being up all night practically every day this week.
Harriet:	You have worked long and hard. I know that. [She pauses and Mitch jumps in.]
Mitch:	Yes, very hard. And not just me. The whole programming team has pushed to get all the testing done on time.
Harriet:	Everyone has been really putting in long hours.

Mitch:	That's just it. I'm not sure how we can do the work under this kind of pressure.
Harriet:	The pressure's on, that's for sure. We have a deadline to meet Friday.
Mitch:	Yeah, I know. We are all aware of it.
Harriet:	Do your best. I know you will.

Harriet paraphrases three times in an effort to show Mitch she appreciates his hard work and is listening to his concerns. As the boss, she could simply order Mitch to work harder "or else," but she wisely demonstrates that she cares about what he has to say. While the problem does not go away, at least Mitch feels that Harriet fairly understands the dilemma.

● **TRAP**   How do you handle criticism? Do you listen calmly and dispassionately, or do you interrupt to defend yourself? A common pitfall for weak listeners is the defensive reflex—the tendency to speak up when criticized instead of keeping quiet and attempting to listen. The next time you are tempted to defend your actions or opinions, close your mouth and consider what's at stake. If you allow a person to finish speaking, then you can gather some extra time to calm down. You can also remind yourself to ask clarifying questions if necessary (*Are you referring to the incident last Monday or are there other examples?*). Best of all, you gain a speaker's respect by showing that you listen. Defending yourself may preserve your sense of rightness or satisfy a stubborn urge, but it rarely accomplishes anything productive, and it risks turning a conversation into an argument.

Many supervisors tell me that they dislike performance reviews because some staffers insist on defending their actions instead of listening. "What's funny is that the handful of people who actually listen to my criticism and at least think it over are the ones that get promoted faster," a personnel manager said. "They may not agree with me, but they don't fight it. I treat what they say with more credence than those who immediately start shaking their heads and interrupting me."

○ **NOW TRY THIS**   Practice handling criticism. Invite a colleague at work to give you honest feedback on some aspect of your performance. Ask, "I'm looking to improve in this area. Do you have any ideas?" The answer, of course, may turn into an ego-bruising critique. That's the point! You will probably grow tense and may react defensively. If you can accept the criticism gracefully and you genuinely appreciate your colleague's openness, then you pass the test. If you start arguing (*But wait...hold* *on...I don't do that...*) or judging the speaker rather than the message, then you suffer from the defensive reflex.

When someone says, "You're wrong" or "That's a dumb idea," do not equate such comments with a personal attack. Instead, demonstrate your determination to listen and learn. Resist the urge to interrupt. Show you are capable of hearing what you don't want to hear.

MEMORY JOGGER

You can choose whether to personalize what someone says. In the face of criticism, detach yourself from the message and listen for its true meaning.

Treat criticism as an opportunity to sell yourself as a fair-minded, thick-skinned individual. Your ability to maintain your composure will be rewarded when you want to exert influence over the speaker. When the day comes to persuade, you will already have earned considerable credibility that will lend force to your ideas.

QUICK REVIEW

- Don't give advice unless invited to do so. Just keep quiet and listen.
- Align yourself physically with the speaker.
- Use occasional listening sounds to acknowledge what's said.
- Use a range of nonverbal cues to show you listen.
- Keep your hands away from your face while you listen.
- When a speaker mentions personal facts, retain these facts and follow up.
- Tie a speaker's stated beliefs to your persuasive message.
- Don't yank a conversation back to you; instead, ask follow-up questions.
- Learn to listen to what you don't want to hear without losing your temper.
- When you hear emotionally upsetting news, detach yourself from the message and double-check the facts.
- Resist the temptation to instantly defend yourself when criticized.

NOTES

1. *The New Yorker*, 4-5-93, pp. 46–47.
2   *Working Mother*, July 1989, p. 74.
3   *The Los Angeles Times*, 12-14-86, p. 33.

CHAPTER 9

Unleashing the Power of Silence to Gain Knowledge and Solve Problems

When you listen well, people tend to talk more. Mike [Wallace] is great at that. A person will give him an incomplete answer, and Mike won't say anything, and the other guy will rush to fill the silence.—Ed Bradley of 60 Minutes, *explaining his colleague's interview technique[1]*

Let me give you two words of advice when it comes to persuasion: Keep quiet.

That's right. You will win over more people when you treat silence as your ally. But tapping the power of silence means fighting an uphill battle.

We live in a loud world. Sounds tend to overlap—speakers talk over one another, conversations turn into screaming matches, and we interrupt to "get a word in edgewise." Background noise, from the music blaring next door to the airplane roaring overhead, makes silence a precious resource.

WHY SILENCE IS SUCH A PRECIOUS RESOURCE WHEN WE COMMUNICATE

Most of us find silence threatening. We grow uncomfortable when a conversation stalls. We feel self-conscious when our questions are greeted with dead air. We panic when we run out of things to say.

177

Why is it so tough to keep quiet and let others talk? After all, you don't have to *do* anything except not speak. We're not dealing with some advanced skill such as rocket science that takes special training. What's the problem here?

Blame it on the mass media (what a relief—it's not our fault!). Radio and television talk-show hosts never stop blabbing. The way they see it, silence equals low ratings. They assume that they will lose their audience if they engage in a calm, unhurried dialogue characterized by pockets of peace and quiet. Watch or listen to a typical talk-show for five minutes and try to count to two whenever everyone stops speaking. Chances are you will not get past one.

Unfortunately, we copy what we hear and see in the media. We want to entertain and be entertained by others. We try to make our conversations clever like those on our favorite television shows. There's no room for silence if everyone's busy attempting to sound witty and practicing their latest joke. Patience, in the form of silence, becomes increasingly hard to maintain for any length of time.

When I was making this point in one of my seminars, a participant told the group about his experience as the volunteer head of his home-owners association. "You're right about how hard it is for people to remain silent," he said. "At our monthly board meetings, it's impossible to stay on track. It's a free-for-all. I mean, people just talk over one another without bothering to listen."

The next time you attend a panel discussion or watch pundits perform on one of those Sunday morning television news shows, notice the lack of silence. If someone asks a question and the respondent wishes to reflect for a few seconds before answering, chances are another panelist will jump in with a ready answer. If you take too long to say something or you stammer a bit, you risk being cut off by a talker who cannot wait for you to finish.

One reason silence poses such a challenge is that many people do not want to listen. When someone else talks, they would rather talk, too. A salesperson confessed to me, "I love to talk. I've always had the gift of gab. The moment someone else stops talking, even if they just want to take a breath or gulp some water, I'm already launching into whatever I want to say next."

What's worse, the task of persuading someone often triggers nervousness. Recall all those fears we discussed in Chapter 2. We may worry about rejection, failure, or humiliation. With our stress level already high, the last thing we want to experience is the self-consciousness of staring at someone in silence. A sound, any sound, spells relief.

When a man meets a woman at a party (or vice versa), casual "small talk" builds rapport and makes for a breezy chat. Asking for a date next

Friday night, on the other hand, ups the ante and introduces the element of risk (She might say no; she might laugh in my face). We want to get it over with—to ask for a commitment and not have to stew in silence awaiting a response. Under these circumstances, silence may reinforce our sense of defeat.

Silence magnifies our thoughts. If we are riddled with doubts, we will feel more unsure of ourselves when the conversation grinds to a halt. If we sense we are losing an argument, we will feel more like losers during bouts of silence. If we are communicating insincerely, we will dwell on our insincerity when it gets quiet.

Memory Jogger

The most effective communicators use silence to focus all their attention on the other person rather than to dwell on their own doubts or anxieties.

USING SILENCE TO STRENGTHEN YOUR PERSUASIVENESS

This might strike you as a decidedly un-Western notion, but silence can speak volumes about what you believe in. You need not open your mouth to make yourself clear. Some cultures, in fact, treat silence as a normal part of communication. Quiet pauses can translate into approval or disapproval, calm reflection or agitated concern, serious consideration or outright dismissal. It all depends on the context of the conversation.

Take the example of Rajat Gupta, the India-born head of McKinsey & Co., a large management-consulting firm. While Gupta was giving a presentation to an important client, someone asked if the turmoil that would result from adopting Gupta's recommendations was worth the risk. According to an eyewitness, Gupta said nothing:

> He [Gupta] just looked them right in the eyes. A minute must have passed in silence. It was quite effective, because the client had to make the decision. It wasn't ours to make.[2]

Admit it: Most of you would have probably chosen to respond to the question by providing facts, observations, and some fancy overhead slides to support your points. You would have explained yourself and justified your self-perceived rightness. Your idea of persuasion is to address the question head-on and show why your view makes the most sense.

But not so fast. Even if you talk a good game, remember that true persuasion rarely results from telling people why you are right: You must make them decide for themselves that your course of action is in their best interest. Here's where silence enters the picture. You let messages sink in and give the audience the time it needs to reach a verdict on the issue at hand.

Sometimes a picture can persuade far more readily than a thousand words. President Gerald Ford repeatedly resisted declaring land in the Pacific Northwest as federal wilderness until someone showed him a picture book on the area. The pictures reminded Ford of his days as a Boy Scout, and without exchanging a word, Ford was finally persuaded to set aside 400,000 acres and establish the Alpine Lakes Wilderness.[3] Glorious silence, along with some pictures, did the trick.

Astute persuaders use silence for a variety of purposes:

- To extract delicate information from reluctant speakers
- To absorb and retain what's been said
- To reduce tension during a heated debate
- To add drama to their remarks
- To move beyond superficial patter and examine the underlying message
- To express empathy and caring.

The most obvious signal you can give to *show* you want to listen is to keep quiet. Bolster your persuasiveness by letting others talk. They will have plenty to say, and you will learn about them in the process. Even the most shy people will eventually fill silence if you give them the luxury of taking their time. The results are well worth the wait.

Diagnostic Self-Test: Can You Keep Quiet?

Each of us has a different comfort level with silence. Some find it easy to listen quietly, while others cannot stop their mouths from racing ahead. Answer the following questions to check your command of silence:

_____ Do you tend to interrupt speakers more often than they interrupt you?

_____ Do you find yourself frequently wishing that a speaker would hurry up and make a point?

_____ Do you enjoy debating a controversial issue in a room full of vocal, passionate people who keep talking at the same time?

_____ Do you rush to fill silence when there is a lull in a conversation?

_____ Would you rather converse with two or more people at once than with one individual?

_____ When a conversation suddenly stops and you begin to notice pockets of silence, do you usually think that something is wrong?

If you answered "yes" to any of these questions, use this as a starting point to examine your feelings about silence. A "yes" response does not mean there is a problem with your communication skills. While it is perfectly acceptable to enjoy loud debates with a group of opinionated people, you will gain a Zen-like tranquility by appreciating the inherent power in peace and quiet.

MEMORY JOGGER

Listening requires silence. You must purse your lips shut, sit still, and give others ample time to express themselves. Then and only then will you persuade them.

KEEP QUIET AND ENCOURAGE OTHERS TO TRUST YOU AND SHARE THEIR SECRETS

The beauty of silence is that it lets you learn about others. People will open up to you if you give them a chance to talk. The longer you listen responsively, the more you will hear. A speaker who does not want you to know something will have trouble keeping it a secret if you remain silent and attentive. That's one way Mike Wallace gets his interview subjects to squirm in their chairs and confess their sins.

As any top negotiator will tell you, the key to successful deal making is to learn as much as you can about the other party's position without revealing too much about your own. Are they desperate to sell? What motivates them to act now? What are they hoping to gain from the deal? When someone completes a point and expects you to jump in, you can simply nod your head and signal understanding. The speaker then thinks, "This person has nothing to say, so I'd better continue."

Silence ensures that you learn more from others than they learn
from you.

Salespeople need to pay special attention to silence. All too often,
they may crush their persuasiveness by making potential buyers feel bored
and ignored. Imagine how you would feel if a car dealer played the role
of carnival barker and began pitching products, "I get so excited when I
think of all the benefits of these fine vehicles—the safety features, the great
mileage, the flexible payments, the manufacturer's rebate, the amazing war-
ranty, the stylish design, the free add-ons..."

Why can't this salesperson shut up? Someone who cannot handle
silence may simply take a deep breath and charge, firing nonstop fusillades
of words like a gangster in a shootout. By rambling on, salespeople convince themselves they are selling. They assume that the more they can say
without being interrupted, the more likely that they will win you over. They
also figure that by shifting into verbal overdrive, they don't give you a
chance to say "no." A few patient customers may face this onslaught in
good humor and buy anyway. But I bet most of you would turn away from
such an obnoxious babbler.

An insurance agent confessed that "the hardest part for me in the
interview is to try to keep my mouth shut at certain times during the close."
With practice, he learned to unleash the power of silence. "After I've made
my presentation and said everything I can say, I keep quiet. It may be fifteen seconds, it may be thirty—it may seem like the world is coming to an
end. But I learned that whoever talks first loses."[4]

Used properly, silence can help you elicit vital information that
you can use to persuade.

How Silence Makes It Easier to Sell Something

Suppose an insurance agent is pitching his policies, and after an exchange
of pleasantries, the prospect (P) says to the agent (A):

P: I'm looking for a life insurance policy, or maybe an annuity that pays a high interest rate.

[The agent, A, needs to know how much money P has to invest, but A knows P may be uncomfortable if asked to reveal such personal data.]

A: To review what's available, we need to discuss the amounts involved.

[Silence. The agent pauses briefly to set the stage for what follows. This first moment of silence is a respectful warning, as if to say, "I realize money is where our interests may diverge. But my delicacy in raising this shows I'm sensitive to this issue." The groundwork is laid for the next question.]

A: (continuing) How much do you want to invest?

[Silence. P does not answer. A, unfazed, lets the question hang out there as the seconds tick away. The agent, A, maintains supportive, earnest eye contact, implying, "I'm asking because I need to know in order to cut the best deal for you." Yet P does not want to commit to a number; he would prefer to hear a menu of possibilities without taking the idea too seriously now. Unnerved by the silence, P buys some time.]

P: (musing) Well, I guess that depends...

[P's voice trails off—he expects A to jump in with some examples, to warn of the dangers of inaction, to trash the competition, or to press for an immediate sale. Yet A wisely taps the power of silence, thus subverting P's expectation and gently forcing P to continue. P, surprised that A remains quiet, finally speaks.]

P: (continuing) Let's say $100,000.

[Bingo. The agent can proceed to sell a $100,000 package, perhaps persuading P to spend even more. Armed with a figure tossed out by P, A has shifted the field of discussion from whether insurance is a good idea to how much works best. A's skillful use of silence allows P to respond, and A can now propose a plan to fill P's needs rather than drowning P in a wave of wasted words.]

The interesting part is, now P feels he's talking to someone who really understands him. A, after all, lets him mull things over and respond to questions at his own pace. Furthermore, A breaks up his sales presentation with periodic inquiries. P's answers let A tailor the product to fit P's expressed needs. By judiciously keeping quiet, A can more easily grant P the pleasure of buying something rather than being sold something.

What to Do When You Are No Longer Willing to Remain Silent

As you have read throughout this book, persuasion is built around fact gathering. To win over people, you must learn about them first. By unleashing the power of silence, you invite others to admit, share, and confess their innermost thoughts. You allow them to take their time, to speak at whatever pace they want, to repeat themselves or go off on tangents as they wish. Every minute that you are able to keep them talking makes you a stronger persuader, because you gain insight into how they think and feel.

But sometimes we can no longer stand to let others babble away at our expense. Some participants in my seminars wonder how they can remain silent and let others talk when they have something "really important" to say.

"I don't see why I should just sit there while my husband drones on about his beloved Giants," Martha said. "I need to discuss something very serious with him, but I feel as if I have to wait before he's willing to listen to me. That's not right."

Martha agreed to bring her husband, Barry, to my next workshop. It soon became clear to me that Barry, like so many others, loved to hear the sound of his own voice. It would take some reshuffling of his priorities for him to appreciate silence.

"Barry, let's try an experiment," I suggested.

"Sure. I'm game," he replied.

"Good. I hear you're a Giants fan. Is that right?"

Barry's face lit up. "You bet. I just love 'em. Grew up watching the games and collecting the trading cards. I would sneak into the stadium in the late innings to catch the ending. I loved those guys on the team like brothers. I would yell and scream and carry on. Still do, in fact. I'm not what you would call a 'fair-weather fan' or anything. I mean. . ."

Like a runaway train, Barry's mouth just would not stop. I could appreciate Martha's frustration. It was time to cut him off.

"Barry, BARRY," I exclaimed.

"Yeah?"

"I hate to interrupt, but I get the feeling you could discuss the Giants for a while longer."

"Sure, as I say, I love 'em," he announced with feeling.

"Okay. Fair enough. Now let's try a different approach. When I ask a question, you must answer yes or no and that's it. Nothing else. Let's start again. I hear you're a Giants fan. Is that right?"

Barry looked sullen. "Yes," he muttered.

"Do you enjoy talking about the team?"

"Yes."

"As much as you enjoy talking to. . .say. . .Martha about what's on her mind?"

Barry thought about this for a few seconds. "I have to answer yes or no?"

"That's right," I said.

"No."

Martha shook her head in disgust, but I felt we had made a breakthough. Barry soon realized that he was more comfortable talking about his favorite topic rather than letting his wife change the subject.

Barry turned to his wife. "I guess I talk too much about something you're just not interested in, honey. I'm sorry," he added with a sheepish smile.

The couple left the session arm in arm, and Barry promised to keep quiet and be a more attentive listener.

If you identify with Martha's plight, I recommend that you try the same experiment. Play a game in which the other person must answer yes or no. Ask a few *closed questions* (with yes or no answers) and guide the conversation forward. You may find that the respondent experiences a healthy, eye-opening dose of self-awareness when he or she is forced to keep quiet and listen!

Chop Away Verbal Fat and Captivate Others

Most people use at least 30 percent more words than necessary to express ideas. No wonder we rarely find time to enjoy a moment of silence.

Speakers may repeat themselves or toss in extra words that do not enhance their message. When President Lyndon Johnson said, "I do not genuinely believe that there's any single person anywhere in the world that wants peace as much as I do," he hardly won over a skeptical America. As Michael Geis writes in *The Language of Politics*, "It is, I fear, highly probable that a president who says that he is more peace-loving than anyone in the world is getting ready to send troops to fight a war."[5] Johnson could have made the same point with far fewer words by declaring, "I believe in peace."

● **TRAP**   Silence becomes a chore if you like to insert filler words into your speech. Try going one day without using words and phrases that say nothing. Examples:

if you will	*frankly*
to be quite honest	*basically*
for all intents and purposes	*essentially*
genuinely	

Such words add nothing and only call attention to your inability to speak concisely. You will have less time to listen if you are overdosing on words. Master the art of brevity by using the fewest words possible to express yourself and then keep quiet.

Even monosyllabic grunts mar silence and make it harder for your audience to absorb your message. A team of Columbia University researchers found that college professors of art and literature were more apt to fill silence during their lectures than math and chemistry teachers. Speakers in English literature classes had the most trouble with silence, averaging over 6.5 "uhs per minute."[6] A possible reason is that there are many more ways to discuss a wide-open topic such as literature than a precise subject such as biology.

You need to chop away the verbal fat. Sandwich key words (such as someone's name) between glorious pockets of silence so that the most evocative words stand out. Do not, uhhh, fill pauses, ummm, when silence will suffice. As you search for that "right" word, keep quiet!

Silence helps you elicit the juicy stuff.

DEVISING ONE-WORD TAGS TO MAKE LISTENING EASIER

I know, I know…it's hard to close your mouth when you have an overpowering urge to speak. Each second of forced silence feels like torture. You want so badly to propel the conversation forward, to blurt out what you really want to say. If you're like Barry in the preceding example, you would rather talk about sports than listen to your spouse!

Many people tell me they find it especially hard to remain quiet at certain times:

- When they converse with a slow talker who doesn't have much to say
- When they are stuck with a boring, rambling talker

- When they want to steer the conversation in a more interesting or appropriate direction.

In each of these examples, the temptation is to do one of two things: interrupt or escape. If you cut speakers off, you risk alienating them. If you claim that you are "short on time" or "need to use the rest room," you lose an opportunity to listen and learn. Don't assume that listening to a boring speaker is a waste of time. The benefits of silence almost always outweigh your desire to flee.

How do you pay attention to a slow-paced or boring speaker? Use one-word tags to help yourself absorb their ideas.

Say you're stuck listening to a babbler. Instead of tuning out or interrupting, generate a mental list of the speaker's points. Use one-word tags to remind yourself of what the rambler says.

For instance, if an irate caller takes twenty minutes to scold you because the price is too high, you're never in the office, and your secretaries are rude, listen and label while the caller rants and raves. Select such words as *price, office,* and *secretary* to represent the caller's specific complaints. When you finally get a chance to respond, you can address each point with the help of your tag words. You can impress even the most demanding customers when you show that you listen to them.

Let's take another example of how you can "tag" others' remarks. Say you manage your firm's purchasing department. A vendor calls and drones on for ten minutes to tell you your phones do not work properly, your payment is past due, and the new product line is ready for your review. You could interrupt (*Hold on now—the phones were just repaired*). You could hang up (*We've got a bad connection—I'm afraid I'm losing you*). Or you can keep quiet, listen, and label the vendor's points (*phone, payment, product*) to help you identify the specific concerns. When the caller finally takes a breath and lets you respond, you calmly address each point with the help of your simple mental list. Remember that *list* helps spell *listen*.

By attaching labels to what you hear, you let silence work for you. Better yet, you retain what others have said (even if they promptly forget).

MEMORY JOGGER

Create trigger words to remind you of the speaker's remarks and add a new label whenever a fresh point comes along.

Selecting one-word tags works in personal as well as professional situations. Say a friend wants to bounce an idea off you and get your input.

Your friend, unfortunately, has trouble expressing himself clearly and concisely. You struggle to remain silent and listen while he explains his plan to travel the world, take photos, describe what the photos reveal about a culture, and then publish the results as a book. You label the main elements of his idea (*travel, photos, book*) while showing, through your silence, that you want to understand what he's saying. When he finishes speaking, you can summarize his proposal by retrieving your three tag words.

Now let's take a tougher case. Some people talk too much and are boring to boot. You can spot these marathon mouths with little trouble. When you ask a question and the reply consumes a full minute without answering your question, get ready for a long and one-sided exchange. Whenever you hear "to make a long story short…," expect the opposite. When someone asks a question, rephrases it, repeats it, and then begins to answer it (all without stopping to exhale), you are stuck with a Talker.

When you come face-to-face with chatty speakers, you probably give them a fair chance to make their point. But you hit a threshold, maybe after a minute or two, when you lose your patience and refuse to listen any longer.

No matter what I advise, of course, you may elect to tune out when someone fails to keep your interest. That decision might cost you. Consider what happens if a nugget of meaning gets lost because you did not listen long or hard enough.

Salespeople may find themselves missing buying signals when they jump ship after a halfhearted attempt to listen to a babbling prospect. A job recruiter may give up on a candidate who brags too much in the early moments of the interview, thus failing to notice the exceptionally wise remarks that the individual makes later on. A student may deem a teacher a windbag, only to struggle during exams for not heeding the instructor's advice about how to study.

● **TRAP**   Do not let your mind wander while you remain silent. Silence will not help if you present a hollow shell to the outside world where you pretend to listen while you daydream at will. Mentally preparing one-word labels can help activate your mind so that you do not fall into the trap of using silence as a reason not to pay attention.

How can you put up with a boring speaker and keep the yawns to a minimum? Listen and label. Use one-word tags to represent a talker's key ideas so that you generate a running list of substantive points. Even the most soporific speaker may surprise you and make a valid observation or express an intriguing opinion. You can capture these comments by mentally choosing a word that will help you remember what was said.

Many boring speakers know that they ramble. Experience has taught them not to expect others to listen when they hold forth. As a result, they may overcompensate by talking faster, repeating themselves, or hopping from topic to topic to cover everything in rapid-fire fashion. Aware of their inability to get others to listen to them, they view conversation as a *Beat the Clock* game. They rush to have their say before they are cut off.

Five Benefits of Using One-Word Tags to Stay Silent and Listen

Using one-word labels offers many advantages that strengthen your communication skills:

1. Confidence   You will no longer have to worry about forgetting what someone says. You can stay silent for as long as you wish, all the while generating your mental list of one-word labels. This frees you from wondering how you are going to remember so many points.

2. Winning A Debate   If you find yourself in an extended discussion or debate, you need to keep quiet to ensure that you understand the opposing points. One-word labels help you isolate each claim made by the speaker. When the time comes for your response, you can address only those points for which you have the best comebacks. Few speakers will recall each and every claim they made, so you can win them over without having to confront their strongest arguments.

3. Showing that You Listen   Recall from Chapter 8 the importance of showing others how well you listen. Some chatterboxes talk so much that they routinely forget almost everything they say. You can score points by reminding them. This sends a message of attentiveness and helps you earn a speaker's trust. Persuading irate callers, frustrated customers, or hysterical friends that you understand their feelings and want to help works best when you are equipped to respond to the main points they make.

4. Conquering Your "Listening Prerequisites"   If you are like most people, you carry around a mental list of prerequisites that determine whether you listen. Such prerequisites may include the physical attractiveness of the speaker, the tone and pitch of the speaker's voice, the topic, and your history of interacting with the speaker. Mastering silence and creating one-word tags help you listen under substandard conditions when your prerequisites are not met.

A participant in one of my workshops identified his personal "requirements" as follows:

1. The speaker must be concise and state a point quickly.

2. The speaker must look me in the eye or speak clearly on the phone. I'm not willing to guess what somebody's trying to tell me.

3. If someone brings up something that makes me mad, I just cut 'em off or don't bother to listen. So they better talk about something I want to talk about.

Many conversations, of course, will not meet all our prerequisites. This helps explain why listening can be so difficult. By adapting to circumstances that do not fit your preferred mode of communication, you can expand your range of persuasive opportunities and develop an affinity for silence. Boring speakers help us become better, stronger, more flexible listeners. As they say in the weight room, "No pain, no gain."

5. Closure   A final reason to listen and label is that *all* speakers, from nonstop motor mouths to soft-spoken whisperers, crave closure. Closure is the act of closing or completing something. When you begin to share an anecdote with friends, you warm up to your topic and enjoy relating the story. Think how frustrated you feel when someone interrupts you midway through your comments, tugging the conversation in another direction. Heads turn away from you, and suddenly you are forgotten. You have been blocked from attaining closure.

When we let speakers complete their thoughts, we lay the groundwork for persuading them. Most talkative people know that they tend to overdo it, and they are accustomed to being interrupted. By patiently allowing them to talk and furnishing them with precious silence, you stand out. They appreciate you. This appreciation translates to success when you set out to win them over.

How do you display the patience of a saint and let blabbing speakers reach closure? In addition to devising one-word labels, try these techniques:

- Pretend they are telling a good, long joke. You would not interrupt a joke before hearing the punch line.

- Listen for details that reveal how they think and feel. Such details make listening interesting as you gather insight into the speaker. Imagine you are a detective, say, Lt. Columbo.

- Resist the urge to prod the speaker along with monosyllabic grunts. Just as such sounds can help draw out a reticent speaker, as we discussed in Chapter 8, they will encourage a talker to drone on.

All too often, listeners trapped in a boring conversation will inject *aha, umm,* or *hmm,* as if such sounds will encourage the speaker to stop talking. Instead, they invite the speaker to continue. Silence signals neutrality.

It takes a leap of faith (and an extra few minutes) to let others direct a conversation. This is particularly hard if you are the type of person who dreads waiting at red lights, curses traffic jams, and detests long lines at the supermarket. You may not enjoy the long wait as others steer a conversation in circles, but your patience in the form of silence shows that you want to understand the speaker.

THE STOP RULE: MAKING SILENCE WORK FOR YOU WHEN YOU WANT AN ANSWER TO YOUR QUESTION

In an ideal world, we would ask questions and promptly receive satisfying answers all the time. We would never have to wait around for a response or grow restless while others evade our queries. We would never have to repeat ourselves or rephrase the question. We would never have to worry about staying silent, because our conversations would flow smoothly without choppy pauses or abrupt breaks.

So much for ideals. Reality intrudes. When we ask questions, we rarely hear full, accurate answers. Think about the last time you posed a question and were greeted with silence. What did you do?

If you were trying to persuade someone, you probably were impatient for a response. If you did not receive a quick answer, you may have answered your own question, asked another question, rephrased or repeated the same question, or simply ignored the question and filled the silence with whatever else was on your mind, perhaps moving on to another topic. I bet you did not let your question hang there and calmly await a response.

Here is a tip that works whenever you ask someone a question: Stop talking. Wait for an answer. Do not feel obliged to fill the silence if you do not hear a quick response.

I call this The Stop Rule: STOP after you ask a question.

Respondents may prefer to take their time, digest a question, and plan an answer before uttering a sound. Remember that some people communicate more deliberately. They choose their words with care and hold themselves to high standards of precise expression. They may want to review the facts in their head first or mentally rehearse what they want to say. The Stop Rule ensures that you furnish the respondent with ample time to come up with an answer.

MEMORY JOGGER

Maintaining silence after asking a question shows that you really
want to hear the answer.

If you talk too soon after asking a question, you send the implicit
message that you did not care that much about the respondent's answer.
The Stop Rule lets others know that you actually *want* to learn from them
and that you will let them respond at their own pace.

Say a lifeguard, Bruce, must discipline a teenage swimmer, Ronnie,
for horseplay around the pool.

Bruce asks, "Why are you running around?"

Ronnie looks at him with a guilty expression on his face. He hopes
that Bruce will continue talking, perhaps lecturing him about poolside rules
and then leaving him alone. But Bruce keeps quiet. Ronnie, growing
uncomfortable, feels as if he better say *something.*

"I don't know...I wasn't really running, just playing," Ronnie mutters.

Bruce remains silent. Rather than scold Ronnie, he keeps staring at the
kid. Bruce wants a better answer. Ronnie, feeling more uneasy with each
passing second, finally admits, "Okay, so I was running a little. I took something from my sister and didn't want her to notice. What's the big deal?"

By allowing Ronnie to talk, Bruce gathers more information and puts
Ronnie on the spot. Bruce is now in a better position to warn Ronnie about
violating pool rules.

Effective job interviewers also play by The Stop Rule. They ask a candidate a question and then stop talking. This works especially well with
delicate questions such as:

How much money were you making at your last job?

What is your minimum salary requirement?

Can you elaborate on why you left your last job?

What did you do between 1992 and 1993?

The best interviewers have a high tolerance for silence. They do not
fidget, doodle, or look out the window after they pose a question. Instead,
they sit back, observe the candidate, and wait for an answer.

Same goes for investigative journalists. As Mike Wallace explains,
"The single most interesting thing that you can do in television, I find, is to
ask a good question and then let the answer hang there for two or three
or four seconds as though you're expecting more. You know what? They
get a little embarrassed and give you more."[7]

○ **NOW TRY THIS**   The next time you are on the receiving end of a nasty or insulting question, repeat the question using The Stop Rule. Do not lash out, or you might fan the flames. Instead, let silence work for you. If you are asked an angry question such as, "Why do you insist on always contradicting me?" simply repeat the question in your normal voice tone (free of hostility or rage) with the pronouns reversed, "Why do I insist on always contradicting you?" Then stop. This places the burden on the speaker to communicate in a more fair and less accusatory manner. It also ensures that you do not get stuck answering emotionally loaded questions.

Same goes for heated statements—repeat them as questions. If an associate tells you, "I don't need to listen to this," say, "You don't need to listen to this?" and then stop. If your son tells you, "I won't take out the garbage," say, "You won't take out the garbage?" Force speakers to confront the consequences of their remarks by tossing their comments right back on their lap.

Try The Stop Rule for a few days and evaluate the results. You will soon discover how much more people trust you and appreciate your attentiveness. They will open up to you, and they will be more apt to follow your advice and agree with you.

Questions sound best when sandwiched between two slices of silence. When you ask for something, provide enough silence to show that you want and expect an answer. Maintain a pleasant facial expression or lean toward the respondent slightly as if to say, "I'm eager to hear what you have to say, and I don't want to miss a word of it." If you are on the phone, ask questions in a voice turned up a few decibels so that the question stands out from the rest of your remarks.

MEMORY JOGGER

Among the mistakes that poor persuaders make, perhaps the easiest to correct is simply to shut up and let people talk.

Silence works wonders in the persuasive process. Sure, it can be boring and downright uncomfortable for two people to stare at each other without making a sound. But in an increasingly noisy and argumentative world, silence exerts even greater power.

For example, *The Los Angeles Times* reported that the Santa Monica City Council decided to take a "retreat" to "learn how to listen." As one councilman told the *Times,* "Maybe if we learned to listen more carefully to each other, we could get through a calendar item in fifteen minutes instead of spending an hour debating things that often don't need debate. We could get through work faster." Another councilman added, "On some issues, like development, after two hours of rhetoric, we sometimes realize we really weren't that far apart."[8]

Whether you are part of a divisive group trying to reach consensus or engaged in a one-on-one dialogue with a loved one, silence helps you influence others. Practice the techniques in this chapter so that you can learn to love the glorious sound of silence.

● **TRAP** As you remain silent, you need an outlet for your nervous energy. So you scratch yourself, crumple paper, click your pen, or engage in some other distracting activity. Silence works best when you maintain eye contact along with a supportive, nonthreatening facial expression. Showing impatience by tapping your fingers or constantly fidgeting can make the respondent feel rushed or pressured. If you are uncomfortable handling silence and you want to unleash energy, wiggle your toes while you wait for an answer. No one will ever know.

AVOIDING INTERRUPTIONS, WITH SILENCE AS YOUR CONVERSATIONAL ALLY

While silence is often perceived as an unpleasant conversation stopper, it actually serves as a wonderfully empowering way to persuade. You must learn to love silence, to treat it as an ally whenever you communicate.

To embrace silence, you must avoid interrupting. You may think that you never interrupt, but others may beg to differ. Think of the last few times that a close friend confessed something or shared intimate news with you. Did he or she start by warning you not to interrupt? A father of five told me, "You know, every time I ask one of my kids how they're doing, they say, 'Let me finish and I'll tell you.' I figured out that I was not very good at listening to them."

The odds of interruption soar during an argument. Voices overlap as both parties want to drown out their adversary. Listening becomes the last thing on either person's mind. As Catherine the Great told Denis Diderot in the eighteenth century, "You have a hot head, and I have one too. We interrupt each other, we do not hear what the other one says, and so we say stupid things."[9]

Looking for a sure-fire way to win an argument? Sit still and shut up. Okay, I'll put it more gently: Maintain silence while the speaker blows off steam. Never cap someone's fury prematurely.

● **TRAP** When standing face to face with a screamer, you make every effort to calm her down. You interrupt her to say, "I understand" or "Enough already." Guess what? That only makes it worse. Arguments are inflamed when both parties insist on talking at once. Some hot-headed types need to vent their rage before they can be persuaded of anything. What they say doesn't matter (indeed, when you listen to a tirade, you realize just how irrational people can be). Don't fall into the trap of trying to shut down a furious speaker. Rely on silence.

There is a moment that occurs early in a confrontation or argument when you must make a choice to act as sender or receiver. The sender keeps talking, defending, and yelling. Never lock yourself into that role. As a sender, you will feel obliged to keep up a constant war of verbal aggression. As your temper flares you will let slip comments that you will later regret.

Have you ever realized too late that your remarks were better left unsaid? The only way to prevent that from happening is to view yourself as a receiver who maintains control through silence. Just hearing the other person out dissipates much of the negative emotional energy that would otherwise get you in trouble.

There's another reason to love silence: It is therapeutic. If you keep interrupting, shouting, or defending yourself, you engage in a futile exercise. You probably know what it feels like to argue with someone who refuses your request because of "company policy" or because they are "not allowed to give out that information." Your entreaties don't help, and the conversation goes nowhere. Meanwhile, your blood pressure skyrockets.

Silence serves as a healthy coping mechanism. It can help you relax regardless of what conflicts swirl around you. Rather than unleash a tidal wave of emotions, you can savor the peace and quiet. A social worker who mediates lots of screaming matches said, "Whenever I'm with a family at each other's throats, I purse my lips shut and don't say a word. I can tell that they are trying to get me to react, but I don't. Soon, they give up and quiet down. And I feel just great, because I don't let all their craziness get to me."

○ **NOW TRY THIS** Introducing The Three-Beat Rule. This rule states that you should silently count to three before responding to a speaker.

First, wait for the person to stop talking. Now mentally count to three (if you prefer a physical rather than a mental reminder, slowly tap your toes three times). Then and only then should you open your mouth. Providing these extra three seconds gives the speaker one last chance to continue talking. This is when you learn what is truly on someone's mind. As an added bonus, giving yourself these extra few seconds buys time so that you can think before you talk. You can also make sure the listener is ready to listen to you.

The Three-Beat Rule works particularly well when a conversation reaches a momentary lull. The last thing you want is to start talking again just when someone else decides to do the same. Both parties may open their mouths simultaneously. (In intimate conversations, of course, this is harmless and often funny, but if you want to persuade someone, you need to establish a speak-listen rhythm rather than talk over each other.)

Finally, as you put silence to work for you, you will sharpen your powers of observation. You give your senses a chance to work at full capacity. You will notice how people dress and you will learn to "read" their nonverbal language. You will detect when their breathing becomes shallow and when their nervous tics set in. Ambient sounds, such as the clock ticking or the radiator humming, contribute to the scene. As you capture each moment more fully, you harness all your listening skills to maximize your persuasive power.

QUICK REVIEW

- Keep quiet if you want to encourage others to reveal themselves to you.
- Don't feel obliged to fill silence with wasted words or monosyllabic grunts.
- Use silence to let others speak at whatever pace makes them comfortable.
- Never miss a chance to listen and learn because you decide to interrupt or flee.
- Use one-word tags to help you pay attention to a slow-paced or boring speaker.
- Resist the urge to tune out when you are dealing with a motor mouth.
- When your "listening prerequisites" are unmet, use one-word labels to retain what's said.
- Allow speakers to attain closure to their remarks. Don't cut them off.

- Follow The Stop Rule: STOP after you ask a question, and await an answer.
- Let people blow off steam. Never cap a speaker's fury prematurely.
- Follow The Three-Beat Rule: Silently count to three before responding to a speaker.

NOTES

1. Mike Wallace and Gary Paul Gates, *Close Encounters,* William Morrow & Company, New York, 1984, p. 358.
2. *Business Week,* 4-11-94, p. 36.
3. *The New York Times*, 5-30-93, Section 4, p. 1.
4. *Life & Health Insurance Sales*, May 1992, p. 7.
5. Michael Geis, *The Language of Politics,* Springer-Verlag, New York, 1987, p. 45.
6. *The Sacramento Bee,* 4-19-91, p. A17.
7. John Brady, *The Craft of Interviewing,* Vintage Books, New York, 1976, p. 83.
8. *The Los Angeles Times,* 1-3-88, p. 2.
9. P. N. Furbank, *Diderot: A Critical Biography,* Knopf, New York, 1992, p. 379.

Distortions
How to Avoid Listening for the Wrong Messages and Crushing Your Persuasiveness

Ever play "Telephone"? In this popular summer-camp game, a message is whispered from player to player until it reaches the last person. Inevitably, the message gets twisted to the point where it loses all traces of its original meaning.

Same thing happens in real life. From idle gossip to talking "on the record" with journalists, conversations are rarely reported faithfully as they travel from person to person. Instead, each individual who relays the comment changes a few words or adds a new idea. This does not mean that people intentionally distort what they hear and pass along incorrect information to others. As much as we may try to summarize what we hear Norm say and express it accurately to Joe a few minutes or hours later, we are unable to function like tape recorders. We cannot reproduce Norm's exact message at will.

Even if we do not need to report a conversation to someone else at a later time, we still might distort what a speaker tells us. At any moment, whether at home or at work, our listening skills can fail us. We can end a conversation *thinking* we know what was said, but actually capturing the wrong message. We then draw conclusions and make recommendations based on faulty data.

Winning people over is hard enough without subverting what they're trying to say. I know a conspiracy theorist who thrives on twisting around what he hears to fit his preconceived notions. No matter what topic you discuss with him, from American aid to a developing country to national health care, he suspects a conspiracy. Rather than taking at face value what others say, he says he tries "to find a conspiracy in everything." He distorts what he hears to match his view of the world.

Even if we resist the urge to mangle others' remarks to fit our own beliefs, we remain susceptible to distortions when we want to talk about ourselves. If we want to brag about an accomplishment, for example, we await a conversational opening to announce the big news. We may feel it is bad form to simply blurt out *I got a raise today* or *The committee accepted my proposal.* We wish that the other person would ask us about our day, but that does not happen. So we listen half-heartedly until we hear something that in some way relates to what we want to say. If a friend discusses *her* job, we jump in about *our* promotion.

MEMORY JOGGER

When you can barely contain your excitement about something and you cannot wait to talk about it, then you are prone to distort what others say until you get your chance to speak.

THREE EXAMPLES OF HOW DISTORTIONS BLOCK CLEAR COMMUNICATION

Poor listening habits result in misunderstandings and lost opportunities to win people over. Distortions threaten to disrupt almost every interaction, as illustrated in these examples:

- Tammy has dated Gary for two years. Eager to get married, she frequently tells Gary about her friends who have married and how happy they are ("They both said that if they knew marriage was this great, they would've done it a year ago rather than waited"). It's her way of hinting to Gary about their wonderful future together. Gary, on the other hand, dismisses Tammy's repeated comments about marriage as part of what he thinks is her tendency to romanticize the lives of others and inflate their happiness ("You always want what you don't have"). As a result, Tammy keeps bringing up marriage, and Gary keeps ignoring her.

- Tom, a vice-president at a property-management firm, works for Stan, the president of the company. Stan tells Tom to try to double the number of clients who use the firm's services. Tom, who is closer to the day-to-day operations of the organization, knows that the thin support staff is already overworked and cannot process a wave of new business. So he tries to tell his boss, albeit indirectly, that in order for the company to properly service new clients, they must first hire more staff. "I'll work with personnel to beef up our back office to get ready for the expansion of business," Tom says. Stan shoots back, "No, don't worry about hiring more people now. Do as I said and bring me more paying customers." Stan hears Tom's comment and thinks his vice-president is noncompliant. Stan does not realize that Tom intends to generate more clients as soon as he feels internal staffing needs are met.

- Denise seeks her father's approval, but she rarely gets it. After graduating from high school with honors and giving the valedictory speech, she approaches her father after the ceremony. He says, "What a special day." She replies, "Oh, Daddy, I'm so happy I could make your day special." Denise hears her father say, "You made this day special for me," but her father was making a general comment about the event.

These examples expose some of the underlying dangers of distortion. First, it becomes harder to persuade others when we falsely interpret their remarks to make ourselves feel better. Denise craves recognition from her father, so she considers his statement "What a special day" as praise for her achievements. Stan, who is used to barking out orders and having his underlings follow them, hears Tom's response as different from what he wanted to hear ("Sure, boss, I'll get right on it."). When we are overeager to hear what we want to hear, conditions are ripe for distortions to take hold.

It also becomes apparent from the preceding examples that indirect communication may lead to trouble. Tammy wants to get married, but she resists having a heart-to-heart talk with Gary about her feelings. Instead, she resorts to hinting (which he perceives not as hinting but as part of her pattern of romanticizing others). Tom feels that his boss has overlooked the need to hire more staff. Instead of expressing his opinion, however, he angers the president by not playing the "yes man" role.

Finally, Gary, Stan, and Denise remind us that we tend to listen based on our own frame of reference, not the speaker's. Distortions often result when we assume that we know why a speaker says something. We read between the lines of a conversation and conclude that we know the "real reason" that led the speaker to speak. The most astute persuaders know how to listen (free from distortions) by stepping into the speaker's world and adopting the speaker's frame of reference.

PREVENTING DISTORTIONS BY LISTENING
FOR THE TRUE MESSAGE

So what can we do to steer clear of distortions when we listen?

If we seek to persuade with consistency, we need to accurately listen and retain what's said. A message gets distorted because we do not soak up what we hear in an unbiased, nonjudgmental frame of mind. Our fears, anxieties, and prejudices get in the way. Or we want to hear something so badly that we overlay our own preferred version of what was said on the actual words coming out of the speaker's mouth!

Most of us realize we have something to lose when we listen. Our ego and self-esteem are on the line. We might be criticized, ignored, or insulted. Some people find that the more they fish for compliments, the less they find. The more they crave approval, the more they are greeted with disapproval. No wonder we misinterpret what we hear: We are trying to preserve our fragile sense of self.

MEMORY JOGGER

The more you want a speaker to say something specific (from *I love you* to *Yes, I'll buy from you*), the more likely you will listen with rigidity. Keep an open mind and be prepared to accept whatever someone tells you, even if it's not exactly what you want to hear.

To combat distortions, you must take preventive steps to ensure that you listen for the true message. This means learning to absorb all types of comments, even the ones that do not immediately captivate you. A friend of mine loves to discuss baseball. No matter what you say, he'll relate it to base hits, home runs, and pitch-outs. As he readily admits, he has trouble listening to what people actually tell him *on their terms* because he's so busy trying to connect it to his favorite topic. He bores easily when the topic strays far from baseball.

MEMORY JOGGER

When we insist on adding our own "spin" to everything we hear, we lose the capacity to fairly comprehend what others say.

We also need to identify the times when distortions arise. For example, many people find it tough to listen in a large group or during an early morning meeting. We have already noted how hard it is to hear what you do not want to hear. By knowing what situations pose the greatest difficulty, you can bring the full force of your communication skills to work for you when you need them most.

As you gain awareness of how distortions interfere with your listening, you can develop strategies to overcome them. Distortions usually occur when we let our guard down and fail to concentrate. If you do not give a speaker your undivided attention, then your chances of persuading that person plummet.

We may find ourselves trying to listen and persuade despite suffering from mood swings, nagging preoccupations, or lingering worries. If you are too distracted to listen well, then you should either postpone the conversation to another time or muster enough discipline to shove aside your distractions for the greater good of engaging in pure communication.

Whatever you do, don't lapse into sloppy habits out of laziness. Take charge of your conversations. If you are unwilling or unable to listen free from distortions, then do something to correct the problem. That's what this chapter is all about.

We will examine the three most common distortions—*exaggeration, leveling,* and *erasing*—and then present solutions that allow us to listen accurately and receptively all the time.

EXAGGERATION:
BLOWING UP A MESSAGE AND MISSING THE POINT

Exaggeration falsely inflates the importance of a message by intensifying it. This usually happens when a comment strikes a chord and we dwell on it or enlarge its meaning. The result? We focus on something the speaker said even as the speaker proceeds to cover other points. Examples:

- A friend mentions a summer cabin that he has already paid for but cannot use. You home in on that cabin ("How can I get the keys?") while your friend continues to discuss other vacation plans.

- A colleague who suggests a product innovation wants your "buy in" when telling you about the plan. You respond, "Sounds good." Your colleague, suffering from a severe case of exaggeration, hears instead, "What an excellent idea. I'll help you sell it to upper management."

- A teacher opens the class by promising to "return your exams today."
  You are so eager to see your score that you cannot concentrate on
  anything else the instructor says. So when the teacher adds, "I've
  decided not to count your exams toward your final grade," you miss
  this crucial piece of information!

When someone gives us a compliment, we may exaggerate it and
downplay everything else. A young woman told me, "When asking me out
on a date, this guy said I looked like a beautiful model. I was so thrilled
that I kept repeating what he said to myself because it made me feel so
great. Of course, I accepted his invitation." It turns out that he also asked
her to wear a costume because he planned to take her to a Halloween
party. She missed that part, and when he picked her up she was stuck without a costume.

Aside from compliments, we invite personal trauma when we react to
our own exaggerated sense of what we hear. When a supervisor discovers
a work-related error and says to you, "You know, I couldn't help but notice
that these files were misplaced," you might recoil in horror and think,
"There I go messing up again" or "Now they must think I'm dumb."
Meanwhile, you didn't bother to listen when your supervisor added, "No
big deal. I'm just thankful you make so few mistakes."

If you insist on mentally scolding yourself for screwing up, then do it
on your own time—not while someone is continuing to speak to you. The
speaker might say something critical about you, only to brush it off
moments later or even dish out a compliment. But if you exaggerate the
negative comment, you will not listen for what follows. Our internal gloom-
and-doom messages (*How can I be so stupid?, I'm so careless; I'm not smart
enough; I can't do anything right*) can immobilize us.

A married couple shared with me how they got in a verbal brawl by
distorting what each other said. The husband couched a problem (his
wife's long hours at her job) in exaggerated terms. "I lost my temper and
told her that her work was a waste of time, that she was throwing her life
away at that corporation," he recalled, wincing at the memory. "I could tell
how harsh that sounded, so I immediately brought up how much talent she
had and how I felt she could maximize all her skills in another line of work
that did not demand so much time."

His wife added, "The minute you said my 'work was a waste of time,'
I didn't hear another word. Whatever you said after that, I wasn't listening.
Those words really hit me hard. I took what you said as the ultimate insult,
when you consider how hard I've worked over so many years to get where
I am today."

Whether someone insults us or compliments us, we may magnify the meaning of what's said and shut off our mind to everything else.

If we're not careful, we may exaggerate a message based on hearing just one word that tees us off. When someone calls us *selfish*, for example, we may replay that word in our head and tune out the rest. Our rational side realizes that we are not always selfish, that we are being unfairly labeled, but we still have trouble listening because of the hurt or anger caused by the speaker's negative characterization.

If we assign blame while we listen, we increase the odds of exaggeration. Our minds resort to accusations or fault finding instead of remaining open and dispassionate. Distortion serves as a handy, albeit dangerous, coping mechanism. It allows us to blur what we hear in order to support our interpretation of who deserves blame.

How to Prevent Exaggeration

To prevent exaggeration from distorting messages, compartmentalize what you hear. Mentally file a speaker's remarks under certain categories. In the preceding example involving the bickering couple, the wife could have visualized a folder labeled "job criticism" and filed her husband's angry comments away. This would enable her to continue listening and engage in further conversation. Although she still might take offense at what her husband said, at least she would hear the subsequent positive statements as well.

Whenever you find yourself tempted to dwell on a word or phrase that stings, think in terms of Teach Me, Teach Me (discussed in Chapter 7). Try to learn from what someone says even when it hurts. Ride a conversation through its ups and downs to its conclusion. The temptation to exaggerate may die down if you replace the impulse to *interpret* what people say with a determination to *understand* them.

You choose whether to inflate the significance of a particular comment. If you do, then you risk losing the entire message. You must understand the full meaning of what people try to tell you before you seek to persuade them.

Another way to guard against exaggeration is to acknowledge that there is a problem or a point of disagreement and then tell yourself that you need to solve it. This will encourage you to keep listening so that you absorb the full, accurate message. Your goal, to identify a problem and then devise a solution, will allow you to keep quiet and listen attentively. You will have little mental energy left over to dwell on how hurt or upset you feel by something the speaker said.

A middle-aged participant in my workshop told the group about a time when his marriage was on the rocks. He vividly remembered the first time his wife used the word *divorce* when discussing their future. "We were talking about our careers and how that might affect having a child, when she said that a divorce down the line would change everything," he said. "She kept talking for awhile, but I couldn't believe she had brought up divorce. So I immediately told myself 'We've got a problem, let's solve it.' And so I listened some more and finally got to the bottom of things. I'm thankful that I was able to let her continue, because she gradually opened up about what troubled her in the marriage."

Have faith in yourself to solve problems rather than allowing them to fester. This way, you can listen patiently and resist the urge to intensify a particular comment so that it crowds out everything else.

LEVELING:
THE OPPOSITE OF EXAGGERATION

Leveling means we deemphasize what someone says until nothing stands out. The entire message is leveled off so that it arrives in the listener's mind without any highlighted points. Rather than exaggerate what someone tells us, we flatten the entire message to the point where it has no meaning.

We may comprehend others' comments, but we do not prioritize their importance. For a leveler, *This house is on fire* and *It's a nice day* are interchangeable. By not attributing more importance to what is clearly an important statement, we distort what is said. Examples:

- Your birthday approaches, and you express enthusiasm for a new computer. "That new model looks fantastic," you tell your spouse. Hint, hint. Your mate, who cannot afford to buy you a computer, hears your comment as, "This computer is alright, I guess. I can take it or leave it."

- A friend raves about a Vietnam War film. You don't like war movies, so even though he's effusive in his praise you hear him say, "It was so-so."

- A colleague speaks highly of a training seminar, but you don't like training programs so you hear her say, "The class was okay."

The Twin Causes of Leveling: Boredom and Biases

Leveling usually results from either our boredom or our biases. If we are uninterested in a speaker's opinion or experiences, we will discount what we hear. This makes it easy to downplay a speaker's enthusiasm.

MEMORY JOGGER

Apathy invites distortions. If you don't care what is said, you will have less incentive to listen for the true message.

Listening requires intense concentration. If you lack the motivation to pay attention, then you will surely distort what you hear. The prevailing attitude of some levelers is, *It's all the same to me* or *I don't care.*

Our biases can prove even more troublesome when we try to listen. If we make snap judgments and jump to conclusions, we might deny a speaker's insights if they do not match how we see things. If we are inclined not to trust the government, for instance, we may not attribute much importance to a political candidate's stump speeches. As candidates blaze the campaign trail, making promises and stating positions along the way, we may dismiss their comments with a wave of the hand. Our skepticism prevents us from listening to their views and attempting to understand what they intend to accomplish. Levelers often think, *I don't need to listen to someone who has nothing to say*; they decide not to listen without giving the speaker a chance.

The Best Way to Avoid Leveling Is to Prioritize What You Hear

You can avoid leveling by prioritizing what you hear. The best persuaders can rank, in order of significance, how we feel about our jobs, our relationships, our families, our hobbies, and so on. They appeal to us by offering ways for us to achieve what we want. They seem to know what we value most in life. They persuade us by helping us fulfill our top priorities.

When you listen, try to identify the speaker's priorities. How? Look for cues that indicate how he or she feels about a particular subject. You can tell speakers care about what they say when they:

- Lean forward or move closer to you while making a point
- Raise their eyebrows
- Smile or otherwise loosen their facial muscles
- Gesture emphatically
- Remove their eyeglasses
- Give you uninterrupted eye contact
- Suddenly start talking louder and/or faster
- Emphasize or repeat certain words
- Reach out to touch you as they make a key point
- Prevent you from changing the topic

When you notice speakers exhibit any of these signs of interest in what they say, pay rapt attention. Assign degrees of importance to their comments. This takes time. You will not learn someone's priorities after a five-minute chat, but with careful listening over time you can develop an understanding of what they hold dear.

A salesperson told me that, after a series of discussions with a new client, he concluded that his client's priorities were as follows:

1. Family
2. Job
3. Golf

"He kept telling me that his family comes first, that he was always looking for ways to put his career in perspective and not get too caught up in office politics," the salesperson said. "He was also a golf fanatic who never missed a tee time. I mean, this guy would write golf into his schedule every few days and insist that nothing interfere." Armed with this information, the salesperson listened to what his client said without leveling.

MEMORY JOGGER

It is hard to deemphasize what people say when you know how they prioritize their lives.

A young doctor complained to me of never having enough time to spend with his patients in a fast-paced managed-care environment. "What winds up happening is that I'm so rushed I don't have time to respond to the patients' concerns," he confessed. "I'm so busy asking questions and gathering information that I seem to ignore what's on their mind." After getting the answers he needed to make a quick diagnosis, he leveled off everything else that his patients told him.

I suggested that he prioritize the concerns of each patient. In order to do this, he had to look up from his notes and observe how they behaved in the examining room. Did they dwell on one worry? Did they seem ill at ease when answering certain questions (such as drug use or sexual habits)? Did they seem more interested in getting better or getting back to work? By observing his patients, the doctor was able to identify the one or two most pressing issues on their mind. Although this took a bit more time, he felt he could help patients stay healthier by understanding them better as individuals.

Another form of leveling occurs when you discount a compliment. In an effort to appear modest, you might disagree with praise that is directed your way. Examples:

- A colleague at work greets you in the morning by saying, *You got a haircut! Hey, it looks great.* You reply, *Huh. Yeah. It's okay.*

- A friend gazes out the window at the panoramic view from your new apartment and declares the place *totally fantastic.* You reply evenly, *It's a place to live.*

- A stranger notices your shoes in the elevator and says, *Hey, those look great on you.* You respond, *I don't like them.*

When someone compliments you, acknowledge the remark appreciatively before you beg to differ. Do not instantly shrug it off.

MEMORY JOGGER

Modesty is attractive, but contradicting someone who sincerely praises you is not.

ERASING:
WHEN YOU INDULGE IN PAIN AVOIDANCE AT THE SPEAKER'S EXPENSE

If a message is threatening or harshly negative, we may block it out by erasing—or not acknowledging—what was said. Some people think that verbal threats exist only in spy movies, where extortionists possess incriminating photos of corrupt public figures engaged in sordid affairs. But in truth, threats creep into everyday conversation far more than we may realize. Distorting these nasty messages helps to soften the blow.

Phrases that begin on a threatening note may lead us to erase whatever the speaker says next. Examples:

I'd hate to...

You don't want me to...

You're forcing me to...

You better do this or else...

You're gonna be sorry if you...

When hearing these ominous openers, who wants to continue listening? It is easier just to shut out the message because we do not want to be bullied into anything.

Same goes for phrases that trigger immediate resistance. If you are the kind of person who questions authority and a speaker begins a sentence with, *You have to cooperate...* or *It is our policy to...,* you might erase whatever follows. You distort the rest of the message because you are too busy thinking, *No, I don't have to do anything!* or *I don't care about your policy!*

Other examples of phrases that may lead us to erase what we hear:

You cannot...

That's against the rules...

It's required that you...

We must insist that you...

Children learn to erase with pain avoidance. They shut their eyes at an unpleasant sight or cover their ears in a sign of defiance. This sends the message, *If I don't listen, I don't have to deal with it.* Adults are usually not as demonstrative as kids, but they also seek pain avoidance with fake smiles, canned nods, and glazed looks of feigned interest.

At least faking it is better than interruption. The moment you jump in, you harm your cause by showing impatience, disinterest, and arrogance. Speakers, their voices silenced to make room for your unwelcome interruption, feel violated and neglected. If you interrupt frequently, you will find that speakers withdraw from you and show little enthusiasm when talking with you. Rather than engage you in conversation, they will move to the other side of the room or simply keep quiet and avoid eye contact.

Memory Jogger

The ultimate form of erasing is simply refusing to listen by terminating the conversation.

When you interrupt, you create an adversarial climate where distortions run rampant. Honest communication turns into defensive maneuvering. Tempers flare. The parties talk without thinking, only to regret their remarks a moment too late. You crush any opportunity for establishing mutual trust

This does not mean that interruption is always bad. Ted Koppel, host of *Nightline,* routinely cuts off his guests and persuades them to address the topic at hand. He explains:

> I think it [interrupting effectively] has to do…with what I think is the key to interviewing: listening precisely to what your interviewee is saying. If you do, you come to a set of extraordinary conclusions. One, you realize when they're being repetitive. Two, you realize when they're dodging the questions. Three, you eventually realize when they've said what they basically need to say. Since people rarely have the capacity of deciding that for themselves, at least in the context of a live television interview program, I have to do that for them. In each of those instances, that constitutes interrupting, but it's not as if I'm sitting there waiting to interrupt them.[1]

Most people equate interruption with talking over someone else. Generations of parents have scolded their youngsters for failing to "sit still and wait your turn to talk." But there are other, equally distracting forms of interruption such as gesturing in an inappropriate manner while someone speaks. Erasing, of course, represents a terrible kind of interruption because you block from your mind whatever the speaker has to say.

Physical interruptions, such as standing up to leave in the middle of a conversation or abruptly hanging up the phone, are just as bad. This harsh type of erasing often occurs in a busy workplace where "controlled chaos" rules. I know a chef at a fancy restaurant who tells me it is normal for the owner to simply walk away in the middle of a sentence if something else requires attention. "You are lucky to have ten seconds with him at any time," she says. "Normal rules of civility don't apply in the craziness of the kitchen as dinner time approaches."

Mental Interruptions: Erasing What Someone Says Because You're Thinking of What to Say Next

Let's not forget mental interruptions. They occur when you think about what you want to say next or when you allow distortions to infiltrate the conversation. Just as erasing screens out an unpleasant message, exaggeration presents problems because it is hard to listen when you remain fixed on something the speaker said five minutes ago. Like some invisible toxic gas that has no odor and no warning signs, mental interruptions can be silent but deadly.

While I was discussing the dangers of mental interruption in one of my workshops, a tall lawyer with a clipped, staccato voice said, "What you're saying won't work for me. I *have* to think about what to say next. If I pace myself to match my clients' slow speaking, then I would be wasting their time and mine. I need to race ahead and figure out whether I've got a case. If that's what you call erasing, so be it."

An elderly woman on the opposite end of the room responded, "That's the problem with you young people nowadays." She jabbed her finger in the direction of the attorney. "You are always rushing, never taking the time to see what's really going on. You should not think about what you're going to say next while people are talking to you. You miss so much. And you start thinking you're the only one that matters."

A lively debate ensued. About half the class claimed it was acceptable to mentally interrupt at times, while others argued that all forms of interruption are destructive.

Changing Times Affect How We Communicate

This debate on interruption underscores how interpersonal communication habits are changing along with changes in the economy. As more professionals are compensated based on productivity, *time* plays a greater role in influencing how people communicate. Doctors joining managed-health-care plans need to see more patients in less time. Attorneys racking up billable hours need to bring in more clients and somehow squeeze more lawyering into an already tight twelve-hour day. Consultants who sell their time will need to work faster to make money in an increasingly competitive marketplace.

It is easier to avoid mental interruptions when you are free of pressures. High-stress activities make listening and persuasion far more difficult. But I believe stress should not be used as an excuse to cut someone off. You have a responsibility to establish mutual understanding whenever you engage in conversation.

Two Factors that Determine Whether We Should Erase a Speaker's Remarks

We decide whether to listen to a speaker by considering two factors—competence and trust. If we judge the speaker as incompetent or untrustworthy, we may erase whatever is said. The words go in one ear and out the other. Even if we retain a tiny piece of the message, we distort it so much that comprehension is lost.

To assess a speaker's competence, we use scales such as experienced-inexperienced, informed-uninformed, trained-untrained, and professional-amateur. These indicators help us determine whether a speaker is in a position to know what's true or right.

Trust is associated with honest-dishonest, open-minded-closed-minded, just-unjust, and straightforward-evasive.

MEMORY JOGGER

When we conclude that a speaker lacks competence and trust, we tend to erase what we hear.

You might think erasing makes sense when you are subjected to a less than credible speaker. I don't blame you. Listening is tough enough when you *like* the speaker, much less when you deem the speaker undeserving of your attention. But your persuasive skills soar when you discipline yourself to listen to any and all speakers.

Cut through all the distortions to unearth the accurate message, and you will position yourself to win over anyone.

FIGHT OFF DISTORTIONS BY KNOWING YOUR DANGER ZONES

To protect yourself from distorting what others say, it helps to know when you are most vulnerable as a listener. We may distort messages more frequently when we are tired, upset, anxious, excited, or confused. Like a scientist conducting a study, you need to spot distortions when they arise and determine what causes them.

Your "research" might lead to conclusions such as:

I can't stand to be around perky people who are always "on." They drive me crazy with their high-energy theatrics. I just level off everything they say by denying their enthusiasm.

After a long day in the office, I am hardly in a position to use any more energy to listen carefully when I get home. So when my family talks to me in the evening, I am happy if I can stay awake, much less understand what they're telling me.

I love talking to people with deep, beautiful blue eyes. It really doesn't matter what they say—it's a thrill just to look into their eyes.

You can prevent distortions by knowing when they threaten to block your listening skills. If you are entranced by blue-eyed people, for example, then you need to make an extra effort to listen to what they say. Physical attractiveness can pose a problem if it stops you from listening to the speaker's actual message. To take another example, if you find that you erase volatile emotional appeals (such as when someone raises his voice at you), then you must at least try to capture the underlying message of even the most explosive, loudmouth-type speakers.

MEMORY JOGGER

Know your danger zones. Look for cause-effect relationships so that you can identify what factors cause you to distort what you hear.

Remember from the discussion earlier in this chapter that we may reconfigure a message so that we hear what we want to hear. If we are looking for support from our friends to quit our job, we may read into their comments to find the approval we seek. If we want reassurance from our mate that the relationship is sound, we may discount troubling comments and exaggerate any positive, future-looking remarks as signs that everything is fine.

When I started investing in the stock market, I discovered that brokers would read me like a book. They would ask me all sorts of personal questions, gauge my tolerance for risk, and then tell me exactly what I wanted to hear to persuade me to buy a certain stock. Rather than listen objectively, I distorted their remarks because the prospect of big winnings overpowered my desire to remain calm and attentive.

I knew that they made money whenever I bought and sold stock, but that didn't stop me from distorting what they said. They sensed my eagerness to "make a killing," so they promised me that "this stock is guaranteed to pay off in six months" or "this stock is so safe, I bought it for my whole family." As a rookie investor, I fell for these lines and regretted it later.

Some of our political leaders, like unscrupulous stockbrokers, also try to feed us what they think we want to hear. They know that Americans prize democracy, patriotism, and liberty, so they drown us in these themes to curry public favor. The actual message, of course, gets buried in the process.

In John F. Kennedy's inaugural speech, he made the now-famous declaration, "Let every nation know, whether it wishes us well or ill, that we shall pay any price, bear any burden, meet any hardship, support any friend, oppose any foe, in order to assure the survival and the success of liberty." Sounds great. But upon closer inspection, we realize that such a promise is impossible to keep and potentially destructive (as in the Vietnam War).

No wonder Americans today vote less and are more skeptical of politicians' promises. Some of us count the lies whenever we listen to a President give a speech. But despite our cynicism, we must resist the urge to distort what our Commander in Chief says. It is tempting to brush aside the underlying message when it comes wrapped in layers of flowery rhetoric. In fact, some politicians *prefer* that we listen half-heartedly to them rather than critically analyze their statements. But by lopping off the fatty tissue (the cheap appeals to patriotism, the self-congratulatory fluff, the sugary smiles and baby-kissing), we can expose the true issues and fairly evaluate the job performance of our elected officials.

○ **NOW TRY THIS**   Here's a way to fight back and sharpen your listening skills when you might otherwise resort to distortion. Summarize the speaker's comments like a journalist reporting a news event. Strive for objectivity. Say, "This is [your name] for Channel 2 News at 6 o'clock. Bill Jones, my boss, has just said that...". This may sound a bit crazy, but it works. Summarize as soon as possible after the conversation ends by hopping into your car or an empty room where you can talk out loud freely. If you cannot slip away, you can apply the same technique *during* the dialogue by mentally paraphrasing the speaker.

When my friend Peggy tried to persuade me not to eat meat, I knew that I might distort her comments because I was exhausted at the time and the topic did not interest me. So I summarized what she said:

> This is Morey Stettner with the evening news. Peggy insists that I stop eating meat. She supports her argument on two grounds: the health benefits of avoiding fat in meats and the ethical implications of how we raise and slaughter cattle. She suggests I try to go one month without red meat and then decide whether to extend the ban.

The benefit of this exercise is that it forces you to uncover the speaker's true message. Despite the fact that you might be tired, angry, or otherwise unable to listen well, you can still call upon your powers of concentration if you strive to sum up the speaker's main points. Summarizing what's said also helps you to strip away misleading rhetoric or faulty premises so that you listen critically rather than sloppily. You enhance your persuasiveness when you listen more openly and attentively to gather the true message.

GIVE SPEAKERS SOME CREDIT, AND YOU WILL NOT DISTORT THEIR WORDS

It is easy to distort speakers' remarks if you doubt their credibility or question their right to address the topic at hand. I recall a manager who was brought in to run the information systems division of an insurance company that I advised. As an outsider to the insurance industry, he was ridiculed behind his back by his staff. "He knows nothing about this business," they said. "What's he doing here?"

As much as he tried to earn their respect, he was never able to win their trust and prove his competence. When he proposed changes in the division, his underlings erased what he said and simply ignored him. They thought their jobs were safe, so they never bothered to listen to him or educate him about their department. They resented his mere presence at the firm. But as productivity continued to fall, management resorted to layoffs.

This story serves as a reminder that if you want to avoid distortions and improve your listening, give speakers some credit. Search for some reason to value their input or respect their views. If you do not like the speaker, strive to find some common ground or at least a basis for establishing mutual understanding.

Here are some characteristics to look for in a speaker to help you treat what they say more seriously:

LEADERSHIP QUALITIES

Inspiration	They inspire you to work harder or achieve more.
Vision	They present a grand vision or design for a better future.
Moral authority	They operate on a high standard of morality and set an example.

PERFORMANCE QUALITIES

Excellence	They perform tough tasks effectively or demonstrate a mastery of highly specialized knowledge.

Information	They have access to material or data that you otherwise lack.
Help	They want to assist you or support you in a shared task.

RELATIONSHIP QUALITIES

Acceptance	They appear to accept you as you are rather than judge you.
Support	They provide emotional uplift.
Understanding	They try to understand you through empathy, sensitivity.

I suggest that whenever you feel reluctant to listen to a speaker, review the preceding list and determine whether the speaker meets any of the criteria. If you find just one reason why the speaker deserves your attention, then you will be more motivated to listen. Distortions get in the way when we discount a speaker's credibility or deny their legitimacy. If you want to strengthen your persuasiveness by listening better, then you need to identify what makes a speaker worth listening to in the first place!

Diagnostic Self-Test: Reviewing What It Takes to Listen

Now that you have learned how to prevent distortions from interfering with your listening, how to use nonverbal cues to show that you listen, and how to train yourself to pay attention when others talk, take the following test to assess your skill level.

Read each of the following statements. Rank each statement on a scale of 1 to 5.

1 = Always
2 = Almost always
3 = Sometimes
4 = Rarely
5 = Never

_____ I look at people when they talk to me. My eyes do not wander away.

_____ When in doubt, I question people to clarify what they are saying.

_____ I appreciate the role of silence and let people blow off steam as needed.

_____ I react responsively to speakers with nods, smiles, and other non-verbal cues that signal that I understand what they're saying.

_____ I distinguish between facts and opinions when I listen.

_____ I keep my back straight and do not slouch or tilt my head when I listen.

_____ I know my danger zones, or when I'm most vulnerable to distorting what I hear, and I have strategies to handle these situations.

_____ I let slow talkers finish their sentences even when my patience is tested.

_____ I do not let judgments about a speaker cloud my ability to listen for what's said.

If your total score is less than 16, consider yourself a top-flight listener. You probably find that you can persuade others with the same high degree of power and precision with which you listen.

If you scored from 17 to 27, your listening is not too deficient, but your persuasiveness will increase as you apply the tools in this book.

If your total is over 28, you need to make listening a higher priority if you want to improve your ability to win people over. Distortions may be blocking your comprehension. A lack of patience or curiosity may also be working against you.

As you strive to listen better, apply as many of the tools in this book as possible. Then measure the results. Note how much insight and information you gain by keeping quiet. Chart how much more persuasive you become and then decide if it was worth the extra time required to listen. You will find this a revealing experiment. If you are like most of my workshop participants, you will conclude that the benefits outweigh the costs.

I have watched far too many potentially great communicators fail to sell themselves and their ideas because they turned obstacles into excuses. Do not blur this distinction; valid obstacles are not the same as manufactured excuses.

EXCUSE: I'm so tired that I cannot listen.

OBSTACLE: I'm so tired. It's tough to listen now, but I will.

There is no way to avoid obstacles, but you can overcome them. An extra ten minutes a day of attentiveness and patience may save you hours of hassles that result from preventable misunderstanding and conflict.

Among the most common excuses is to convince yourself that you lack the sensitivity and attentiveness of "natural" listeners. A majority of my students openly admit that they "have never been much of a listener" or that they "need plenty of help." I respond, "Hold on. By declaring yourself a poor listener, you let yourself off the hook."

Good listeners do not possess some special talent that most people lack. You may not be a natural athlete or a born musician, but anyone can learn to listen. The techniques discussed in this book work for anyone who makes a commitment to apply them.

MEMORY JOGGER

Each and every one of you can become a "natural" listener.

QUICK REVIEW

- Don't falsely inflate the importance of a message by intensifying it.
- Learn from what someone says, even when a word or phrase stings.
- When someone compliments you, do not dwell on it and ignore everything else.
- Don't distort what you hear to support your predetermined conclusions. Listen with an open mind.
- Don't deemphasize what someone says until nothing stands out.
- Prioritize what others tell you to avoid exaggerating and leveling.
- When you receive a sincere compliment, acknowledge it. Don't argue.
- Resist the urge to erase, or block out, an unpleasant or negative comment.
- Don't interrupt, or you may crush any opportunity for establishing mutual trust.
- Know your danger zones—when you are most vulnerable as a listener.
- Be careful of distorting messages so that you hear what you want hear.

NOTES

1. *The Los Angeles Times,* 12-14-86, Part VI, p. 1.

STEP THREE

Speak to Sell

Plugging in Power Phrases
to Easily Get Your Way

Talk is the sea upon which all else floats.—James Britton

Never use two words when one will do.— Harry Truman

A government agency issued a blackout order during World War II when Americans feared the possibility of Japanese air raids at night:

> Such preparations shall be made as will completely obscure all Federal buildings and non-Federal buildings occupied by the Federal government during the air raid for any period of visibility by reason of internal or external illumination. Such obscuration may be obtained either by blackout construction or by termination of the illumination.

When President Franklin Roosevelt learned of this order, he substituted his own command to "tell them that in buildings where they have to keep on working to put something over the windows; and where they can stop work for awhile, to turn off the lights."[1]

Which approach sounds more persuasive?

The first order, filled with wasted words, puts the burden on the listener to sift through the bureaucratic mess to uncover a message.

Roosevelt's order uses shorter words in a conversational manner to make the same point. Better still, FDR humanizes the message by involving real people in a real process (workers covering windows).

We respond more favorably to ideas that are simple and direct. Persuasive speakers know how to get their points across in a clear, compelling way. They want their listeners to easily grasp the message, so they use familiar words and speak in a friendly but firm voice. They appeal to our senses with vivid imagery. They bring plenty of enthusiasm to the table. They express an underlying confidence that their idea deserves the listener's acceptance or approval.

Clarity comes with knowing exactly what we want to say and choosing the fewest words possible to say it. Former Secretary of State Alexander Haig would overcomplicate his remarks with phrases such as "careful caution," "caveat my response," "epistemologicallywise," and "definitizing an answer." It's hard to trust a guy who talks like that.

If you ramble, then your chances of persuading decrease. Not only do you bore your listeners, but you also invite them to jump to conclusions and dream up reasons to reject your proposal. Smart persuaders send a clear, crisp message with the fewest words possible. If you need a ride to the airport, ask for it! If you want to sign up magazine subscribers, ask for the orders! If you want an employee to change a certain behavior, clearly state the benefits of your suggestion. Do not evade when you want to persuade.

Salespeople who do not believe in what they sell may let their doubts creep into their delivery. They will be more apt to use qualifiers that weaken their persuasive power. To cover their backsides, they will hide behind a bureaucratic wall of words. Listening is already hard; talkers who waste words make it harder.

If you have read this far in the book and practiced your ability to prepare and listen before speaking, you are well on your way to mastering the art of persuasion. You are no doubt discovering how much work it takes to organize your ideas and remain attentive before saying a word. Talking, by contrast, is easy. All the effort that goes into preparing and listening pays off now that you are ready to say something.

THE SECRET OF PERSUASIVE SPEAKING: KEEP IT SIMPLE

Whenever you have an important persuasive goal, hammer it home by keeping it simple. Stick with topics that people care about. Don't be afraid to come right out and say what you want.

MEMORY JOGGER

Speak the same way you would write a newspaper headline: subject, verb, object.

Make it easy for your listeners to retain your central point. Repeat the key idea. Use the fewest words possible to express yourself. Think about youngsters who repeatedly beg their parents for a bicycle. They make themselves clear: They want that bike. Kids have a talent for voicing their wants and needs over and over until their exhausted parents relent. Some call this nagging. I call it persuasion.

Keep the theme consistent over time. If you want a bike one day and a video game the next, your parents will learn to say no; they figure you will change your mind soon enough. Same goes for an executive who wants a better office. I met a manager at an accounting firm who asked for a pay raise in June, a new company car in July, and a bigger office in August. Instead of targeting the same goal month after month, he coveted different things at different times. This made it easy for his boss to say "no."

Advertisers, who are paid to persuade the masses, appreciate the value of chipping away at a consistent theme. For instance, Pepsi's battle with Coke for the top spot in the cola wars did not begin overnight. Pepsi's ad slogan in the 1980s ("Choice of a New Generation") echoed its campaign of the 1960s ("For those who think young"). Here we are in the mid-1990s, and Pepsi continues to air commercials aimed at youth. Pepsi has challenged Coke over the years by relentlessly pursuing the same market segment of young consumers.

MEMORY JOGGER

Express your persuasive goal as a single theme that you continually reinforce with zeal.

During Harris Wofford's successful campaign for Pennsylvania senator in 1991, *The New Yorker* reported on political consultant James Carville's advice to Wofford:

> Carville, to convince Wofford that he was not making him less than human by forcing him to focus on one message—middle class anxiety, especially about health care—proposed Abraham Lincoln as a model. He gave Wofford, the college president, a homework assign-

ment—to read Lincoln's speeches of the late eighteen-fifties and try
to find one in which he did not hammer at the need for a Union.[2]

A dutiful pupil, Wofford accepted Carville's challenge and proceeded
to score a stunning upset over former Governor and U. S. Attorney General
Richard Thornburgh. The lesson: Strip away extraneous matter so that you
deliver a simple, action-oriented goal.

Just as Lincoln pounded away at the importance of preserving the
Union, Marcus Cato persuaded his Roman compatriots nearly two thousand
years earlier with the rallying cry "Carthage must be destroyed." He repeated this phrase in speech after speech, building a rhetorically stirring plea
with just four words.

When a speaker inflates a persuasive request with too many words,
the odds of misunderstanding and rejection soar. If listeners cannot easily
grasp a message, then they may not take the time to think through what
they are asked to do. The mind shuts off. The path of least resistance is to
just say no.

Keeping it simple does not mean your idea must be simple-minded.
Many participants in my workshops worry about oversimplifying or insulting their audiences by treating them like little kids. I say, "Go ahead."
Pretend you are talking to a youngster. Resist the urge to use fancy words,
inscrutable jargon, or foreign phrases. You wouldn't rephrase a request five
different ways when pleading with an uncooperative child, each time
resorting to subtle shifts in meaning. You would state yourself clearly and
concisely, repeating the point if necessary until you were understood.

People want to understand what they are told. Whenever they are
asked to do something or think a certain way, they consider whether it is
in their best interest to act or think accordingly. This decision is made easier when they comprehend the message.

MEMORY JOGGER

Your job when you persuade is to concisely let listeners know
what you want and what's in it for them.

A large part of persuasion is knowing what you can and cannot control. You have no control over other people's comments, but you can command your own language. When you speak, you choose what words to
use, how to you string those words together, what tone of voice to use, and
what attitude to take. It is not enough to say, "Oh, I'll just be myself." Yes,
you want to communicate in a natural, genuine way. No, this does not
mean you should let your mouth run free.

This chapter will show you how to blend word choice and verbal imagery to captivate any audience. Rather than telling you what to say and how to say it, I will present a range of strategies that apply to different situations. Practice these tools and select the ones that work best for you. Get comfortable using them. Take advantage of the fact that you can control how you communicate.

OPENING WITH THE WORD THAT KEEPS ON GIVING

Many of my friends are getting married these days. We're all pushing thirty, so it seems like a good time to settle down.

Communication plays a particularly critical role in the early years of a marriage. Because spouses are so eager to make each other happy, they spend plenty of time wondering what their mate is thinking. But not everyone feels comfortable reporting what's on their mind at any given moment. Stoic breadwinners may not want to confess that they are worried about money. A new parent may hesitate to admit that he or she is terrified of all the responsibility of rearing a child. An individual who is naturally underexpressive poses a special challenge, because the spouse rarely has a clue how best to communicate.

"My husband is a clam—the strong, silent type," a woman told me. "Most of the time I have no idea what he's thinking, so it's hard for me to try to talk him into anything. I don't know what angle to take."

○ **NOW TRY THIS**   A great way to draw out a bashful communicator without talking too much about yourself is to use If-Then Statements. They are structured like this:

If you [desired action], then [benefits].

This direct approach eliminates ambiguity and prevents misunderstanding. If Rhoda wants her husband to reveal more of his feelings, she could say, "If you tell me what's on your mind more often, then I promise not to ask you what you're thinking all the time." If Jeff, a volunteer at a youth center, wants to befriend a shy youngster, he could say, "If you shake my hand, then I will show you a secret handshake that only my friends know about." If a manager wants to encourage entry-level clerks to suggest ways to improve the file room operation, she could say, "If you come up with an idea, any idea, come see me. Then we can see about implementing it." An alternate approach to If-Then statements is,"*By [taking the desired action], you'll gain [result].*"

Miriam Arond and Samuel Pauker write in *The First Year of Marriage*[3] that newlyweds fight about the way they communicate more often than they clash over sex, religion, friends, or other matters. To prevent these verbal duels, young couples must nurture open, respectful dialogues.

The beauty of honest, personal communication is that it forces us to focus on the other person. Rather than trying to convince someone of what *we* want or how *we* see things, we speak in terms of the other's concerns, views, and needs. With so much energy invested in understanding someone else, we are less apt to waste time dwelling on our own fears or self-doubts. The most confident, charismatic communicators never seem stiff or self-conscious; instead, they envelop the audience with passion and excitement.

Persuasive speakers shower their listeners with attention. Their favorite word is *you*. They keep the conversational spotlight riveted on the listener. Their sentences begin:

You will find...

You can benefit by...

Imagine your...

You may enjoy...

It is hard to ignore a speaker who discusses our wants and needs. When the conversation revolves around us, we tend to listen up. Our minds are activated and our interest is aroused. Think about the last time you overheard someone mention your name. You probably tried to eavesdrop to figure out what was being said about you. There is no better way to capture an individual's focus than to make that person feel like the most important person in the world.

Beware of *I*. Red flags should wave in your head whenever you begin a sentence with *I*.

I think...

I believe...

I have found...

I want...

I'd like to...

You have to earn the right to discuss yourself. Think of the last time you were trapped in a one-way conversation with a spouting pontificator.

You did not listen because you were probably too busy planning an escape. You must show the audience that you prefer to learn from them rather than to preach to them.

MEMORY JOGGER

Remember the cardinal rule of handling any audience: They will care about you only if you show that you care about them first.

Top salespeople know that positive selling phrases containing YOU can sway even the most resistant prospects:

This may help you…

You will find…

Based on your comments,…

These phrases build alliances and establish credibility. They can soften a hard-sell pitch and make the speaker sound friendly and responsive. Best of all, they signal to the potential buyer that the salesperson is thinking less about closing the sale than about filling a need.

How to Make Others Stop Whatever They're Doing and Listen to You

Many professional women in my workshops discuss how they need to repeat themselves before male colleagues will treat their remarks seriously. This may happen (regardless of gender) if you are a lowly subordinate, a newcomer, or an outsider. A handy way to get others to listen to you is to plug in the following *you*-based power phrase:

You think [summarize speaker's point] and I think [insert your point].

If Kathy hears a co-worker argue for a better employee carpool policy, she might respond, "You think strengthening our carpool policy makes sense, and I agree. I think we can go further and establish a four-day work week to help us attain your goal of devising better commuting plans."

She opens with *you* and acknowledges the speaker's remarks. She even adds "I agree" to build an alliance. Now that she has everyone's attention, she proposes her idea (a four-day work week) as an extension of what's already been said. Kathy shrewdly reframes her idea so that it complements, rather than conflicts with, her colleague's comments.

Notice how Kathy avoids using *but*. Whenever you summarize what someone says, do not signal that you disagree with a *Yes, but* approach. A *Yes, but* statement paves the way for an argument. Replace *but* with *and*. "You say that carpools make sense, and I think..." works better than "You say that carpools make sense, but I think..."

Opening with that pleasing word, *you,* can get you out of some jams. A New York City beat cop told *The New York Times* about how he used "the gift of gab" to enforce the law. A woman pointed to a muscular guy on the street who slapped her and stole her money. She warned the policeman that the suspect had just gotten out of jail and that it took ten cops to lock him up the last time ("His arms were so big they couldn't get them together to cuff him. They needed two sets," she told him.)[4]

The policeman realized that it might not work to threaten the suspect by saying, "I'm going to lock you up if you don't give her the money." Instead, he said, "Excuse me, fella. Could you come here for a minute? Look, I heard you just got out of jail. Here are the charges you face so far: robbery, assault three, and if you want to fight me, it will be assault on a police officer. Why don't you give her the money and you can walk."

The guy said, "OK, officer" and gave back the money.

The policeman persuaded by focusing on the suspect's situation, by suggesting a way to cooperate rather than ordering him to submit to authority. The moral of the story? Appeal to others' best interests (not your interests) if you want to win them over.

Three Exceptions to the Rule: When *I* Works Better than *You*

While *you* works better than *I* most of the time, there are three exceptions to the rule:

- Using *you* to make accusations.

  Coupling *you* with *don't, can't, always, never,* or *didn't* may trigger defensiveness. *You didn't do what I asked you* or *You don't help around the house* sound more harsh than *What made you do that?* or *How much do you help around the house?* We do not like to hear lectures about our failings. We also fight back when someone characterizes our behavior in absolute terms (*You never care about what I say. You always think of yourself first*). We may respond by exclaiming, *How dare you!* or *How can you say that!* Transform accusations into questions and save yourself some grief.

- Allowing youngsters to avoid accountability for their behavior.

  Calling all parents! When teaching your children to act assertively, it is okay for them to use *I* more than *you*. When kids fight, they often deflect blame and say, "You did that to me." Children learn to take responsibility for their actions when they start sentences with *I* (*I guess I ate all the cookies; I was playing with his toy*) rather than pointing the finger at someone else.

- Expressing judgments or opinions.

  Beware of opening with *you* when rendering a judgment. If you wish to express your thoughts, preferences, or opinions, then do not open your sentence by saying, "You are..." or "You make me..." In such cases, go ahead and say "I think..." or "I feel..."

  Apart from these three examples, *you* is generally a stronger word than *I* when it comes to persuasion. Focus on the other person and you will establish rapport.

EMPHASIZING *GLOW WORDS* TO ELECTRIFY YOUR SPEAKING

Glow words radiate energy. They enliven a dialogue and generate excitement. When we talk someone into something, our success depends partly on our ability to choose positive, high-octane words that drive home our points. Relying on cliches will deaden the message.

One word can make a big impact. In Barry Goldwater's 1964 acceptance speech for the Republican presidential nomination, he declared, "Extremism in the defense of liberty is not a vice." The stormy reception that greeted his speech surprised him. It turns out many Americans feared an extremist president. Goldwater later admitted he should have substituted "dedication" for "extremism."[5]

On the financial front, economists devote months of careful analysis to determine whether the nation is in a *recession*. When a recession is first declared, the national mood plummets. Most consumers already know the economy is hurting, but to hear it made official in the morning newspaper makes it worse. The recession label is like a skull and crossbones that poisons our economic outlook.

Yet words can also brighten a message. When those same economists decide that a *recovery* has occurred, the nation celebrates with a jump in spending. Changing from a *recession* to a *recovery* can transform a pessimistic populace into a surging wave of happy shoppers. Because of its positive connotations, *recovery* is a glow word. It makes us smile.

What's the universal glow word—the one sound that automatically sparks the interest of almost everyone? A person's name. People simply like to hear their name. But do not go overboard and endlessly repeat someone's name. You can spot graduates of the Dale Carnegie course by the way they open a conversation:

> *Well, hello, Theodore. What a pleasure to meet you, Theodore. That's a very dignified name. Theodore, tell me, how're you doing on this wonderful day?*

If you are going to use someone's name, pronounce it clearly. Do not mumble the name or recite it using a preprogrammed script. Some telemarketers have developed an obnoxious way of repeating our name three times in the opening seconds of a call:

> *Is this Bill Jones?*

Yes.

> *Mr. Jones?*

Yes, this is Bill Jones.

> *Great. Mr. Jones, I am calling you about an exciting offer...*

Many sales training courses now teach this mechanical approach to launching a conversation. The theory goes if you say someone's name three times right off the bat, they will like you.

I say limit the number of times you use someone's name, but take full advantage when you do by uttering the name with clarity and force. Let those vowel and consonant sounds ring out with reverence. Imagine that you chose the name and you are verbally savoring it. Pause just before and after you say it so that it stands out. Flood yourself with happy thoughts when you say it. Your physiology will reflect your fondness for the other person: your face will radiate warmth, your body will relax, and your voice will sound rich and welcoming.

Beyond someone's name, there are other glow words you should use to enliven your speaking. They can be verbs or nouns. Because they engage the senses, stir mystery, or illuminate the topic, they may fit a variety of conversational roles. Examples:

- Effective salespeople use phrases that begin with *imagine* to plant positive images in a listener's mind, "Imagine yourself sailing this beautiful boat along the coast at dusk."

- Vin Scully, the legendary play-by-play announcer for the Los Angeles Dodgers, describes the action with phrases such as, "Russell *sparkles* at shortshop."

- Glow words can even make something as destructive as an atomic blast sound appealing. An observer of the 1945 Trinity Test in Los Alamos, New Mexico, recalled, "I looked outside and saw a luminous, billowing fireball—peach, blue, green—a magnificent ball of colors going up and up."[6] The deadly bomb sounds downright pretty.

Speakers use glow words to excite their listeners. It is hard to ignore an eyewitness to an atomic bomb blast who talks about the colors he sees flash before him. With the audience captivated by his remarks, he can proceed to either argue for the elimination of such weapons or for the need to build more powerful bombs to fortify our national defense. Either way, his opening comments arouse images of strength and beauty that make us want to hear more.

○ **Now Try This**   If you want to incorporate more glow words into your vocabulary, flip through a newspaper or magazine and read the ads. Look for words that make you stop and smile. Record these words or phrases on a notepad and use them in your conversations. Beware of trite phrases such as *fully guaranteed, once-in-a-lifetime chance,* or *free trial offer.* Avoid puffy words that do not activate the senses. Jot down any expressions that pack energy and excitement. Examples are *capture the pulsating energy, enjoy a soothing sleep, catapult yourself forward.* Carry these glow words around with you whenever you need to persuade.

Make your words come alive. Plug in power phrases that inspire your listeners and drive them to action. Flat nouns and verbs kill a persuasive presentation. Glow words, by contrast, evoke images of security, virility, longevity, and beauty. They are underappreciated and underused. More examples:

- Describe the "*spectrum* of choices" available rather than say "you've got a lot of choices."

- Characterize a business venture as a "*shining* example of a great deal" or an opportunity that "*glistens* with promise."

- Promise to "reveal an *electrifying* secret" to gain an audience's attention. (Television ads are filled with glow words. Announcers tell us not to miss "the world premiere movie that *sparked* a national debate" or "never-before-seen *explosive* footage.")

Emphasize the freshness of your remarks to maximize their appeal. Information is more likely to persuade someone when it is perceived as new. Don't merely "try a different approach"—"uncover a new angle" or "introduce a fresh perspective."

SAY WHAT YOU SEE:
VISUAL SNAPSHOTS ARE WORTH A THOUSAND WORDS

One of the first lessons of good writing is "show, don't tell." This same principle applies to verbal communication. The way to build your persuasive speech can be summed up in four words: Say what you see.

Speak in visual pictures. Glow words work because they conjure up vivid imagery. Don't just tell your friends you are angry—show them what caused the anger. Instead of relying on overused adjectives (*My trip was great, just great*), describe it (*I visited ancient caves filled with skeletons*). Listen to how the best sportscasters avoid clichés such as *He looks aggressive today* in favor of reporting what they see: *He's approaching the net a few seconds faster than last week.* Use your words to relate what you see so that you enable others to see the same thing.

Share crisp, relevant details (colors, unusual objects, sounds) that provide descriptive precision. Stay away from stale adjectives (*That was beautiful; What a nice day; That design looks super*). Like a journalist, stick to reporting facts.

In a business story about investing in "socially responsible" companies, for instance, the reporter describes firms that sell ice cream and beauty supplies, "These are great businesses and here's why: They use vats to mix up big batches of glop—ice cream, shampoo, or lip balm—and sell the glop in tiny packages at a big markup." The image of vats filled with "big batches of glop" offers a fine example of descriptive communication.[7]

On a more personal level, rather than label someone "a glutton who just can't stop eating," you can report what you see:

> At lunch I saw a person rapidly consume three double cheeseburgers, one after another. Then, reaching into another bag, this person grabbed handfuls of six or seven fries and ate them in bunches until the bag was empty.

While some may think, "What a pig," others may reflect on how "unhealthy it is to eat so much." By saying what you see, you allow listeners to draw independent conclusions. This paves the way for persuasion. You do not let your personal views get in the way of the facts.

MEMORY JOGGER

Report what you see before you interpret what you see.

Judgments can provoke disagreement. Issuing pronouncements of good-bad or right-wrong can ignite conflict or injure feelings if someone begs to differ. Persuasive speakers use descriptions to reduce the risk of needless argument, since it's hard to disagree with objective data or empirical facts.

Diplomacy and persuasion go hand in hand. Growing up in Beverly Hills, I learned not to criticize a new movie too loudly at school because someone's mom or dad may have worked on it. You do not want to declare the film a worthless piece of garbage within earshot of classmates. Instead, you describe your favorite scene, "The whole part about the space landing was fascinating." If you do not have a favorite scene, then you pick a particular moment in the film and summarize it, "When we see the murderer's shadow in the moon's reflection—that's quite a scene."

By speaking visually, you activate your listeners' minds. They assess the subject matter based on your reports, summaries, and observations. Their judgments thus come from within: They do not feel as if they have been talked into anything against their will. They sell themselves.

Your role is to plant the seeds by stating verifiable facts, describing details, or supplying relevant evidence or testimony that upholds your persuasive goal. Examples:

- Rather than say, "Mary looks so relaxed," say what you see, "She sits with her left leg crossed comfortably over her right, head tilted slightly to the right, breathing evenly and rhythmically."
- Instead of describing something as "quality work," cite the qualities themselves, "The workmanship on that antique desk shows meticulous design and a hand-crafted finish."
- Avoid declaring that "this is a dreadful day" or "what a terrible situation." Instead, provide concrete facts that lead you to such a conclusion, "You should know about the accident I had with your car. Let me tell you exactly what happened."

Persuasive speakers capture details that most people miss. Their comments are not weighed down by dogmatic pronouncements or opinionated ravings. The policeman we met earlier in the chapter knew how to change the suspect's behavior, *not* by commanding him to obey the law, but by accurately describing his behavior (and the consequences) and then introducing the benefits of altering that behavior. (Parents and teachers, take note. Telling kids what to do will rarely persuade them to behave, but letting them know all that they can gain by cooperating may win them over.)

Descriptions Help Bring Your Words to Life, While Inferences Can Kill

Descriptive words capture specific events, actions, and observable characteristics. When you say what you see, you speak in term of descriptions.

Inferences, on the other hand, are judgments, interpretations, or reactions to a situation. Inferences do not report actual events or activities. You can observe a worker who arrives at 6 A.M.. daily, but you cannot observe *initiative*. You can describe how someone dives into a swimming pool to save a drowning infant, but you cannot observe *heroism*. Initiative and heroism are inferences—conclusions based on facts or premises.

○ **NOW TRY THIS** Underline those words that are descriptions rather than inferences:

consistent	loyal
reliable	guilty
efficient	lazy

Answer: you should not underline any of these words. All are inferences. Here are examples of descriptions to support each of the above inferences:

wins nine out of ten cases	has worked here seventeen years
arrives on time	has sweaty palms and shifty eyes
uses color-coded filing system	naps on office couch

While these descriptions support the inferences listed above, they do not prove anything. A seventeen-year employee with Acme Corp. may have spent the last ten years searching desperately for a new job—hardly a *loyal* worker. A manager who naps may be tired due to putting in so much over-time—hardly a *lazy* worker. When you persuade, say what you see and allow listeners to draw their own conclusions. Stick to the safe world of observable behavior. Lay off the inferences and judgments.

You may wonder what's the harm in inferring something that seems obvious. If a team wins ten games in a row, calling them *consistent* seems a safe bet. If you repeatedly arrive on time, you certainly qualify as *reliable*.

But think about the boss who says, "You take work from Jackie's desk when you finish your own work." That's a simple description. Consider how many inferences you may draw from that remark:

A. You're too aggressive and you shouldn't be taking work off someone else's desk.

B. You're working too fast and you'll make mistakes. Slow down and complete your own files accurately.

C. You're wonderfully aggressive, just the kind of hard worker we like to promote. Keep up the great performance.

D. You're operating independently and not waiting around to be told what to do. Great job!

A patient listener would allow the boss to elaborate before concluding whether taking work from Jackie's desk was good or bad.

Follow the example set by effective teachers who prod students to produce better work. An instructor will meet with a pupil to review past assignments, remarking on the quality of writing, the depth of analysis, the use of evidence, and so on. The teacher makes specific observations, not general criticisms (*See in this paragraph how the supporting points do not match the thesis? Here your writing shifts to past tense; This section is based on a faulty premise*).

Rather than criticize the student personally, the persuasive teacher will typically ask such questions as, "How would you characterize your work, and how do you think it will improve in your upcoming assignments?" The student offers a self-critique (*I suppose my work has been a bit sloppy*) and decides to perform on a higher level (*I will work harder to tighten my writing and strengthen my reasoning*). The instructor persuades without having to issue commandments or resort to threats.

Smart managers use the same technique when conducting performance reviews of their staff. By describing the subject's behavior and work product (*Your ability to talk Dr. Hanson into buying the whole package was impressive; Your report on the branch offices offered some excellent ideas*) rather than making general inferences (*Your sales ability is impressive; Your research has been helpful*), a supervisor can give more meaningful feedback to an employee.

You can avoid conflict with an underachieving worker if you focus less on judgments (*It seems you're not working up to your potential*) and more on supplying hard evidence (*Your presentation at today's regional meeting left out key details of our new product that you explained so well last month; Your analysis in these two papers is not as thorough as your exceptional work on last year's merger*). During a performance appraisal, give employees plenty of examples that explain how you feel about their work. Beware of making general statements that you cannot back up.

◯ **NOW TRY THIS**   Stop yourself the next time you start to state an opinion. Typical opinion phrases begin, "They are. . ." or "He is. . ." Replace your judgment with the facts that led you to reach your conclusion. For example, if you want to tell someone how much you dislike your dentist, avoid issuing an opinion (*My dentist isn't sensitive to patients' needs*). Instead, state the basis for your opinion (*My dentist begins drilling without any warning, and when I hold up my hand indicating that I want him to stop, he drills deeper*). Explain the evidence that leads to your conclusion. Stick to the facts and leave out your opinion.

Many participants in my workshops ask me how they can train themselves to replace inferences with descriptions. After all, inferences are easy to make, while descriptions require keen observational skills and a rich vocabulary. *Inferences are more common*, they tell me. *It's hard not being able to state an opinion or judge a situation.*

How true. Many speakers find inferences a natural part of communication. In law school, where students are taught to analyze fact patterns in rigorous detail before offering a conclusion, professors often scold the class for being "too conclusory." It takes most budding lawyers years of practice to extract the core issues from a case, analyze the facts, and think in logical sequence—all before concluding whether a party is guilty or innocent. Another reason inferences can spell trouble is that judgmental speakers lose their intellectual edge. Their brains soften as they resort to simple-minded labels (*You're so ___*) instead of documenting their feelings with precise observations. Each time you render a judgment, the doors of your mind close just a little bit more. Your sensory perceptions weaken, your awareness fades, and your speaking loses its spark. Loading up on inferences can deaden your mind and chip away at your persuasiveness.

● **TRAP**   Watch for the infamous verb *to be*. Excessive use of *is, was,* and *are* should tip you off that you are relying on dead words. What's worse, when you say *Doug is dumb,* you make it sound as if Doug possesses an inherent trait. The *is* serves as an equal sign: Doug=dumb. Rather than say *Doug is dumb,* say *Doug left the party after having six drinks. Then he insisted on driving home.* Let your listeners decide from the facts whether Doug is dumb.

How Comedians Make Us Laugh:
Provide Stories with a Time, Place, and Activity

To improve your ability to speak in pictures, try giving listeners a time, place, and activity to associate with your message. Comedians understand the importance of telling jokes with a definite setting: naked men relaxing in a steamy Jacuzzi, harried motorists stuck in rush-hour traffic, parents trying to awaken their kids at dawn on a camping trip. Each scenario provides a clear action, a distinct atmosphere, and a cast of readily identifiable characters. Punch lines pay off when the audience visualizes what's going on.

You can train yourself to talk visually by addressing *when* an action happened, *to whom* it happened, *where* it happened, and exactly *what* happened. Supply answers to each of these questions. While writing a senior thesis in college, I was repeatedly told to "flesh it out a bit more." One day I asked my instructor just what he meant by that. He said, "It's like making good wine. Give your narrative a full-bodied taste. Fill in what's going on in the background, the people moving around, the events affecting them. Show us more, analyze less."

Wise advice. By saying what you see, you keep the spotlight on the events swirling around you. You persuade by adding sights and sounds to your listeners' world. You watch the tennis players drenched in sweat, the executives huddled around a mahogany desk, the shoppers dangling their oversized bags. You describe ducks flapping in the pond, the soft touch of a baby's skin, the bright white snow blanketing rooftops. Imagine your eyes are cameras taking snapshots.

○ **NOW TRY THIS**   Here's a way to sharpen your ability to talk in pictures. Select a banner event from your past (a marriage or honeymoon, winning an award, moving to a new town). Recall images from the event. Now reminisce out loud. Say, "I remember..." and keep talking. Capture the smells, tastes, and sights. Use simple words and provide lots of details. Every time you complete this exercise, you learn to speak with more visual impact.

Reduce Lofty Concepts to Concrete Facts, Anecdotes, or Analogies

One of my workshop participants, a director of development for a large nonprofit organization, said that successful fund raising depends on how the speaker communicates the value of giving. Appeals to goodness, brotherhood, or generosity mean little to an audience. "Lofty concepts don't translate into lofty checks," he explained. "Abstractions don't sell. What does sell is when I introduce a few kids who have been helped by the program or show the audience specifically what their money will buy. That motivates them to give."

Abstractions do not persuade people. You must speak in more down-to-earth terms. The best way to illustrate your points and produce the desired action is to provide anecdotes or analogies.

Anecdotes serve as excellent vehicles to relate visual images. They can also add a dose of humor. One of my favorite stories was told by South African Archbishop Desmond Tutu when I saw him speak in Los Angeles not long after he won the Nobel Peace Prize:

> When the missionaries came to our neck of the woods, we had the land and they had the Bible. They said, "Let us pray," and we foolishly closed our eyes. And when we opened our eyes, we had the Bible and they had the land.

This anecdote works well because it is short and to the point. Rather than lecture about the dangers of colonialism, Tutu told a simple story that gently reinforced his message.

You may think that as long as you present a logical argument, you need not waste time telling stories. One participant in a recent workshop said, "I am persuaded by people who present well-reasoned positions. If they tell anecdotes or discuss their experiences, that doesn't move me." Fair enough. Some of us enjoy critically analyzing a situation. But you are safer if you do not rely exclusively on logic to persuade. After all, your airtight argument may not translate into a lively, persuasive presentation.

Anecdotes add a human touch to your abstract, logical messages. Stories communicate the qualitative rather than the quantitative side of experience. They enable you to tie emotion to your rational analysis.

Analogies work the same way. I know a fellow who loves science. He attracts a crowd at parties because he enthralls his listeners by making complex scientific principles easy to comprehend. One time I heard him explain Galileo Galilei's formula for the distance of falling objects by comparing "a peanut dropping on the carpet to the roaring cascades of

Niagara." By establishing a likeness among a range of objects, he made us aware of the underlying meaning of scientific discovery.

You can use analogies, too. Whenever you want to express a persuasive point, ask yourself, "How is my persuasive goal similar to something else? What can I compare it to?" Examples:

- You have a suggestion to streamline your back-office operation, and you want to win over your staff to your new approach. By comparing your idea to dialing a rotary telephone, you make everyone aware of the benefits, "When we dial with a rotary phone, it takes maybe ten more seconds to get through to the other party compared to a touch-tone phone. That doesn't seem like much time savings, but when you think about the hundreds of calls you make every month, then those ten seconds add up to many hours! Same goes for my idea to..."

- You want to persuade your spouse to act differently. Rather than criticize, you try an analogy to make your point, "You know when we take those long walks on the beach and the sand seems to stay in our shoes for days afterward? Well, that's how I feel when you tell stories about my mother to our friends. Like that sand, it stays with me for days when you say those things. I find it hard to forget."

Through anecdotes and analogies, you can strengthen your persuasive speaking by providing listeners with visual images.

THE ART OF FRAMING: SEVEN WAYS TO EXPRESS YOUR IDEAS

Framing is how you define your persuasive message to others. Some salespeople, for example, frame their presentations as a hard-sell plea for your business. They begin by proclaiming *what a great deal* and force-feed all the benefits to a bewildered prospect who takes the stance of a resistant cynic.

The same prospect, however, would respond favorably to a low-key, attentive salesperson who listens and strives to fill needs.

In this section, we examine seven popular frames. As you become familiar with their uses, you can select the best one to enhance your persuasive appeal.

Frame 1: Let Me Help You Solve a Problem   How can you frame your message to maximize its acceptance? Based on careful listening and preliminary fact finding, you can place the other person in an appropriate setting and then plug in power phrases as needed. If someone reveals a difficulty to you, then your persuasiveness grows when you offer a way out of that difficulty. When you hear complaints such as *This bothers me; Something is wrong;* or *I've got a problem,* then your job is to paraphrase the difficulty and prescribe a solution.

But framing is not always as easy as *Let me help you solve your problem.* Many people do not know they have a problem. They live in a state of denial or ignorance. Persuading such people requires that you make them aware of the difficulty and then get them to both acknowledge that difficulty and accept responsibility to change.

I still cringe when I recall a story an office manager told me about a file clerk with terrible body odor. It fell upon the manager to suggest that the clerk shower before work. "Persuading him was really hard, especially since I felt embarrassed even raising the issue of b.o.," the manager said. Finally, after days of procrastination, the manager walked up to the clerk, smiled supportively, and asked him softly if he could find time to shower before work. The clerk smiled back, visibly relieved. "I've felt pretty bad about that," he confessed. "I have to rush to get here on time, and I wondered whether anyone noticed. Now I know."

Frame 2: Let's Dig a Bit Deeper or Try Something Different   Another frame applies to situations where someone has a feeling that something is wrong, but cannot identify the precise problem. To achieve your persuasive goal, you must shed light on the unfocused difficulty and introduce a solution. For instance, psychologists often encounter patients suffering from a general malaise or a mental block. The doctor frames the situation like this: *Let's dig a bit deeper to uncover precisely what's going on, and then we can work together to come up with a solution.* This nonthreatening approach puts the patient at ease so that the doctor can propose ways for the patient to constructively change behavior.

Unfocused difficulties can plague frustrated corporate managers, who sense morale is down but cannot specifically isolate the cause. Sometimes the numbers indicate a drop in productivity, but the manager cannot identify the bottleneck in the system that accounts for the alarming downward trend. Supervisors may want to rally the troops to perform at a higher level, but their entreaties fall upon deaf ears. Even after managers join employees in the trenches where the real work gets done, the source of the problem remains a mystery.

In these situations, leaders persuade by breathing new life into the organization, usually in the form of fresh incentives, realigned work teams, or simply changing some aspect of the workplace. As the famous Hawthorne studies found in the late 1920s, any change in the work environment—from painting the walls a different color to modifying the intensity of the lighting—increases productivity. The researchers concluded that as long as interest is shown in workers, then they will be persuaded to work harder. Today, a "Hawthorne effect" refers to improved performance by the mere fact of change.

Frame 3: Let's Correct Past Mistakes or Build on Past Success The theme of change carries over into another frame: *Let's correct past mistakes.* Bill Clinton won the 1992 presidential election by framing his campaign speeches in this fashion. He attacked twelve years of Republican leadership as a lost opportunity for the nation, and he stirred the voters' restlessness with the status quo. His economic message boiled down to "If we don't act now, it'll cost us more to fix later." This kind of change appealed to Americans worried about how the huge budget deficit would harm the next generation. Clinton's opponent, George Bush, relied on a different and more dubious frame: *Let's build on past success.* The results of the election showed that voters were ready for change. The candidate who framed his message to best appeal to voters won.

MEMORY JOGGER

If your audience favors the status quo, try to sell your ideas as a continuance of past success. If they clamor for change, frame your message as a break with the past.

Frame 4: Think Big Other persuasive challenges do not involve problem solving; rather, they require motivating someone to reach further to attain a more ambitious goal. This is my favorite type of persuasion— prodding others to Think Big. Sales managers often remind their staff that *complacency is the enemy.* They persuade the group to sell, sell, sell, by describing growth opportunities (build your book of business), personal fulfillment (provide more for your family), ego gratification (who wants to be Number One this week?), financial security (double your sales and enlarge your nest egg), professional obligation (the customers need you), incentive rewards (who wants to qualify for the Hawaii trip?), and corporate objectives (we must triple production by 1997).

Yet framing messages to motivate others to set higher goals can backfire. A basic rule of persuasion is that the individual must feel some internal need to change. We fight back when someone tries to talk us into something that doesn't fill our immediate needs. Educational theorist John Dewey found that the best way to motivate students in the classroom is to introduce a tension and help them resolve it. Instead of having the teacher explain how the war started, students should examine *why* it started when prospects for peace appeared strong. Similarly, successful sports coaches let players decide for themselves what action is missing that prevents victory; the coach then encourages the team to commit to performing at a higher level. This works better than telling the players to improve their conditioning or play more aggressively. The well-coached team figures out for itself what's wrong and how to fix it with the help of a wise leader.

When you persuade someone who is already satisfied with the status quo, then you may want to introduce a healthy tension that spurs them to want *more* money, *more* victories, *more* physical well being—more of whatever they value dearly.

Frame 5: The Few, The Proud...   An alternative approach to persuade people to Think Big is to frame your message as a personal challenge. When you tell someone *It takes exceptional talent to succeed, Only a select few can do it* or *This is a test of your mettle,* then you may spark the kind of superior performance you seek. Coaches might prod their teams to play better by appealing to their pride as champions or asking them what price they are willing to pay to excel.

When I started my business, I read in a business magazine that only a handful of consulting enterprises made money in their first year of operation. That motivated me to set a goal of earning my way into the black within the first year. I still remember the day when I opened my mailbox and received two sizable checks from clients, rushed to the bank, and found that I was finally making a profit—eleven months after setting up shop.

Frame 6: You're the Kind of Person Who...   Some individuals can be swayed by an appeal to their sense of identity. You can frame your persuasive goal by reminding people how they view themselves and then presenting points that are consistent with their current values, behaviors, and interests. Examples:

- You've said you want to give back to your community. Here's a great way to do it.
- You've told me that you think of yourself as a leader, not a follower. Leaders pave the way for others to follow, and that's why I'm asking you to be the first to...
- You're always so excited about attending the school board meetings, and you've said how much you see yourself as an activist for change.

That's why I think you will be a great asset as a member of our planning council.

With this approach, you invite people to uphold or reinforce their positive sense of self by accommodating your request.

Frame 7: I Need Your Advice

Among the simplest, most effective ways to frame your suggestion is to *ask for advice, get your input,* or *bounce something off you.* Persuasion need not require complex negotiations or elaborate strategies. The direct appeal is often the best form of communication.

During the first year of my consulting work, I met with senior executives to solicit their feedback on my business plan. I found that framing my requests in blunt terms (*I need your help*) worked because they knew exactly what I wanted and appreciated my candor. You will find that most people are willing to provide assistance if you come right out and ask for it. Sure, some will say I'm too busy and hang up the phone, but there's always someone else to call. If, on the other hand, you tiptoe around your request and waste their time, they may grow restless and shoo you away.

Like a beautiful frame that complements a stunning painting, you can choose the design that enhances your persuasive idea. Whether you ask for help, appeal to someone's identity, or solve a problem, you are establishing the context within which you can persuade.

QUICK REVIEW

- Don't waste words. Speak clearly and repeat key points to hammer them home.
- Shower your listeners with attention. Use *you,* not *I.*
- Call others by their name. Just don't overdo it.
- Use glow words to engage the senses, stir mystery, and illuminate the topic.
- Speak in terms of crisp, relevant details that provide descriptive precision.
- Say what you see and allow your listeners to draw their own conclusions.
- Describe observable behavior. Lay off the inferences and judgments.
- Give your listeners a time, place, and activity to make your anecdotes come alive.

- Rather than express opinions, try describing the basis of your opinion.
- Don't tell people how to act: Let them figure out for themselves what's wrong and how to fix it.
- Choose a frame that provides the best context for your persuasive request.

NOTES

1. *CSAE Update,* April 1992, p. 10.
2. Quoted in *The Wall Street Journal,* 10-27-92, p. A16.
3. Miriam Arond and Samuel Pauker, *The First Year of Marriage,* Warner Books, New York, 1991.
4. *The New York Times* magazine, 12-12-93, p. 76.
5. Wallace C. Fotheringham, *Perspectives on Persuasion,* Allyn & Bacon, Inc., Boston, 1966, p. 69.
6. *Brown Alumni Monthly,* February 1994, p. 30.
7. *Worth,* February/March 1992, p. 76.

Ask, Don't Tell
Posing the Right Questions So That Others Persuade Themselves

It's not what you tell them that's important. It's what they hear.
—Red Auerbach

Most of us hate being told what to do. We resist when someone orders us around. Rebellion is not just a teenage rite of passage. Any of us, regardless of age, would probably fight any force that threatens to encroach on our free will. Even if we know we're wrong, we prefer the freedom of making our own decisions. It can be hard to simply roll over and do as told.

Almost every child reaches a moment in life when it becomes clear that Mom and Dad were right. This realization may not settle in for years, when chastened adults grudgingly admit that their parents actually knew what they were talking about. One reason so many children reject parental input is that Dad plays dictator and Mom plays enforcer. Only the most enlightened parents persuade by gentle questioning.

MEMORY JOGGER

Asking, not telling, is the surest way to sway opinion and produce the desired action.

Just as master persuaders "listen to learn", they also "speak to seek." Persuasive probing applies to almost any situation, from the bedroom to the boardroom to the courtroom. On the bench, for example, Supreme Court justices may ask a question not to learn the answer but to sway another justice's wavering vote. By posing questions rather than barking orders, persuaders invite others to participate in the decision-making process. The respondents take away more self-esteem and emotional "buy in" than if forced to play the role of order-taker.

You cannot persuade if you feel apathetic. Indifference kills a conversation. If you lack curiosity, then your speaking will suffer. Questioning will become a chore—an exercise in futility. The publisher of a financial newsletter told *The Wall Street Journal,* "We often have dinner with portfolio managers. The weak portfolio managers spend the whole dinner telling us what's going to happen. The best managers spend the meal asking questions." Curiosity pays off in more ways than one.[1]

The best way to enliven your communication skills is to stimulate an exchange of information, a snappy dialogue filled with interesting questions that lead to fascinating answers. It is hard to tire of a fluid debate or an honest sharing of opinions, where entrenched beliefs break free from their moorings and fresh ideas splash around like waves.

Back in the real world, however, such invigorating chats are rare indeed. Persuasion never stands a chance when speakers recite the same stale scripts or ask predictable questions with the charm of an android. In telemarketing, for example, the repetitious nature of cold calling can crush even the most resilient spirit. Turnover within the telemarketing ranks is high because only a handful of individuals can call hundreds of strangers, day after day, without letting the rejection drag them down.

I spent a summer during my college years making calls for an investment firm, figuring that talking on the phone could be no worse than waiting tables. My job was to generate leads for a team of stock brokers by plugging whatever "exciting investment opportunity" was the flavor of the day (*Would you be interested in discussing zero-coupon bonds with our broker, Tim Cash?*). The experience hardened me. It hurts to annoy people and hear them curse and hang up on you.

That's when I discovered the magic of asking the right question. Instead of mindlessly reading off the well-worn script that the brokers gave me, I started asking, *What do you look for in an investment adviser?* This got people talking. Some bragged that they did all their own investing (sometimes telling me a success story about how they bought a stock "at 7 and now it's at 43"), others confessed that their current broker (while a "good friend") charged high commissions. I found that the more they talked, the more they complained. As any effective salesperson knows, getting a prospect to complain is like hitting the jackpot. All you have to do is fill their needs by addressing their complaints, and you've earned a sale.

By asking questions, you can light a spark to ignite any interaction. You can turn a disinterested listener into a lively participant. Responding to questions gives people a chance to think, reveal their feelings, and reach their own conclusions.

LAY THE GROUNDWORK FOR PERSUASION BY INVITING INPUT

Individuals usually like to be asked for their opinions, and they grow closer to someone who appears sincerely interested in their responses. Asking questions is a great way to build rapport. When you invite people to discuss their ideas, you make them feel important. All of us like to think our views matter.

If you want to persuade someone, lay the groundwork by asking for input, feedback, or guidance. Listen intently to the answers, and extract key points. When they are finished giving you their advice, ask for more advice! You gain the twin benefits of learning from others *and* showing them that you are genuinely interested in what they have to say. When the time comes for you to persuade them, they will be more inclined to go along with you because you have already demonstrated that you value their insights.

In any customer-driven business, smart salespeople do not try to pitch their products until they ask potential buyers what they think. The best sales representatives listen for information and respond to anxieties that threaten to block the sale. As the head of a furniture company reports:

> It's the probing and listening approach, and it seems to be sorely lacking in American industry. Actually asking questions like, What kind of growth plans do you have?...What could the company be doing better?...What could we be doing differently to help you? We ask it that way, instead of asking, Are we doing well? or something where they could give a yes or no answer—and the answers we get are fascinating.[2]

Most customers appreciate the opportunity to share their insights about how a vendor can provide better service. It makes them feel as if they have a say in how the company operates. Perhaps this explains the spectacular growth of customer-satisfaction surveys, where companies write or phone buyers to follow up on a purchase. Just posing the right questions can send a message of caring and curiosity, a great mix if you want to pave the way for a stronger relationship.

A CUSTOMER SATISFACTION STUDY

Service companies that seek feedback on their performance must ask the right mix of questions to encourage customers to respond. A typical survey looks like this:

Please take a few minutes to answer the following questions. We value your opinion as much as your business. Thank you for helping us know how we are doing.

1. How satisfied were you with our customer service in each of these areas?

   Courtesy:

   Professionalism:

   Technical Ability:

   Responsiveness:

   Helpfulness:

2. Which one of the following statements best describes your feelings about the action taken by our company?

   _____ I was completely satisfied.

   _____ I was partially satisfied, and the action taken was acceptable.

   _____ I was not satisfied, but I did get at least some acceptable action.

   _____ I was not at all satisfied with the action taken.

   _____ I was not at all satisfied and no action was taken.

3. Would you refer your friends to our service?

4. How can we improve our service?

5. Do you have other comments?

There are right and wrong ways to ask for something. If a survey asks too many questions, it can be intimidating. A harried customer may choose to ignore a long or wordy questionnaire. If it looks as if it will take more than a few minutes to complete, many people will simply toss it in the trash.

Same goes for one-on-one communication. Badgering can backfire. Nagging can drive even the most patient person crazy. Intrusive questions risk violating people's privacy. Questions loaded with thinly disguised biases or negative phrasing can alienate a potential ally. When I asked my plumber why it took two hours to fix a simple faucet leak, he shot back *That's not fair* and began defending himself. I realized too late that he interpreted my question as an accusation: *Hey, you're overcharging me!* I should have asked instead, *What exactly did you do?*

● **TRAP** Do not invite someone's input unless you want to listen to the answer. There's nothing more frustrating than taking the time to answer a question in an honest, thoughtful manner, only to find the questioner visibly distracted instead of listening. "It's like I'm wasting my time," said a mother of three who felt ignored. "Someone asks me a question. I answer it. Then I look up and they're turning the television on or scratching lottery cards or something. It's rude."

How to Question a Shy Person

People often ask me how they can solicit input from someone with a bashful personality. Shy, quiet types tend to answer questions with the fewest words possible. They would rather sit back and let others do the talking. (At least they have no trouble harnessing the power of silence, because they *prefer* to stay silent!)

If you want to persuade someone who does not enjoy speaking, then you must first learn to love silence. Review Chapter 9 and train yourself to welcome long pauses in the conversation. Do not feel obliged to jump in when you do not receive a prompt answer to your question. Remember to apply The Stop Rule, and stop after you pose your question.

○ **NOW TRY THIS** Here's an exercise to help you draw out a quiet individual. Ask for input with the same words that the other person uses. This lets you phrase your inquiry in a way that makes the respondent feel comfortable. It also prompts the speaker to continue. A therapist might use this technique with a patient:

> *Patient:* I feel like I'm falling into a hole, a big black hole.
> *Doctor:* You feel like you're falling into a hole?

This approach also works in everyday conversation, especially with a shy person. Repeat a speaker's phrase in the form of a question. This will keep the person talking so that you can learn even more.

Give others a chance to speak at their pace, on their terms. When you ask for input or guidance, some respondents take their time and select their words carefully. After all, they do not want to steer you wrong. They may want to mentally rehearse what they are about to say or predict how you might react to their advice. Let them take their time, and don't interrupt.

How to Question a Repetitive Speaker

If you grow antsy listening to a repetitive speaker, develop questions that help you propel a conversation forward. The specific question will depend on the situation, but you can prepare a range of possible inquiries that encourage the speaker to move on. Examples:

How does this relate to the issue at hand?

What needs to happen for us to move ahead?

What's your desired outcome?

What do you want me to do?

Weave these types of questions into your discussions with repetitive talkers. With practice, you will soon find yourself naturally incorporating them into your conversations as a way to direct the focus, gather facts, and save time while developing rapport.

When you pose questions that encourage a speaker to elaborate, you allow the other person to drive the dialogue. We are more likely to be swayed by someone who does not insist on controlling the conversation. Someone who asks questions and awaits our answers earns our trust. This is particularly true in physician-patient encounters. As *The New York Times* reported, "The physician who typified the good interview repeatedly asked questions that directly referred to what the patient had just said, a questioning style that researchers said invited a response, rather than demanded an answer, and gave the patient a sense of some control over what they would be talking about."[3]

● **TRAP** Do not expect someone to give you substantive answers to your questions after just meeting you. Asking for input works only after you establish some rapport. Beware of trying to ask for too much, too soon, especially on the phone. Never ask for input or feedback during the initial moments of a call (unless your sole purpose is to gather information for a survey). Instead, introduce yourself and launch a friendly conversation. Don't interrogate someone you barely know.

Finding the Right Person to Ask

When you invite input, find the best person to answer your question. The ideal respondent has the ability, expertise, or experience to help you. This underscores one of the many benefits of mentors and role models—they are in a great position to provide meaty answers to our questions with our best interests in mind.

If you question the wrong person, then you may not receive accurate feedback and you will reduce your chances of persuading that person later. For example, let's say you want to talk several neighbors into sharing the cost of replacing the fence that runs along the back of your properties. You begin by posing questions to your neighbors about the current situation (*What do you think we should do about a fence? Do you have any plans to build a fence around your home?*). They tell you how much they would like to have a new fence, but each one has a different opinion of the kind of wood or the color that should be used. It soon becomes clear that the neighbors cannot agree on what to do.

Try a different approach. Ask an objective outsider, a recognized expert, to recommend a fence. Let's say that you and your neighbors use the same real estate agent who is widely regarded as a knowledgeable professional. You ask her to suggest what kind of fence would look best and boost property values. Her input helps everyone reach a consensus.

You will waste time if you ask questions of people who are ill-equipped to answer. A talkative rambler may use your question as a springboard to dive into an entirely different topic. A philosopher may prefer to challenge you with more questions rather than dish out easy answers.

The search for the right person to ask can take a while. Have you heard the joke about the boy who wanted to know the sum of one plus one? First he asked a biologist, who said, "Are we talking bacteria, mice, or whales?" Then he asked a physicist, who said, "Are we talking matter or antimatter?" Finally, the boy hired an accountant, who said, "One plus one...tell me, how much do you want it to be?"

THE OPEN-CLOSE BALANCING ACT: WEAVING DIFFERENT TYPES OF QUESTIONS TOGETHER TO PERSUADE

Questions can be neutral, leading, skeptical, fact finding, insistent, or just plain friendly. To win over others, you need to select the best type of questions for your particular audience.

Watch any Senate confirmation hearing for a lesson in how to ask (and not ask) questions. A nominee for a Cabinet post sits at a long table as senators, seated regally on an elevated platform, ask away. Senators who support the nominee lob softballs and let the respondent hit home runs (*You have a wonderful record on civil rights: Among your many accomplishments, could you pick a few triumphs that you are most proud of?*). Adversaries ask piercing questions that expose apparent inconsistencies (*You have praised the role of greed in the marketplace: Can you explain how you reconcile your love of greed with altruism?*). Yet the majority of senators resort to self-serving speechifying, attaching an obligatory question simply for show. The most revealing answers stem from questions that both clearly frame a topic while providing the nominee with enough wiggle room to craft a thoughtful response.

Like an inquisitive senator, an effective persuader fosters a healthy dialogue by asking open questions that invite free-flowing answers. *Open* questions encourage the respondent to express ideas or opinions, while *closed* questions require a yes, a no, or a specific piece of information. Examples:

Open: What did you think of the movie?
Closed: Were you bored by the movie?

Open: How does it feel to have another birthday coming up?
Closed: How old are you?

Open: How do you set your financial goals?
Closed: Are you satisfied with your financial goals?

Open: What do you do when you are faced with a tough decision?
Closed: Can you make decisions quickly?

Open and Closed Questions

An OPEN Question:

- Invites the respondent to express feelings
- Allows for longer and more revealing answers
- Asks for subjective responses
- Opens up a subject under discussion to new areas
- Usually starts with *how, what* or *why*

A CLOSED Question:

- Requests specific information or facts
- Seeks out "needed" data
- Asks for objective responses
- Involves short answers such as yes, no
- Usually starts with *when, do, where,* or *who*

Both types of questions play a vital role in persuasion. As people open up to you, their thoughts and feelings add color to the canvas of the conversation. You can learn why they think a certain way, how they arrive at a conclusion, or to what extent they are willing to reassess a decision. You can gain insight into their likes and dislikes, hopes and dreams, fears and defeats—all by asking the right question.

My favorite open questions:

What's the view like from your window? (great for a long-distance phone call)

What do you expect you'll be doing twenty-four hours from now? (good to ask on Friday to learn how someone spends the weekend)

How does this month compare to last month? (This works both on personal terms [I'm doing much better.] and professional terms [Business is booming.].)

The selective use of such questions offers a great way to establish a connection before you try to persuade. As people share details with you, you are in a better position to understand their moods and behaviors in both business and social situations. For instance, a speaker who talks about the beautiful old oak tree outside her window finds this image appealing, so you may wish to recall this type of natural image when you persuade her.

How Smart Salespeople Mix Open and Closed Questions

Knowing which kind of question to ask is particularly important for salespeople. *Are you off to a good start today?* works well when checking in with clients. Someone who reports that the day is off to a rousing, productive start may be riding a wave of good cheer. The answer gives an immediate indication of whether this is a good time to mention a new product, request referrals, or otherwise ask for something. *What do you usually do in the morning before going to work?* is a great way to learn details about some-one's daily routine. A salesperson can contrast the sameness of entrenched habits with the benefits of positive change.

Let's say a financial planner pitches her services to a wealthy prospect. Her first goal is to build rapport by encouraging the prospect to do most of the talking. This approach also gives her a chance to assess the prospect's needs and explain how her services can fill those needs. She asks such open questions as:

> *How satisfied are you with your existing financial goals?*
>
> *What would you change, if you could, about your situation?*
>
> *What are your feelings about taking financial risks?*

Note the difference if she were to ask closed questions instead of open ones:

> *Are you satisfied with your existing financial goals?*
>
> *Are you happy with your situation?*
>
> *Do you have a high tolerance for taking financial risks?*

If you want to persuade someone, asking *What would you like to change about your situation?* is better than *What do you like least about your situation?* Allow others to define the parameters of the conversation. Let them interpret your question as they wish. The more comfortable they are answering your question, the more they will tell you.

Using Open Questions to Get Others to Reveal Themselves

The best kind of open questions make a respondent stop and think. During the 1992 presidential debates, a young woman asked President Bush how the deficit affected him personally. Taken aback, Bush rejected the intro-spective nature of the question and recited a canned response about his plan to improve the economy. In an electrifying moment, the questioner interrupted the president to repeat her question, "How has it affected YOU?" Bush, exasperated and confused, feebly answered that he could identify with the less monied classes in the same way a healthy person could feel for a cancer victim. Bush's you-don't-have-to-have-cancer-to-care argument did not win over many voters.

Prospective jurors during the federal trial of four Los Angeles police officers accused of violating Rodney King's civil rights faced a battery of questions intended to gauge their views on race relations and law enforcement. As reported in *The Los Angeles Times,* lawyers for both sides asked such open questions as:

> *What was your personal reaction to the verdicts in the state court trial?*
>
> *What do you feel caused the civil unrest and riots that occurred in Los Angeles in April and May of 1992?*
>
> *How serious a problem do you think racial discrimination against blacks is in Southern California?*

Along with these concerns, the lawyers asked such closed questions as:

> *Did you, or any friend or relative, participate in the civil unrest?*
>
> *Do you fear the prospect of social unrest following a verdict in this case?*
>
> *Do you believe police officers make mistakes in the performance of their duties?*

By mixing open and closed questions, the defense lawyers and prosecutors sought to find twelve people who seemed fair and impartial. As one of the lawyers told the *Times,* "Some of those are unusual questions, but they are designed to elicit responses, and we're going to look carefully at how people answer."[4]

How do you feel about that? is the most generic open question. Journalists, physicians, therapists, and just about everyone else can fall back on this all-purpose inquiry. While overused, it almost always gets people talking.

MEMORY JOGGER

Ask open questions to encourage others to talk, and then use closed questions to gather facts or establish agreement.

○ **NOW TRY THIS** Well-phrased open questions almost always make you look smart. Really. Just asking, *What if...?* or *Why do we continue to...?* can persuade others that you are a visionary—a creative, conceptual thinker who does not think in terms of narrow boundaries. Draft a list of three *what if* questions that you could ask someone, from a boss to a friend. Think big. You will not only enhance your credibility and persuasive power, but you may also help someone see things a new way.

Closed questions are restrictive rather than expansive, thus giving the respondent little space to wander from the topic. In law school exams, for example, professors warn students to address "the call of the question." A typical essay question will present a thicket of facts with a question attached at the end: *What evidence would the defense attorney favor most/least? Should the defendant file a claim? Under a California jurisdiction, how would the court proceed?* If the test question asks how a judge would rule on a set of facts, then the entire response should be delivered from the judge's point of view. Answers that fall outside the scope of the question receive no credit.

○   **Now Try This**   Having trouble getting a conversation started? Looking for some dependable open questions? Remember that persuasion begins with fact gathering. A successful insurance agent, Art, once taught me how to collect information in a way that made selling easy. He would ask potential customers two questions:

What do you like most about the policy you already have?

What do you want in terms of costs, coverages, or service that you don't have?

By asking these "have-want" questions, Art learned how to top the competition. How? The first question puts prospects in an upbeat frame of mind by encouraging them to discuss what they like. The next question lets them identify any unmet needs, thus saving Art from having to guess his way toward a sale. You can apply the 1–2 punch of have-want questions to almost any topic. Examples:

What do you like most about the job you have now? What would you want in a job that you don't currently have?

What do you like most about the stereo system you have now? What would you want in a sound system that you don't currently have?

The Job Interview: Interrogating Candidates with Open Questions

Open questions work particularly well in interviewing job applicants. Most recruiters find that such questions yield more information and allow them to better assess candidates' skills and attitudes. If you interview people, you may want to use some of these questions (and if you're job-hunting, rehearse your answers in case these questions arise):

What does it take for you to perform your best work?

How would you describe your last job?

What approach do you take to working on a team project?

What strategies do you use to manage your time?

How do you feel about advancement?

How would you describe the ideal job for you?

How has your past experience prepared you for this position?

What are three examples of problems you've faced on the job before, and how did you handle them?

Compare the narrower scope of these closed questions to the preceding ones:

Can you perform your best work even when you have to do three things at once?

Would you describe your last job as a success?

Do you work well when assigned to a team project?

Are you good at managing your time?

Would you consider yourself ambitious?

Have you ever thought about what would be the ideal job for you?

Do you feel your past job has prepared you for this position?

Have you had problems with your prior job(s)?

Beware of asking closed questions that hint at the answer you seek. For instance, *Do you enjoy handling three things at once?* implies that the job involves multiple assignments. *Do you like to be on the road?* implies that the position requires travel. When you ask a closed question, make sure your wording remains neutral so that you do not reveal the answer you prefer to hear.

Let's switch roles. Say you are the candidate trying to impress the interviewer. Most recruiters will end the formal part of the interview by

inviting you to ask questions. Prepare some closed questions that demonstrate your knowledge of the company. Examples:

Are you on schedule with the new product roll-out?

Does the company expect to match last year's profits?

Did the company settle that lawsuit I read about last month?

These types of specific questions show that you have taken the time
to research the firm. If you ask open questions, on the other hand, an interviewer may not want to answer. Stick to safe, fact-based questions and
learn what you can about the company.

GAINING COMPLIANCE WITH QUESTIONS

Most of us will happily answer nonthreatening questions about ourselves.
That's why you are almost always on safer ground trying to persuade with
questions rather than with statements.

Statements, especially negative ones, rarely sway people. Lecturing,
accusing, or attacking can poison a message and polarize those you wish
to win over. When tempted to let your mouth run, remind yourself of the
ugly consequences (namely, the permanent repercussions of antagonizing
or boring someone). Then rein yourself in and rely on the dependable art
of asking.

Questions serve as magnets that attract the other person's attention.
They work wonders in helping us gain compliance. The skillful use of
questions can sway even the most stubborn people to act on our suggestions or respect our wishes.

When someone asks you a direct question, you must come up with
some kind of answer. Even if you choose to stall, evade, or ignore the
question, your mind must grapple with the issue before you decide how to
respond. There is no way to escape. On the other hand, if someone bab-
bles endlessly, you can get away without listening to a word.

MEMORY JOGGER

You can ignore statements, but it is much harder to tune out a
question. Why? Someone is sitting there waiting for you to
respond.

If you want to ensure compliance, get people in the habit of saying "yes." Establish a rhythm of asking questions that the other party is likely to answer affirmatively. If respondents agree over small points early in the discussion, then they will be more likely to keep bobbing their heads up and down when you ask for a larger commitment later. This is called the "foot in the door" factor.

As early as 1930, in their book *Strategy in Handling People*, E. T. Webb and J.J.B. Morgan wrote, "The first step in persuading people to act as you wish, is to present your plans in such a way as to get a 'Yes Response' at the very start. Throughout your interview, but above all at the beginning of it, try to get as many 'Yesses' as you possibly can."[5]

Dale Carnegie reinforced this point six years later in *How To Win Friends and Influence People*. "Get the other person saying 'yes, yes'," he wrote.[6]

As you try to keep them saying "yes," listen with special care to their reservations and objections. Give them room to roam. Home in on your persuasive goal by gradually narrowing the focus of your questions so that you subtly lead the respondent closer and closer to the core issue. Look for each incremental "yes" as another step toward gaining compliance or agreement.

○ **Now Try This** Here's a wonderful way to persuade with questions. First, you need to understand the difference between *conditional* and *disturbing* questions. Like a closed question, a conditional inquiry seeks specific information or quantifiable data. Examples include:

How much money did you make last month?

What are your major financial assets?

How long have you been aware of this?

Disturbing questions are open-ended and elicit feelings, thoughts, reflections, or anxieties.
Examples include:

Are you happy with that?

How concerned are you with protecting your assets?

How long will you let it continue?

Tie a disturbing question to a conditional question to gain compliance. Ask the conditional question first, followed by the disturbing one.

Consider Ron, a sales manager, with a persuasive goal of motivating Bob, one of his agents, to increase production. Ron asks, "How many sales did you make last month?" Bob looks dejected and mumbles, "Not many. About seven."

Ron follows up with a disturbing question, "Are you happy with your production?"

Bob starts to chastise himself and offer excuses.

Undaunted, Ron asks another disturbing question, "What would happen if you continued at the rate of seven sales every month?"

Through gentle but persistent questions, Ron allows Bob to evaluate his own performance and talk himself into doing a better job.

MEMORY JOGGER

When you want to persuade, use questions to gather facts. Follow up by asking others how they feel about those facts. Then sit back and let them persuade themselves.

You can also use questions to test the waters to check how you're doing. Salespeople trying to close a deal will pepper their presentation with questions such as, *Have we addressed that point? Are we ready to sign the papers? Aside from the price concern that we've discussed, is there anything else preventing us from moving forward?* The key is not to oversell. Questions serve as handy reminders so that we do not ramble on too long.

TAMING YOUR TEMPER WITH QUESTIONS

You may recall Ozzie and Harriet cautioning the kids, "If you don't have something nice to say, don't say it." Easy to say, tough to do. Our personalities do not come packed with 100 percent sweetness and light. Almost everyone stores away a shameful memory of hurling insults in an uncontrollable rage. When emotional runaway takes over, there's no stopping it, and we might regret what we say later.

Questions can save the day. Even if you don't have anything nice to say, you can rephrase statements as questions to soften the blow. *I'm really getting tired of your whining* becomes *What's all this you're talking about?* Similarly, *You're just lying again* becomes *Why should I believe you?* and *You've got a lot of nerve saying those things to me after all I've done for you* becomes *After all I've done for you, how can you say those things?*

These types of questions, while hot to handle, are far less inflammatory than declarative statements. Long-standing relationships can be severed with just one nasty word or hurtful phrase. When you lash out with verbal attacks instead of asking questions, you do so at your own risk.

A father in his mid-sixties told me he went five years without talking to his only son. "It started with a phone call. One day he called me out of the blue to say he was leaving his corporate job to try sales," he said. "I yelled at him, 'You'll never make it as a salesman.' I knew how much it hurt him to hear his father say that." Reflecting on the pain that one statement caused him, the father confessed to me with tears in his eyes that he wished he had simply asked his son why he chose sales.

○ **NOW TRY THIS** Questions persuade most effectively when you look for an affirmative response. By opening your question with *when,* you signal to the respondent that you fully expect your action to be enacted. The only uncertainty is *when* your request will be met. Many questioners undermine their persuasiveness by needlessly asking *if* the respondent will act as requested. "Iffy" statements sound wimpy. While setting up my consulting business in New York, much of my time was spent asking executives and politicians to meet with me. At first I would say, "If it's at all possible, I'd like to arrange a time to meet with you." Their response was lukewarm. Then I tried, "When would you like to meet?" and filled my appointment book.

No matter how optimistic your questions may sound, they may not be greeted with satisfactory answers. Don't get upset if that happens. Swim with the current of the conversation. An evasive respondent may prefer to address another subject. A preoccupied worrier may need to express some fears or misgivings about something said earlier. A well-intentioned person may simply misunderstand or have trouble hearing you and respond to the wrong question. No problem. Sometimes you can learn all kinds of things from these "mistaken" answers.

ASK AWAY! DON'T BE BASHFUL ABOUT QUESTIONS

During my high school years, I worked part time at a doctors' office. Despite the fact that my employers—four warm, friendly internists—had likable, down-to-earth personalities, some of the patients were embarrassed to ask questions. They would ask *me* their medical questions on their way out, and I was a lowly file clerk! I encouraged them to ask their doctor, but they would say *Oh, it's such a silly question* or *He's so busy, it doesn't matter.*

If you take away just one point from this chapter, remember to ASK AWAY. Do not stop yourself from asking what you want or need to know. Sure, the answers may annoy or upset you. So what? At least you will learn.

Lovers of safety, security, and the status quo may lack the will to "speak to seek." They settle for whatever comes to them. They prefer to operate on autopilot, reacting to the world around them rather than charting an independent path.

Almost everyone feels nervous when asking for something. Few salespeople enjoy watching a door slam in their face or feeling their pride shrivel up like a prune. Few employees enjoy asking their boss for more money. Few political candidates, even haughty incumbents, enjoy the humiliation of having to grovel for campaign contributions from wealthy supporters.

Nervous persuaders may not realize that with each rejection they grow stronger and more resilient. Asking for something and not getting it is the ultimate learning experience. There are hundreds of stories of persistent persuaders who "ask until"—they learn from each failure and keep on plugging. From Edison and the invention of the light bulb to Colonel Sanders and his travails trying to pitch his fried chicken recipe, visionaries have faced years of setbacks before they achieved their goals. They asked lots of questions, heard "no" far more often than "yes," and finally prevailed.

Prepare yourself for anything. Some people will not give answers like *yes, no,* or *maybe,* preferring to toss in qualifiers, tangential data, and irrelevant commentary. Listen with patience, and the rewards will come.

Accept the fact that you will not always get the kind of clear answers you seek. You may hear offensive, upsetting, or shocking responses to your seemingly innocent questions. Do not let fear or intimidation stop you from asking. I have met many people who refrain from questioning because they do not want to appear rude or nosy. They may also worry that the intent of their questions will be misinterpreted. A lobbyist told me she was uncomfortable asking for so many favors on the job until she received some advice from a legislator: People in the Capitol expect you to ask for something, and they may think it odd if you don't.

FINISHING WHAT YOU START:
MAKE YOUR INQUIRIES CLEAR AND BRIEF

You are now ready to ask more questions to increase your influence skills. Great. Just one more thing: Keep those questions brief and simple. Finish what you start.

From my experience teaching communication skills, I have observed that many people have trouble asking concise questions. They tend to ask away without stopping when they reach the question mark at the end of their sentence. They may string three or four questions together or rephrase the same question five different ways before anyone has a chance to answer. If you've ever been on the receiving end of a never-ending question, you know how aggravating it can be to sit there and not get a chance to respond.

A confident communicator comes right out and asks for something without hesitancy. There are no abrupt mid-sentence corrections and no stop-and-start sputterings that test a listener's patience. Perfectionists who hold themselves to unrealistically high standards of precise expression may launch a question several times until they approve of the wording. This wastes time and tends to irritate the respondent.

The irony of all this dilly-dallying is that most listeners immediately comprehend the gist of the question. While speakers repeat themselves and try to communicate with the utmost clarity, the respondents are nodding endlessly and thinking, "Enough already—let me answer." They are all set to jump in, but they do not get a chance because the questioner can't seem to shut up or even stop for a breath.

MEMORY JOGGER

Limit your questions to one sentence.

Watch any presidential press conference, and you will see how long it takes some people to ask a question. The President of the United States will call on a journalist, who will drone on for at least a minute or two. Instead of asking a simple, compelling question, the reporter might opt for an elaborate hypothetical. Almost always, the Commander in Chief will silently wait his turn and then say, "I prefer not to respond to hypotheticals. Next question." I bet our political leaders love these convoluted "questions," because the more journalists babble, the less time remains for presidential gaffes.

Some reporters insist on asking layers of questions. They pile a hypothetical on top of two or three fact-finding questions. They connect the dots like this:

> Mr. President, if your answer is "yes" to my first question, then how do you explain the inconsistencies with the panel's report? And how about the members of the panel? Were they impartial? And if your answer is "no," how do you justify all the taxpayer money spent on this commission? The cost has been estimated at $7 million. Would you have done it differently now that the panel's findings have been announced? And I'd like a follow-up, if I may.

No wonder presidents grow weary of the White House press. It takes supreme concentration merely to remember all the questions that are asked at once, much less prepare level-headed responses to each part.

● **TRAP**   Do you censor your remarks while you are making them? Avoid editing what you are trying to ask people. Never "start over" once you begin posing a question. Spit it out and be quiet. If you are unhappy with the way it sounds, you will probably have a chance to ask again later. Do not continually chop away at what you're trying to say or you will stretch the patience of your listeners and receive less complete, forthright answers.

Think about the last time you were asked a long-winded question. You were probably ready to answer it well before the questioner stopped to let you respond. Most of us do not like multilayered questions that go on far too long. We remember simple questions and find it easier to answer them.

HOW TO ANSWER A QUESTION TO REINFORCE YOUR PERSUASIVENESS

What happens when you are the one answering, not asking, the questions? How do you stay out of trouble? Questioners usually do the persuading by driving a conversation and framing the debate. Respondents can try to advance their own position, but they are constrained by the need to address incoming inquiries. You may think it is tough to persuade when you are busy fending off a series of tough questions.

Whenever you find yourself under interrogation, whether at a police station, on *60 Minutes,* or in the comfort of your own home, remember that you hold some aces yourself. The questioner needs an answer from you, so you possess something of value. You may have knowledge or insight that cannot be found elsewhere. You are under no obligation to provide instant answers. Even in a court of law or a statement under oath, your role when answering questions is simply to tell the truth. (And any lawyer or politician can attest to the various shadings of truth that fall somewhere between full disclosure and outright lies.)

So does this mean you should fib? Absolutely not. Just don't rush to reveal everything you know. As they say around the poker table, keep your cards close to your vest.

The first sentence out of your mouth need not answer the question, but it should indicate that you heard the question. Acknowledge what you understand to be the issue at hand. Repeat the question if necessary. Say,

"Let me make sure I understand your question..." or "Can you run that by me again?" This tactic can also help buy time when you need to choose your words carefully.

● **TRAP** The worst mistake a respondent can make (aside from lying) is not to acknowledge a question. People hate having their questions brushed aside. It makes them feel invisible. Resentment sets in. I recall attending my first homeowners association meeting, where some of my fellow residents asked questions about landscaping or architectural controls. A board member would babble about some irrelevant point as if his mind were housed somewhere on Mars, totally ignoring the homeowners' questions. The sad part is that the questions hardly seemed controversial or tough to answer, but by failing to respond, the board needlessly alienated its constituents. As I walked out of the meeting, my neighbors concluded that "the board must be hiding something from us."

Never let a question pass by without acknowledging it. Successful politicians understand the power of affirming their audiences by respecting their questions. During the 1992 presidential campaign, Bill Clinton responded to open questions with the kind of persuasive flair that swayed millions of voters. He routinely used stock phrases such as:

I'm glad you asked me that.

I've asked myself that very question for years.

That's a good question.

The best way to answer your question is to...

In most cases, he looked the questioner right in the eyes and sounded sincere. Clinton proceeded to rephrase the question to fit his preferred mode of communication: reciting policy positions to reinforce his key campaign themes.

There are other ways to acknowledge questions. You will find these sample responses helpful not only in showing the questioner that you intend to address the issue, but also in buying extra time to mentally plan what you want to say:

That's the first time anyone has asked me that question.

That's tough to answer, but let me give it a try.

I appreciate your question. I'm sure many others wonder the same thing.

Thank you for asking that question.

The quick answer is "yes," but there's more to it.

Another approach is to ask a question right back:

What makes you ask that?

What do you think?

What kind of answer are you looking for?

Warning: Greeting questions with questions can be risky. People want answers. They may suspect that you have something to hide if you deflect their questions. Yet some teachers, salespeople, and senior managers successfully use this technique to persuade people to do their own thinking, to grapple with difficult issues by tackling their own questions.

If you discuss a controversial or emotionally sensitive topic, expect heated questions that come dripping with sarcasm or disagreement. Do not repeat a loaded question. You should not accept questions that come packaged as thinly disguised opinions. Examples:

So it's okay with you if sinners brutally murder?

After bringing so much shame to your country, how can you call yourself a patriot?

Rephrase such questions in neutral terms and then answer as you wish:

Is it okay to conduct abortions? My feeling is...

How can I call myself a patriot? I proudly call myself a patriot because...

Do not inflame matters by growing testy or defensive in the face of an insulting question. Win over your audience by staying cool and restating unfair questions before you attempt to respond.

TIPS AND TECHNIQUES FOR ASKING THE MOST PENETRATING QUESTIONS

The best persuaders can talk us into almost anything because they follow some basic rules when they ask for something. As you apply these rules, keep your eyes on the ultimate prize: your persuasive goal. Well-phrased and properly timed questions are the stepping stones to help you get there.

Here's a checklist of tools to help you ask effective questions:

Be Specific   Ask precise questions that clearly identify what you want. Think like an investigative reporter who poses *who, what, when, where, how,* and *why* inquiries. Vague questions produce vague answers. When Barbara Walters interviewed the mother of Martin Luther King, Jr., she did not ask, *What's your famous son really like?* but *What qualities did you most want to instill in your children?* [7]

Follow Up   Demonstrate what so many effective persuaders do so well: following up after a speaker completes a thought. When someone shares a fond anecdote or proudly boasts of an accomplishment, ask a follow-up question. When people are on a roll, prolong their pleasure—invite them to elaborate. As long as you have a sincere interest in hearing more, then ask for more!

Exploratory Questions   These types of questions can help you build rapport and persuade. Pick a person whom you want to win over. The next time you see this person, casually weave a question into the conversation that begins:

When was the last time you...

What do you look for...

Is it possible...

If you intend to eventually see your manager about a pay raise, ask, "What do you look for when you approve a pay increase?" If you are thinking of asking friends for a donation to your favorite charity, pose this question first, "When was the last time you felt really good about spending money on something special?" Exploratory questions provide valuable information that will help you persuade later, as well as demonstrating your genuine interest in the other person. Sending nonthreatening "feelers" helps you build a foundation for successful persuasion.

What and Why   *What* and *why* work together. Ask *What* questions to build rapport or gather facts. They also help you come across as curious, bright, and a stimulating conversationalist. People like to dispense knowledge. By asking these questions, you legitimize what they know by showing that their insights and opinions matter to you. Follow up with a

why question. Asking *why* produces analysis, discussion, and persuasion
Move from *what* to *why* questions, and you will win people over.

Be Patient   Have you noticed that people rarely ask concise questions? They usually toss in their own opinions or simply babble an extra
few minutes, taking their own sweet time before getting to the question. If
you listen to any radio talk show long enough, you will undoubtedly hear
the host interrupt a talkative caller to ask, "Do you have a question for our
guest?" Show patience when someone takes what seems like an eternity to
let you respond. Avoid excessive nods, smiles, or frowns while you wait
for the questioner to let you answer. Others may read approval or disapproval in your facial expression and assume they know what you think
before you utter a word in response. If time (or patience) runs short, let the
questioner know you are ready to answer by calmly holding up your hand
in a gesture of acknowledgment and understanding.

QUICK REVIEW

- Speak to seek. Invite others to participate in the decision-making
  process.
- Persuade someone by first asking for input, feedback, or guidance.
- When you ask a question, allow others to respond at their pace, on
  their terms.
- Combine open and closed questions to build rapport and sway opin-
  ion.
- Rely on questions, not accusatory statements, when emotional run-
  away strikes.
- Start your questions on an optimistic note with *when,* not *if.*
- Use the incremental "yes" technique to get respondents in the habit
  of saying "yes."
- Ask away. Do not let fear stop you from asking what you want or
  need to know.
- Tie a disturbing question to a conditional question to gain compli-
  ance.
- Keep your questions brief and simple.
- When someone asks you a question, acknowledge it and then answer
  it.

NOTES

1. *The Wall Street Journal,* 12-21-92, p. C2.
2. *Inc.,* March 1992, p. 47.
3. *The New York Times,* 1-21-88, p. B10.
4. *The Los Angeles Times,* 2-4-93, p. A18.
5. Quoted in Giles Kemp and Edward Claflin, *Dale Carnegie: The Man Who Influenced Millions,* St. Martin's Press, New York, 1989, p. 177.
6. Ibid.
7. John Brady, *The Craft of Interviewing,* Vintage Books, New York, 1976, p. 60.

CHAPTER 13

Perfecting the Persuasive Voice So That You Sound Too Good to Resist

A raspy, hoarse, shrill, thin, breathy, throaty, loud or weak voice can misrepresent you.—The Wall Street Journal [1]

When most of us listen, we pick and choose what's most important and discard the rest. Persuasive speakers know this. They try to highlight prominent points and make sure we hear what they want us to hear. They accomplish this not only by plugging in power phrases and asking the right kind of questions, but also by using a tool that is often overlooked: the voice.

Among the three elements that contribute to any message—content, nonverbal cues, and voice—which do you think counts the most toward ensuring that an audience comprehends what's said? If you guessed content, guess again. Nonverbal cues and voice influence interpersonal communication far more than words.

Diagnostic Self-Test:
Does Your Voice Work For or Against You?

Answer the following questions to get a sense of how your voice contributes to your persuasive communication skills.

1. _____ When you deliver a presentation to an audience of five or more people, do you find that someone inevitably asks you to "speak up"?

2. _____ In one-on-one conversation, do you find that others have trouble hearing you or that they frequently ask you to repeat what you just said?

3. _____ When you want something badly, does your voice change (i.e., take on a higher pitch or whine)?

4. _____ Do you prefer to speak at roughly the same tone of voice all the time, regardless of your emotions (i.e., do you tend to avoid RAISING or lowering your voice)?

5. _____ Do others tell you to "speak slower" or "slow down" frequently?

6. _____ Do you find that when conversing in a group, others talk over you or interrupt you?

7. _____ Do you have a habit of clearing your throat or coughing as you prepare to speak?

8. _____ When you give a big speech, does your voice sound shaky to you? Do you fear that you are about to lose your voice?

If you answered "yes" to any of these questions, your voice may not be working for you as well as it could. Questions 1–2 may indicate that your voice volume needs to improve. Questions 3–4 involve tone. Question 5 relates to tempo. Questions 6–8 describe common situations where, in order to sound our persuasive best, we must ensure that our voice is ready to do its job. Read on to gain the tools to bring your voice to life all the time.

Voice Drills: Do They Work?

As a member of my high school debate squad, I studied how the voice works. My teammates and I participated in what at first struck me as silly vocal exercises. In one memorable enunciation drill, my forensics coach asked the class to recite this sentence ten times:

Mumbo Jumbo, God of the Jungle, will voodoo you.

To stand side by side with twenty hot-shot debaters from Beverly Hills High School repeating Mumbo Jumbo is an experience that one never forgets.

Fast forward a few years, and I was teaching communication skills seminars while attending college. At first, I downplayed the voice and focused on the less identifiable but critical role of confidence. Psychology seemed to influence how my participants came across much more than the physiology of their voice.

It soon became clear to me, however, that much of their confidence was directly tied to how they felt about their voice. Because so few individuals were happy with the sound of their voice, they lost confidence whenever they tried to win over an audience. As a result, an hour of vocal drills hardly seemed to matter. I would hear comments such as these:

I speak in a monotone. Always have, always will.

I'm stuck with a lousy voice. I sound wimpy when I want to sound commanding. I get hoarse all the time, and people have trouble hearing me.

Voice exercises might make me enunciate better, but I still hate my accent. I mean, it makes me sound so unpleasant. Pronouncing words is the least of my problems!

Today, I have concluded that voice exercises work to a limited degree for anyone who has the discipline and will to diligently follow them each day for many months at a time. Yet even if you do not want to commit to months of daily drills, you can develop a more persuasive voice by expanding your vocal range. That means sampling a different tone, volume, pitch, and speed. Experiment with the rich diversity of your voice. Do not dismiss your voice as "bad." Play around with it and you will find it can do much more than you may realize to enhance your persuasive power.

LEARNING TO LIKE THE SOUND OF YOUR VOICE

Let me guess: You do not like the sound of your voice. You cannot bear to listen to a recording of yourself. You dread the thought that every time you open your mouth, people hear that nasal, gravelly, or otherwise unacceptable vocal whine. You are convinced that your accent is terrible and your articulation is awful. You worry that you speak too loudly, too softly, or too harshly.

The vast majority of people dislike the sound of their own voice. In almost every workshop, a handful of participants corner me at the break and insist that their voices need "plenty of work" or "a complete overhaul." One woman said she felt so ashamed of her voice that she was reluctant to speak up at work. (She sounded just fine, by the way.)

Time for some perspective. Yes, your voice influences how your listeners react to what you say. Yes, listeners may notice if your voice does not accurately reflect the thoughts or feelings you express. No, your voice is not as bad as you think.

You may view your voice as detached from the rest of your personality. When you hear yourself on tape, you might say to yourself, *I don't talk like that; Where did that voice come from? Why do I sound so horrible?*

Your voice sounds so different on tape because it is different. You are hearing it on tape through your ears, not your head bones. It does not resonate through your skull because it is coming from an external source— the tape machine. It is still your voice, of course, but as far as you're concerned it represents a whole new (and unpleasant) sound.

Listeners do not respond to your voice the same way you do. They do not separate *you,* the fully dimensional individual, from your *voice.* They link vocal sounds with a person. A soft voice indicates a pleasant, nonthreatening speaker. A whisper indicates a secretive speaker. A monotone makes us think the speaker is boring. A shaky, scratchy voice indicates nervousness. Loudness signals aggressiveness.

Your goal is to sound genuine and conversational whenever you speak. But that doesn't mean you must be limited by an uncooperative voice that always seems to work against you. Persuasive speakers know how to control their voice, to modify their tone, and to shift gears as circumstances change. If you want to play the role of aggressor, go ahead and raise the volume. But if you seek to charm a new friend into joining you for a date, then stick to a gentle, inviting tone.

This chapter shows you how to produce a confident, commanding delivery by combining the elements of tempo, volume, breathing, inflection, and variation. Just as you learned how to flex your personality muscles in Chapter 4, you need to tap the full range of your voice in order to win over audiences. The best speakers use a wide range of sounds, like musical notes, to convey their messages and keep their listeners attentive. Like a tool for which you continually find new uses, your voice serves as an instrument for growth and exploration. The more variety, the better.

SPEAKING TO THE BEAT: ESTABLISHING A CATCHY VOCAL TEMPO

Here's a foolproof way to attract anyone's attention: shift your vocal tempo. If you tend to talk fast, slow down. If you speak at a deliberate pace, speed up. When you alter your tempo, you make your listeners do a mental double-take. They cannot help but notice when you suddenly change your rate of speech. They grow used to hearing you talk at one speed, and then you surprise them. Varying your tempo prevents you from sounding too predictable or mechanical.

A trial lawyer explained to me that whenever he gives a closing argument to a jury, he paces himself so that his tempo gradually slows to a crawl by the finale. He starts off fast to wake up the jurors and summarize the facts and evidence of the case. Then he starts to slow down a bit as he analyzes the opposition's side. By the time he approaches the conclusion, he builds drama and magnifies the importance of his remarks with pauses between almost every sentence. The jurors, captivated by his delivery, listen raptly to every word.

Smart persuaders constantly check their rate of speech. They do not want to talk too fast or too slowly. Their goal is to create a smooth rhythm. As one party stops speaking, the other pauses for a beat and then begins.

Watch any "sitcom" on television and you will see rehearsed repartee. The characters know when it is their turn to talk. When two voices chime in at once, there's a reason (in *Moonlighting,* for example, Bruce Willis and Cybill Shepherd would speak simultaneously to indicate their familiarity and intimacy). Most of the time, however, Person A talks to Person B and we see a shot of A, B's reaction, and another shot of A.

Like most kids growing up in the early 1970s, I was hooked on episodic television. I marveled at how *The Brady Bunch* family (nine of 'em, including Alice) could communicate week after week and never cut each other off. In the Brady family, everyone talks equally. There are no wallflowers or loudmouths who speak too little or too much. My personal experience, where you had to interrupt to make yourself heard, did not resemble what I saw going on in the Brady household.

In real life, of course, we talk over each other all the time. We start, stop, then politely invite the other speaker to go ahead. We communicate the way two cars approach an intersection. Both vehicles slow down at the stop sign, both inch forward, and then one driver motions to the other driver to continue.

Successful persuaders talk at a comfortable pace that fits the context of the conversation. They strive to speak in sync with the person they wish to win over. For example, if they want to persuade a fast talker, they talk equally fast at the beginning of the chat. Both parties thus speak at the same beat in the opening minutes of the conversation. But as the dialogue proceeds, the persuader gradually slows down. What happens next? The other person usually slows down, too.

The Dangers of Talking Too Fast

Less effective communicators seem oblivious to the beat of a dialogue. I recall a young man who asked me in rapid-fire fashion how he could increase his persuasive power with his friends and family. Just as I was opening my mouth to respond, he interrupted me to repeat how much he wished he could improve his persuasive skills. I could barely understand him because he strung words together so quickly.

Fast talkers get themselves in trouble for a number of reasons:

1. They trigger suspicion and resistance.   They can make us feel uncomfortable when they rattle away. We tend to shut down when the stereotypical fast-talking salesperson goes in for the kill.

2. They usually make others talk faster to keep pace.   We are less apt to be persuaded if we are struggling to get a word in edgewise. We resent when we must rush to say something because someone else monopolizes the conversation. When we converse at double or triple our normal speed to keep up with a fast talker, our attention is diverted from the issue at hand. We grow preoccupied with simply making ourselves heard.

3. Empathy is lost.   If you speak at a breakneck pace, you cut off any opportunity to establish understanding. You block empathy. You will find it much harder to step into someone else's shoes if you are verbally treading all over them.

4. They waste words.   Fast talkers ramble. Rarely will you meet fast talkers who are also concise, because they just fire away and do not view words as a precious resource. It's like squandering water or gasoline. If you take such things for granted, you will see no reason to conserve.

MEMORY JOGGER

When we waste words and talk too much, we lose time, trust, and countless opportunities to persuade.

---

5. They tend to speak too loudly.   If you talk at a rapid clip, your volume probably rises as your pace quickens. By slowing down, you will develop a lower, richer voice.

When faced with the temptation to rush into a sales pitch or blurt out your request for a pay raise, tug on the reins and slow down. You may find your blood pressure goes down while your persuasive power shoots up.

What can you do if you talk too fast? Set up checkpoints so that you do not launch a verbal fusillade. Silently count "1 and 2" before opening your mouth. Learn from John Wayne, who cut each sentence in half ("I say the first half, stop, then say the second half," Wayne once explained).

○ **NOW TRY THIS** If you want to increase control over your rate of speech, practice reading a passage from a book at different speeds. Speak aloud, preferably into a tape recorder. Start at your natural speed—whatever seems most comfortable to you. Then talk fast, faster, fastest...slow, slower, slowest. Pick up or slow down the pace in increments. Do not rush ahead for one paragraph and then abruptly come to a near halt with the next. Notice subtle shifts in tempo and how those shifts affect your voice.

Slow Talkers Can Get in Trouble, Too

Slow talkers face a different set of challenges. There is nothing wrong with slowness in itself. Unfortunately, however, people's attention spans are pathetically short. By talking too slowly, you increase the chance of losing your easily distracted audience. You face the added danger of boring even those somewhat interested listeners who initially cared about what you had to say but soon realized they did not have the patience to wait around while you plodded onward.

Paul Brountas, the senior adviser to Michael Dukakis during the 1988 presidential campaign, recalls Sam Donaldson complaining to him about Dukakis's lengthy pauses between sentences. Unlike John Wayne, who paused to add gravity and force to his lines, the deadening Dukakis style put people to sleep.

MEMORY JOGGER

> To persuade, your words must penetrate the listener's head and make an impact. A delivery that is too fast or too slow makes it harder for your comments to sink in.

When you seek to win people over, you must ensure that your listeners absorb what you say. Your tempo influences whether others comprehend your message. As one of President Clinton's advisers told *The New Yorker*, "He paces himself, and he's comfortable in delivering a thoughtful idea. He's learned how to let people listen instead of trying to sell the idea."[2]

You, too, can establish a smooth vocal pace. If you sell for a living, whether you canvass door-to-door or do telemarketing, you must resist the urge to speed up when you interact with the prospect. Do not rush ahead because you want to save the listener's time or you feel you are imposing. Do not shift into high gear because you suddenly get the president on the line. Check your attitude. Ensure that you believe in what you are selling so deeply that you see no need to cut a few seconds from your pitch.

"I know that my product is a damn good one," a hair-care salesperson told me. "Although I don't want to waste anyone's time, I'm certainly not going to rush through my presentation. I think that sends a message to my potential customers that I just want to finish my spiel and escape."

When you try to persuade, establish a pleasing speak-listen rhythm. When someone stops talking, count silently "1 and 2" before opening your mouth. Use pockets of silence to cushion your remarks. Try to match the speed of the other party, at least in the early minutes of a conversation. Call attention to your key points by shifting your tempo (from slow to fast or vice versa). Do not allow yourself to fall into a steady, predictable, or fast beat.

● **TRAP**   If someone interrupts you, do not interrupt right back. When two mouths jabber at the same time, neither person can listen. The characters in *Moonlighting* can get away with it because they don't have to persuade each other in real life. If the situation involves a conflict or disagreement, talking simultaneously almost guarantees that the problem will worsen as tempers flare. When two or more people talk at once, we miss contextual cues, and misunderstanding may result. We might hear a phrase and immediately draw a conclusion without hearing the speaker's full comments. Persuasion flows from a balanced conversation where everyone who wants to speak has a turn.

ROAR SOFTLY: ADJUSTING THE VOLUME DIAL ON YOUR VOICE TO MAKE YOURSELF HEARD

Mrs. Allen, one of my junior high school math teachers, usually explained integers and fractions in her calm, normal voice. But whenever our class would get unruly, she would suddenly erupt in a screaming fit. We marveled at her ability to belt it out—to yell so loudly that our desks would vibrate. This mild-mannered woman turned into a raving maniac, seemingly on the verge of a nervous breakdown, as she demanded that we STOP TALKING NOW.

Did her outbursts shut us up? Not really. Actually, most of us enjoyed her overwrought performances. Precocious kids like nothing more than to provoke a teacher into "losing it." There was a certain entertainment value to watching her pale-skinned face turn beet red. At recess, we would compare her decibel level with past explosions. "Last week she blew up a lot louder and longer," one of us would say. "This time, her heart wasn't in it. Her face didn't turn red enough."

Mrs. Allen taught me more than math. She helped me learn that loudness does not necessarily accomplish anything. You can yell at the top of your lungs and still not persuade an audience to act as you wish. In fact, you may antagonize your listeners and spread ill will. Some participants in my programs report that they do not respond well when a screamer rails against them. They say they "freeze up when being yelled at" or "shut down" when others lose their temper.

Volume plays a critical role in persuasion. Win people over by adjusting the volume control on your voice so that you capture their attention in a nonthreatening manner. Turning the sound way up might make others stop whatever they're doing, but bellowing may not pay off in terms of selling an idea.

MEMORY JOGGER

We usually resent it when others raise their voice at us. Although we might hear what they say (how can we ignore it?), we are hardly in a receptive position to be persuaded.

Do not assume that you must speak more loudly to make yourself heard. With his thick accent and nearly inaudible voice, Henry Kissenger makes others listen to him. He roars softly. I have watched him give a speech in a large auditorium where no one dared to cough or rustle paper for fear of drowning him out.

○ **NOW TRY THIS** Whispering works wonders, and it is possible to whisper loudly enough to be heard in a crowd. Experiment with your voice volume by devoting a few minutes to communicating solely through whispers. Gather a few friends and lead a discussion while keeping the dial on your voice turned down to "low." Make sure your whispers are still audible—your voice should be heard by anyone within three yards. This exercise teaches you not to string words together or muffle sounds by not properly opening your mouth to enunciate. To make sure people hear you while you whisper, you must extend your lips, let your tongue accentuate your sounds, and slow the pace.

Whispering requires that you use your lips, jaw, and tongue to help you enunciate. Tongue control, in particular, makes your speech more distinct and adds expressiveness to your voice. Never take your tongue for granted when you talk. Give it a workout by sticking it between your front teeth to say *the* and pressing the back of it along the roof of your mouth to say *king*. Raise your tongue to the gum line behind your upper front teeth when you utter *t, d ,* and *n*. If you have a lazy tongue, you will not articulate words effectively.

MEMORY JOGGER

Use your tongue when you speak. This relieves your throat of pressure so that your mouth can do most of the work in forming clear, sharp sounds.

Sloppy habits such as slurring or swallowing words can set in if you do not loosen your mouth. Monotonous speakers tend to lock their jaws, tighten the corners of their mouth, and barely part their lips, resulting in a strained, tinny voice. Avoid this by freely moving your mouth, dropping your jaw, and curling your lips so that you produce a more crisp, resonant voice.

Your lips come in handy when you make the sounds of *b, p, v, f, m, w,* and *wh*. The rest of the time, relax your lips and let your tongue help you create the sounds you want. The muscles in the throat lead to the lips, so when you overwork the lips you endanger your throat.

Grow comfortable using the highs and lows of your voice. Do not take your voice for granted or you will lapse into a narrow band of sound that will flatten your persuasiveness. Speak softly when you want to emphasize a point. It's okay to turn the volume up every so often, but don't overdo it.

To test your vocal range, find the text of your favorite play and read a few pages aloud. Develop distinct voices to represent each character. Try to find a passage that involves at least three different roles, preferably a mix of male and female parts. Record yourself reciting the lines in your "actor's voice," communicating with theatrical flair and precision. Shed any self-consciousness so that you step fully into the roles. The goal of this activity is to become more confident tapping the highs and lows in your voice for maximum impact.

○ **NOW TRY THIS**   To practice varying your voice volume, pick an object about fifty feet away and talk directly to it. Speak from the stomach and diaphragm, not the throat. Project your words slowly, and do not turn your head in midsentence. Keep aiming your sounds at the object. Ask a friend to stand near the object to test how well your voice carries. Then have your friend move the object about twenty feet closer and twenty feet farther away, continuing to speak to it the whole time. This will help you experiment with the highs and lows of your voice in a controlled environment.

As you pay more attention to the sound of your voice, you will appreciate the beauty of the language. Words with hissing consonants such as *s* and *sh* will sound like sibilant melodies. Your pleasing articulation will make others think of palm trees swaying in the breeze. A public speaker told me that she enjoyed to use words such as *wistful* and *shimmy* because she liked the way they rolled off her tongue and produced a relaxing sound. Or you may like to use low-pitched consonants such as *w, m, n,* and *ng* and extend their sound. Rather than say *magnificent,* for example, you may want to try *mmmagnificent.*

⬤ **TRAP** Beware of drawing unwelcome attention to your voice by excessively clearing your throat or apologizing for its sound. Clearing the throat or coughing just before you speak will not improve your speaking; rather, these actions may reveal your nervousness and discomfort. Just because you detect a bit of vocal quivering or nasality, do not assume your listeners notice or care. *Excuse my voice, but I'm getting over a cold* serves no purpose except to redirect the listener's focus away from your message. Rather than apologizing for what you perceive as your embarrassing voice, periodically check to ensure that you are understood. Ask, *Can you hear me?* or *Am I making sense?* If they tell you no, then you can repeat yourself (and, at that time, perhaps explain that you have a cold or you're losing your voice). Do not needlessly denigrate your voice.

To protect your voice, try not to talk too much on airplanes, where you must raise your voice to be heard above the jet's rumble. You cannot roar softly when battling incessant background noise. What's worse, the humidity of an airplane cabin is usually only about 12 percent. The dry air makes it harder to modulate your volume and endangers your vocal cords. Turn the volume dial up on your headset, if you wish, but keep your voice volume on "low" while in the air!

By continually adjusting the volume control on your voice, you will avoid sounding tedious and increase your persuasive power.

BREATHING LIFE INTO YOUR VOICE

Breathing always struck me as pretty basic. You inhale, then exhale, then inhale again…and so on. What else is new?

Actually, the way you breathe greatly affects the sound of your voice. How do you exhale when you talk? If you do not push air through your abdomen, out of the lungs, and into your larynx, the vocal cords will not vibrate properly. Flat vocal cords spell trouble if you want to perfect your persuasive voice.

Most of the people in my workshops assume that the source of their voice is their throat. They do not realize that a truly resonant sound comes not from the throat, but from the gut. Maintaining a physical posture that allows us to push air vigorously through our upper abdominal muscles contributes to a strong voice.

Another stumbling block when it comes to breathing involves the stomach. Some of my participants suck in their tummy when they speak. They may have been taught to stand up ramrod straight, but this restricts their ability to breathe into their stomach. When I led a seminar in the San Diego area, a contingent of military officers from Camp Pendleton attended the session and seemed determined to tighten their gut at every opportunity. "It's okay to loosen up when you try to win somebody over," I said. "Persuasive speakers are at ease with their bodies. You are making it harder to breathe properly by squeezing in your tummies."

○ **Now Try This**   The next time you seek to persuade, make sure your physical posture facilitates your breathing. If you are face to face, stand up with your weight spread equally on both feet (if you are on the phone, stop reclining in your chair and stand tall!). Straighten your spine and hold your head up so that your chin does not cling to your chest. Don't indent your lower back too much or you will make it harder for your stomach muscles to control breath flow. Wash away any tension from head to toe. Visualize a magnet that pulls away any lingering stiffness that remains around your jaw, shoulders, arms, pelvis, chest, waist, back, and hips. Establish an inhale-exhale rhythm that relaxes you even more. When you speak, remember to exhale from your abdomen.

Air circulates more easily through our chest cavity when we exhale in a relaxed state. Stress caused by internal or external factors can translate into stiffness in our bodies. Examples of physical tension that can inhibit the voice are a locked jaw, a throbbing temple, a sore neck, upper back pain, stiff shoulders, and even the familiar lump in the throat.

Rid yourself of these problems by dwelling less on the source of your tension and more on the actual breathing process. Focus on air flow. Feel the intake of air during each breath. When I'm negotiating over the phone, I sometimes place my hand on my gut as a reminder to breathe evenly in and out. Yawn a few times to relax your jaw. Allow yourself an extra second or two to inhale. Release your breath through your mouth, not your nose (a friend who took yoga class had trouble with this, because her teacher had trained her to exhale through her nose).

Match the rate of exhalation with your rate of inhalation. Like paddling across a lake in a canoe, you want your breathing to reflect even strokes that allow you to proceed at a steady forward pace. You do not have to fill your lungs to capacity before speaking.

● **TRAP**   The prospect of trying to persuade others can unleash much anxiety. In moments of nervousness, we may neglect to breathe evenly. Instead of breathing in a rhythmic, controlled manner, we may take quick gasps and exhale choppily. This results in shallow breaths and occasional hyperventilation. Once we fail to breathe properly, our odds of persuasion drop as our thin, reedy, or otherwise weak voice works against us.

If you have trouble maintaining your natural, steady breathing when you are about to persuade, take preventive measures to prepare yourself for these unpleasant bouts of nerves. Here are some helpful breathing tips:

- A few minutes before you persuade, inhale normally and say *now* or *one* before you exhale. Get in the habit of monitoring each breath by uttering a single word just before each exhalation. This forces you to regulate your breathing.

- Remember the technique of visualization that we discussed in Chapter 3. Visualize a door inside your upper abdomen that opens every few seconds to release the air upward through your lungs, to your voice box, and out your mouth. See the stream of air flowing smoothly through your body.

- Create a relaxed inhale-exhale rhythm so that you guard against running out of breath at the end of a sentence. Stop and breathe before trying to cough up too many words at once. Stopping to breathe may sound easy now, but think of a time when you were panicked, excited, or frightened. The last thing on your mind was to check your breathing. Yet by periodically taking calm, unhurried breaths, you gain the twin benefits of mental relaxation and increasing your vocal clarity. Breathiness can ruin your persuasiveness.

Breathing, after all, reflects our emotional state. A heaving exhale can signal relief after a close call. A sigh can indicate frustration or disappointment. A series of rapid inhalations can reveal nervousness, as in the moments before we take the stage to deliver a big speech. Just as actors take breathing lessons to gain access to different emotions, you can treat your breathing as a tool to help you express yourself.

Poor breathing comes in short, rapid beats, putting a strain on the throat muscles. Your motto for proper breathing should be, "Fill the belly, not the chest." Let the air flow from low in your belly, not high in your chest. Taking quick breaths from your upper chest will make you more anxious, and your voice will lose resonance. You can tell if you are breathing too much from the chest if your tone sounds high-pitched and squeaky.

When Bill Clinton campaigned for the presidency, he "began to sound increasingly froglike," according to *The New Yorker*.[3] Clinton's laryngologist, who took a holistic approach to saving his patient's voice, found that the candidate talked too much, drank too much coffee, and consumed too much food. These habits, along with poor breathing, seasonal allergies, and lack of sleep, resulted in a croaky voice. Because he was gaining weight after a few months on the rubber chicken circuit, his stomach acid was washing up the esophagus to create "acid reflux."

The solution? Clinton slept on an inclined bed to prevent his stomach acid from heading upstream. His breathing was controlled, and, after five days of vocal relaxation, he returned to speech-giving with a renewed voice.

HOW TO UNDERLINE WHAT YOU SAY
WITH VOCAL INFLECTION

Guilty or innocent? When we listen to an accused person present a defense, we wonder whether we are getting the truth or a lie. The vocal inflections of the speaker help us to decide whether to accept or reject what we hear.

Think of a sentence such as "I did not say I did the killing." Repeat it a few times, emphasizing a different word. "I did not *say* I did the killing" leaves open the possibility that you did the killing. "I did not say *I* did the killing" implies that you know who did. "I did not say I did the *killing*" makes it sound as if you did something, but not necessarily the killing.

Whenever I see parents calling out to their children, I listen for the inflections in their voice. *Jimmy, come back here* can sound angry, endearing, or admonishing. *How can you say that?* can sound accusatory or pleasantly surprised. *You know how I feel about that* can sound intimate or guarded. It all depends on what words are emphasized.

MEMORY JOGGER

Inflection conveys meaning. Drill home key points by verbally underlining them.

When you try to persuade, you want to sound confident and authoritative. We tend to say "yes" to speakers who give the impression that they know what they're talking about. Here's where a downward inflection helps at the close of our sentences. Broadcasters are taught to complete each snippet of news with a slight downward inflection. The next time you listen to a newscast, note how the anchor uses inflection to punctuate each sentence.

In general, ending our comments on a downward pitch sends a message of awareness, certainty, gravity, command, or assuredness. Upward inflections, on the other hand, signal questions or wavering, uncertain statements.

● **TRAP**   Upward inflections are appropriate when you ask a question. But beware if you use them when making statements. Ending on an upward note undermines your assertions and softens your persuasive edge. Speakers who do not believe what they say or doubt themselves may fall into this trap. Do not fear sounding sure of yourself. The more definite you sound, the more persuasive you will be. End all declarative or informative statements on a firm downward inflection.

Persuasive speakers use a downward inflection to underscore their most important points. I encourage public speakers to rehearse the last sentence of their speech so that they end on a note of vocal finality—a rousing finish where the audience immediately bursts into applause. This way, there is no doubt in anyone's mind that the speaker is done. Because we remember the end of a speech more than what came before, a powerful close leaves a lasting positive impression.

Emphasizing key words with a downward inflection adds confidence and authority to your delivery. When Clint Eastwood says, *Make my day,* each word leaves his mouth with such understated gusto that you cannot help but get caught up in the drama of the moment. When a professor advises the class to *Write this down,* most students comply because they can tell from the instructor's strong inflection that what follows might be on the test. When a lawyer assures a client *We can win this case,* the primary emphasis on *win* and secondary inflection on *case* can send a message of supreme confidence.

Effective reporters know how to use voice inflection when posing delicate questions. A poor communicator might ask a new mayor, *How can you save this town?* by emphasizing *you.* The implicit message is, *How can you, of all people, save this town?* But if the reporter asks the same question by stressing *this town,* the subtext is, *Can you save this town, with its particular problems?*

MEMORY JOGGER

Your speaking will never lapse into a monotonous drone as long as you take advantage of inflection.

When you want to highlight a word or phrase, prolong the vowels so the words sound more distinct. Recall how the late John Houseman advertised a financial services company, "They make money the old fashioned way. They e-e-e-earn it." Or try saying "I love you" by stretching it so that you say "I lo-o-v-v-e you." Vowels add music to your speech. Try rounding your lips when you say *o* or pushing them forward to say *u*. Compare these rich sounds to saying *o* and *u* with your lips hardly apart. You cannot speak in pleasing melodies with a stiff upper lip.

Inflections can help you colorize your comments. They also make it easier for your listeners to feel the impact of your message.

CHARISMA COMES WITH PASSION: LET YOUR VOICE RING FREE WITH FEELING

Persuasive speakers tap a wellspring of feeling in their audiences. A charismatic preacher, for example, communicates in a lively voice filled with emotion. You will never have trouble hearing an evangelist deliver a sermon. Their voices can fill an auditorium and stir each worshipper to react with fervor.

You have heard it a thousand times: Speak with enthusiasm when you want to win someone over. Why? Because enthusiasm enhances a message. Repeat the same persuasive plea in a monotone and in a robust voice, and you will appreciate the role of passion. The identical words take on entirely different meaning when you utter them with force and conviction.

MEMORY JOGGER

Logic alone rarely persuades. Remember that most of us look for logical reasons to satisfy emotional urges. Speaking with passion plants the emotional seed.

Passion is contagious. When you speak with emotion, you trigger emotion in your listeners.

A Hollywood movie producer once cried in order to persuade investors to buy into his film. The project involved an estranged son making a deathbed confession to his father that all he ever wanted was Dad's love. The producer, describing the plot to wealthy investors, would get so choked up that the buyers would lose their composure as well. Whether the producer's tears were real or not, he was able to speak in a persuasive voice and collect the money he needed to make his movie.

This does not mean you should fake enthusiasm in order to get what you want. Most of us can tell when someone goes overboard with canned excitement or phony feelings. Telemarketers, for instance, may repeat the same stale script all day. Although they may follow many of the vocal rules covered in this chapter (expertly using tempo, volume, and inflection), they still fail to persuade if we doubt their passion. No matter how well you perfect your persuasive voice, it is hard to win over anybody by reading from a script or memorizing your remarks.

We sound most passionate when we speak in our natural voice. Enthusiasm results when we do not hold back our emotions or suppress our spontaneity. We persuade when we express our feelings in simple terms. I know some intellectually gifted individuals who think through every emotion to the point where they lose any trace of impulsiveness or unbridled energy. They tend not to be very persuasive.

The most persuasive speakers, by contrast, are comfortable vocalizing the feelings we were all born with. They express universal emotions that reach out and grab us. Their voices reflect their passion, and we gain access to their hopes and fears, their triumphs and sorrows. Their enthusiasm transforms us from disinterested, partial listeners to full participants in their remarks.

● **TRAP** Do not mistake pleading for passion. True enthusiasm percolates from the core of the speaker and is unabashedly sincere; it is not some device to employ when you desperately want to get your way. We plead for something that benefits *us* first, *others* second. We radiate passion, on the other hand, when we propose something that benefits our listeners first and foremost. Be aware that when nagging or begging, you risk annoying others in your self-centered push to win them over.

Speaking in your most persuasive voice is easier if you drop all pretensions. The more conversational you sound, the better. When you are seated around a restaurant table with a group of friends, your vocal tempo and volume come naturally. You stress those words you want to emphasize. You do not need a series of speech exercises to teach you how to speak in a lively, enthusiastic manner.

But in some business or personal situations, we may feel inhibited. Corporate conference rooms, filled with flip charts and number-laden handouts, are hardly scenes we associate with passionate speeches or heartfelt presentations. Communicating with emotion can prove equally challenging in families where such interaction is not the norm. Yet the truly persuasive speaker never withholds passion. Powerful voices tend to stir our feelings even when we are least susceptible to emotional appeals.

○ **NOW TRY THIS**   Think of a fond childhood memory. Share it with a friend or record your reflections on tape. Express yourself as a child would. Do not play by stiff adult rules of "proper" expression. Do not take yourself too seriously. Now carry over this same conversational voice when you want to persuade someone. Strike the same tone, richness, and vocal variation that you achieved when you were reflecting on a happy time from your past.

You can modify this exercise to fit whatever you want to talk about. If you are deeply involved in a church or a nonprofit group, discuss why you give so much of your time to a cause that you believe in. When you are passionate about what you are saying, your voice exhibits all of the persuasive characteristics we have covered in this chapter. Here's a review:

Tempo   Your tempo varies from fast to slow, depending on your emotions at the moment. If you are recalling a triumphant day (when the new volunteer center was dedicated, when you received an award for your service), your voice may speed up to reflect your pride and excitement. If you are retelling a touching or tragic story, your voice may slow down as appropriate.

Volume   The dials of your voice turn up and down freely. When you share a funny anecdote, you may speak more loudly to enliven the story. When you raise a sensitive topic such as the number of deaths attributed to a disease or the struggles of those who need help, your voice softens to reflect the gravity of the topic.

Breathing   When you are sharing something you truly believe in, you need not worry about choppy breathing. You probably do not swallow your words or hyperventilate. You remember to breathe evenly because you feel deeply about what you are saying. The underlying passion that drives your remarks influences your nervous system and helps you regulate your breathing naturally.

Inflection   If you care about what you say, you will notice that inflection, like breathing, takes care of itself. Listen to how you describe a happy memory or a personally satisfying experience. You emphasize key words to drill home your points. You verbally underline as you speak so that your audience captures the full message.

Your voice reveals your feelings. It tells others who you are. Many people just open their mouths without thinking. They do not attempt to control their tempo, tone, or pitch. They find themselves faking it all day long, pretending to care about what they say while their mind wanders far away.

If you want to persuade, you must reclaim the sincere expression of ideas and opinions that deserve an honest voice.

QUICK REVIEW

- You persuade most effectively by using your natural, conversational voice.
- Shift your vocal tempo so that you do not fall into a predictable rhythm.
- Don't talk too fast, or you will lose your listeners and fail to empathize.
- Set up checkpoints to monitor your speed so that you do not talk too fast.
- Don't talk too slowly, or you will lose your easily distracted audience.
- If someone interrupts you, do not interrupt right back.
- Adjust your voice volume so that you capture others' attention.
- Make your tongue and lips work when you speak to relieve throat pressure.
- Push air vigorously through your gut when you speak. Breathe evenly.
- Verbally underline key points with vocal inflection.
- Your voice is at its most persuasive when you express sincere emotions.

NOTES

1. *The Wall Street Journal*, 8-17-87, p. 20.
2. *The New Yorker*, 10-19-92, p. 39.
3. Ibid., p. 38.

ABOUT THE AUTHOR

Morey Stettner, a writer and consultant, teaches courses on communication skills for private companies, nonprofit organizations, and trade groups. He has worked extensively with insurance companies and financial services firms (such as Merrill Lynch, PaineWebber, New York Life, and Mutual of Omaha). He has also served as public affairs manager for a California-based insurer.

His articles have appeared in *The Los Angeles Times, Sales & Marketing Management, Manage, Management Review, Chemical Engineering, The Toastmaster, The Providence Journal, Providence Business News, Brown Alumni Monthly,* and other publications.

Stettner received a B.A. *magna cum laude* from Brown University in 1986, where he launched his career as a public speaking coach in Providence, Rhode Island.

He is the author of *Buyer Beware: An Industry Insider Shows You How to Win the Insurance Game* (Probus Publishing, 1994).

WANT MORE INFORMATION?

Morey Stettner is available for speaking engagements, seminars, and consulting. A dynamic, crowd-pleasing speaker, he has addressed more than 100 corporations and trade associations. He has also taught three popular courses for The Learning Annex (*Public Speaking, Listening Better, How to Sell on the Phone*) and produced a series of training tapes.

For more information, please contact the author at (212) 330-8319.

Index